The Last Place You'd Look

The Last Place You'd Look

True Stories of Missing Persons and the People Who Search for Them

Carole Moore

ROWMAN & LITTLEFIELD PUBLISHERS, INC.
Lanham • Boulder • New York • Toronto • Plymouth, UK

Published by Rowman & Littlefield Publishers, Inc.
A wholly owned subsidiary of The Rowman & Littlefield Publishing Group, Inc.
4501 Forbes Boulevard, Suite 200, Lanham, Maryland 20706
http://www.rowmanlittlefield.com

Estover Road, Plymouth PL6 7PY, United Kingdom

British Library Cataloguing in Publication Information Available

Library of Congress Cataloging-in-Publication Data
Moore, Carole, 1951–
    The last place you'd look : true stories of missing persons and the people who search for them / Carole Moore.
       p. cm.
    Includes bibliographical references and index.
    ISBN 978-1-4422-0368-6 (cloth : alk. paper) — ISBN 978-1-4422-0370-9 (electronic)
    1. Missing persons—United States—Case studies. 2. Missing children—United States—Case studies. 3. Missing persons—Investigation—United States—Case studies. I. Title.
    HV6762.U5M65 2011
    363.2'3360973—dc22   2010043445

♾™ The paper used in this publication meets the minimum requirements of American National Standard for Information Sciences—Permanence of Paper for Printed Library Materials, ANSI/NISO Z39.48-1992.

Printed in the United States of America

To Ernie

Contents

Acknowledgments

$\mathscr{I}$ would like to thank my editor, Suzanne Staszak-Silva, as well as my agent, Jennifer Lawler. Their belief in this project has provided me with priceless inspiration. I am also grateful to Rowman & Littlefield's Melissa McNitt and Evan Wiig for their patience in answering my endless questions and to Erin McGarvey, whose sharp eyes made this a much better book.

Eileen Brady and my sister, Elaine Sioufi Maxwell, were invaluable as readers and sounding boards. They made my first draft readable.

Barbara Nelson of Fox Valley Technical College in Appleton, Wisconsin, and the staff who produces the school's invaluable annual conference on missing persons deserve both my gratitude and much of the credit for helping this book to fruition.

Kelly Jolkowski, mother of missing Jason Jolkowski and the voice behind Project Jason, has become my friend. Without her and her boundless energy, this book would never have gotten off the ground.

I am always grateful for the friendship of Naval Criminal Investigative Service Agent Cheryl Diprizio, who put me in touch with several key people involved in this project and who also guided me around the Washington, D.C., area. Thanks also to Jerry Nance and Glenn Miller of the National Center for Exploited and Missing Children, and Lou Eliopulos, who shared their time and expertise with me.

To Jacksonville (North Carolina) Police Chief Mike Yaniero, who spent an afternoon explaining his department's position on missing persons issues, as well as Todd Matthews of the National Missing and Unidentified Persons System (NamUs), Michelle Bernier-Toth of the U.S. State Department, and all of the officials, police officers, detectives, and investigators who took the time to answer my questions—I thank you. Thanks also to fellow Yo-Hi graduates who shared their memories of our beautiful friend, Jeannette Kamahele, especially Jean Luza and Debbie Branin Coglianese.

My editors at *Law Enforcement Technology* have been both supportive and generous. You are the reason I love writing for the magazine. Cliff Hill, thank you for rekindling my interest in this project. And to Elliott Potter, my old friend and first mentor, whose lifelong editing of my work has turned me into a better writer—I hope I have done you proud.

There is almost no way to adequately thank the families who have told me their stories. Two in particular—Helen Aragona and her daughter, Jennifer, who lost their darling Phyllis to kidnappers and thieves, and Bill and Ellen Kruziki, whose personal tragedy is almost too difficult to bear—sat down and went over their losses in detail. They are courageous beyond belief. And so are the many, many others who spoke with me about their sons and daughters, their sisters and brothers, their fathers and mothers who remain lost. I hope your stories allow others a better understanding of what it means to not know. I have learned so very much from all of you.

To Kelly Pennell, Jan Bowman, Beverly Haskin, Toní Snyder, Barb Vollick, Glenn Hargett, and Diane Bertrand, my thanks for the constant support and encouragement, as well as ideas. To Sue Nathan, a heartfelt thanks for always being there. And, to my extraordinary writer friends, Jennifer Nelson and Randy Hecht, my gratitude for helping me sort through the issues I faced as I started this project.

Lastly, thank you to my husband, Ernie, and our children, Liz and Evan, who never lacked faith in me, even when I could not say the same.

Land of the Missing: It's a Big Ugly World Out There for Families of the Lost

One missing child is one too many.—John Walsh

$\mathcal{A}$s a sworn police officer and trained criminal investigator, I thought I knew all about missing persons. I had taken reports and worked a number of those cases, but as I started to write this book, I discovered I still had a lot to learn. And I decided to talk to the real experts on missing persons—their families. They were gracious, helpful, and generous with their time, even though they were often still immersed in enormous mental anguish. They shared their stories, their grief, their contacts, and the ways they cope with the uncertainty that colors their everyday lives.

Thanks to them, I learned that what I knew about this subject would fill a thimble—and there are great oceans of information out there. Media outlets tell these stories on a selective basis, using what they think will grab the most headlines; law enforcement either works these cases with great passion or not at all; dedicated agencies and nonprofits devote themselves to the cause or don't exist where they're needed; and civilians volunteer to fill in some of the gaps. The reactions, the resources, and the manpower are all over the map when it comes to missing persons investigations, but things are improving. And the impetus behind that change is due in great measure to the families of the missing: a small army of people determined that their own tragedies should count for something.

Each person started as an ordinary parent, spouse, child, or sibling whose life disintegrated when someone they loved did not come home one day. While I don't share with them the depth of their experiences, my own interest in the subject has a similar connection. It began when I learned that someone I knew had also vanished.

Her name was Jeannette Kamahele. She was pretty, with raven hair, dark eyes, and the kind of personality that made you want to know her better. And on April 25, 1972, when she was twenty years old, she put her thumb out to catch a ride near Santa Rosa Junior College in Santa Rosa, California, and vanished forever.

Jeannette, a fellow military brat and college student, grew up on and around military bases. Like the rest of us, she moved many times. In 1970, Jeannette was a graduating senior at Nile C. Kinnick High School in Yokohama, Japan, where I also attended school.

The high school, known by students and faculty alike as Yo-Hi, served members of the U.S. Navy and Marine Corps stationed in Yokohama and the nearby port of Yokosuka, home to both the navy's Seventh Fleet and a large military hospital. Many of the troops evacuated from Vietnam were brought first to Yokosuka to stabilize before the trip home. My dad was stationed there at the Naval Hospital.

Those of us who attended the dependents' high school existed in a kind of suspended animation. Although students living stateside were involved in war protests and the peace movement in a country divided over the military's role overseas, none of that encroached on our lives at Yo-Hi. We were as protected from reality as if cocooned in bubble wrap.

Yo-Hi students only heard popular music for an hour a day on the Far East Network (FEN) radio. We didn't have to worry about controversial numbers—songs like "Angel of the Morning" with its implicit sexuality were not allowed on FEN. Movies available at the base theaters and the newspaper—the ubiquitous *Stars and Stripes*—were squeaky clean. English-language television did not exist. Those of us who were the offspring of servicemen and civilians who attended Yo-Hi would emerge almost untouched by that era's popular culture.

Outside the base's gates, there was also little to fear: the Japanese at that time were an orderly and even formal society, just beginning to feel the effects of postwar cultural changes. Although everyone seemed to be learning to speak English, the more shocking aspects of the new American revolution of the 1960s and early '70s had not yet bled over into Japanese society. Students at Yo-Hi, like Jeannette Kamahele and me, were immersed in surroundings that were more associated with the 1950s than the late 1960s.

Although the school's classes were small, we did boast some serious overachievers in our ranks. Tina Lutz Chow, a fashion icon who before her death was often on the international best dressed list, graduated in 1968; actor Mark Hamill was student body president in 1969. Jeannette belonged to the class that graduated after Hamill.

With her long, dark hair parted down the middle and short-short skirts, Jeannette wore the uniform of the Yo-Hi girl. Her family had its roots in Hawaii, and she reflected her island heritage with her exotic good looks and almond eyes. Smart, popular, and well-liked, Jeannette had a steady boyfriend and longtime best friend with whom she would share an apartment in college. She had no enemies—who could dislike someone as cheerful and personable as Jeannette? After graduation, she would relocate to California and enroll in Santa Rosa.

The smiling Jeannette, whose raucous laugh echoed up and down the hallways at Yo-Hi, didn't have a suspicious bone in her body. Her graduating class of about one hundred was as close as family. Emerging from our vanilla childhoods in Japan, she saw no evil—not even in hitchhiking, which in the early '70s was in vogue for both young men and women.

Not quite two years after her high school graduation, Jeannette left home one warm spring day and caught a ride near the on-ramp leading to Highway 101, then vanished into the bright California sun. Although authorities found the bodies of several other young women from the community who disappeared around the same time as Jeannette, she has never been located, nor have those murders been solved.

Everyone who knew Jeannette Kamahele—from her high school classmates to her friends—says she would never, ever leave of her own accord. She had no reason to run away. I graduated from Yo-Hi one year ahead of Jeannette, but time scattered our classmates around and it wasn't until an all-school reunion held in 2000 that I found out she had vanished. The news threw me off balance: how could this happen to someone I knew?

I was no stranger to missing persons in my police work. I remember early in my career sitting at the front desk at the department as a patrol officer, when a young man came in to report his wife missing. Not more than a couple of hours before, the county sheriff's office had responded to a call about a woman's body found on a nearby beach. I directed the man to the sheriff's department, and as it turned out, the woman was his missing wife.

The two incidents—Jeannette Kamahele's disappearance and the missing woman on the beach—combined to fuel my drive to learn what I could about missing persons in this country. When I began my research, I discovered a hidden network of families, organizations, civilians, and officials, all linked by one thing: their interest in the tide of people who have disappeared and in unidentified recovered human remains. And the first lesson I learned was that while the numbers don't lie, they also don't tell the whole story.

Each day in excess of two thousand individuals are reported missing in the United States, according to the National Crime Information Center. That total does not include Americans who have vanished in other countries or individuals who disappear and are never reported: the homeless and the children born to them, prostitutes, drug users, foster kids, individuals without families or who have lost touch with their families, and transients.

Most of those reported missing return home. Some turn up in the medical examiner's office. Others, like Jeannette Kamahele, vanish and are never seen again. Most of the families I have encountered while working on this book have spent their time turning over every rock, looking in every crevice. They never quit, as in the case of Dorothy "Dee" Scofield, whose disappearance many years ago set her parents on a lifelong quest to find their child. They lost her in the most ordinary of circumstances—the kind of thing that could happen to any family. In fact, the ordinariness of Dee's disappearance is what haunts me.

When Dee was twelve years old, she accompanied her mother to the Ocala, Florida, highway patrol office, where Mrs. Scofield was obtaining a new driver's license. Dee went to run an errand a few hundred feet away at a nearby department store. The preteen, her hair in pigtails, promised her mom she would return to the station once she finished her errand, but she never came back. Her mother went to the store to look for her.

Unable to find her daughter, Mrs. Scofield returned to the highway patrol office and reported her child missing. It was July 22, 1976. Later, a clerk at a nearby store told investigators that two men came into the store with an upset child matching Dee's description, but the clerk did not intervene and the men left with the girl.

The Scofields did what any parents in their position would do. They spent every penny they had looking for their missing child, but Dee, who would have been forty-six at the time this was written in 2010, has never been heard from again. It is a hard story to read, but the worst part is that it is not unique, demographically, generationally, or geographically.

Far away from the Scofield family, on the other side of the country, another set of parents also faced the unthinkable during an ordinary outing. Today they, too, keep the candles burning for their lost child.

On December 5, 1998, eight-year-old Derrick Engebretson was with his dad and grandfather looking for a Christmas tree in the Winema National Forest located in Klamath County, Oregon, when he became separated from the pair. A massive search was conducted once they discovered the child was missing, but it was called off when a blizzard struck that night, covering the search area in heavy new snow.

Later, evidence suggested Derrick could have found his way to a nearby highway, where he may have been forced into a car by a passerby. Despite his parents' efforts and subsequent searches of the forest and road, no trace of the little boy has ever been discovered. Like Jeannette and Dee, Derrick's disappearance was a tragedy that struck without warning or any type of foreshadowing: each simply vanished.

Jeannette Kamahele, Dee Scofield, and Derrick Engebretson are not household names like that of Natalee Holloway, the blond American teen who disappeared while on a high school graduation trip to Aruba, or Stacy Peterson, an Illinois woman who vanished in October 2007 under mysterious circumstances. I doubt the media was interested in Jeannette's disappearance since she was an adult at the time. I know from press clippings that local coverage following the disappearances of Dee and Derrick was intense; in the pre-Internet days, such cases would fade from the public radar over time, their causes resurrected on the anniversaries of their disappearances or on the rare occasions when a new development surfaced.

In fact, before the Internet, most disappearances not involving small children or celebrities received scant attention from all but their local news media. Families and friends had little help with publicity. They would raise rewards, make posters, run ads, and try to keep the media interested. Some helpful national initiatives emerged: in the mid-1980s milk cartons with photos of missing children on them made their debut, asking, "Have you seen me?" The first child to appear on one of those milk cartons, Etan Patz, a six-year-old from New York who disappeared walking to the bus stop in May 1975, has never been found.

For families like the Kamaheles, Scofields, and Engebretsons, publicizing their loved ones' disappearances proved much more difficult. It's still challenging, but the World Wide Web gives families of the missing additional tools to keep their stories alive and also grants access to more and better resources, one of which is also the resource of last resort.

———∞∞∞———

The young woman who goes by Clark County, Nevada, coroner's case number 80-01221 could be asleep in the photograph, except that the background behind her head is not a pillow, but a metal tray—the kind where bodies are rolled out to be viewed or autopsied in a morgue.

That is where the young girl found in Henderson, Nevada, "sleeps" in this photograph. Her picture, as well as many others, appears on the Web site of the Clark County Coroner's Office.

It is a Web site not for the morbidly curious, but rather it was established to help authorities unite this young girl and the other unidentified dead on the site with their identities. The problem of unidentified remains is not unique to Clark County, but Clark authorities are on the leading edge of finding a solution.

Clark County, the fifteenth-largest county in the nation, is home to the city of Las Vegas and has a population of two million that derives much of its commerce from the tourism industry. Thousands flock from all over the world to visit the area's casinos. Some of them die there, and not all are identified.

I heard Clark County Coroner P. Michael Murphy speak at a conference entitled, "Responding to Missing and Unidentified Persons," which is held each year by Fox Valley Technical College in Appleton, Wisconsin. Murphy says his county has 8,060 square miles of territory, and each year, on average, his office deals with about fourteen thousand deaths. Sometimes the bodies are bones or even bone fragments. Murphy and other staff members work hard to identify the unknown dead that turn up in his jurisdiction because, as he puts it, "they're all somebody's children."

In the case mentioned earlier, number 80-01221, the victim died as the result of a homicide. Five feet, two inches tall and 103 pounds at her death, the girl had fair skin, red hair, and green eyes, as well as a tattoo of the letter *S* on her right forearm. Her body was found on October 5, 1980, with lacerations to her scalp and puncture wounds on her back. She wore no clothes.

The coroner estimates her age at somewhere between fourteen and twenty years. I chose her from among the many who fill the Web site's pages because I found it hard to understand how this girl could remain unidentified and unclaimed for three decades. Someone, somewhere, misses this young woman, but until very recently there was no organized method of sharing this information with the public, law enforcement, or even other medical examiners. Today that is changing: coroners and medical examiners across the nation are not only posting the likenesses and descriptions of unidentified bodies that are found in their jurisdictions, but they are also taking part in a new initiative designed to link civilian and official resources in an effort to identify the more than forty thousand bodies retained by authorities that remain unclaimed in this country.

Called the National Missing and Unidentified Persons System (NamUs), the program allows law enforcement, medical examiners, and families to input information and grants access to the public, except for some investigatory details not released by the police. This unique, citizen-centric approach has already helped officials make several identifications.

"The government finally woke up," says Todd Matthews, a civilian who works with NamUs.

I first heard Matthews speak at the same Wisconsin conference as the Nevada coroner. Later, we talked about his involvement with NamUs, as well as his unique take on working with missing persons and unidentified human remains.

Matthews has a deep and abiding personal interest in both subjects, and he is one of the more interesting individuals I encountered while writing this book. One of the founding members of the Doe Network, a civilian, Internet-based enterprise that works to match human remains to missing persons, his obsession with missing persons began in 1968, when a man named Wilbur

Riddle discovered the body of a woman wrapped in a green tarp discarded near a dirt road in the area of Georgetown, Kentucky. A local newspaper dubbed the young woman—thought to be between sixteen and nineteen years old—the "Tent Girl."

The autopsy suggested she had been rendered unconscious with a blow to the head and placed in a plastic bag, where she asphyxiated. The bag was then wrapped in the tarp and tossed in the woods. Her fingerprint was obtained and an artist drew her likeness, but all attempts to identify the victim failed.

Decades passed and Riddle, the man who found the Tent Girl, retired and moved to Livingston, Tennessee, where his daughter, Lori, had a boyfriend named Todd Matthews. Matthews was fascinated by the story of the girl with no name and began working to identify her. When the Internet became available, Matthews switched his quest to an online search. Now married to Lori, he searched for clues to Tent Girl's identity and one day he found her—Barbara Hackman Taylor, a twenty-four-year-old mother married to a carnival worker. Following exhumation and a DNA comparison with the victim's living sister, a positive identification was made.

Barbara Hackman Taylor's husband, who said Barbara ran off with another man, was by then deceased, and her murder has never been solved. It took three decades to identify her and put a name on her headstone, a step Matthews believes is crucial—all John and Jane Does deserve to be identified and buried with dignity and their families to mourn their losses.

"When I made the identification of the Tent Girl, I really had no idea that I had a better chance of hitting the lottery," he says.

His job now—and that of NamUs and modern, forward-thinking coroners and medical examiners like Murphy—is to make sure the tools exist for more identifications, as well as better cooperation between law enforcement and the civilian community. The reality is that officials have not always been willing or able to cooperate with one another, much less civilians, while working missing persons cases.

For decades, the direction and depth of missing persons investigations have been determined by local jurisdictions, except in cases involving federal or state-level authorities. In fact, the local protocol regarding whether to even take such a report has varied. Some jurisdictions treat with seriousness every report of a missing person and start an immediate investigation. When a Jacksonville, North Carolina, man was reported missing by his family, county deputies completed a report and started backtracking the man's movements. Within days it was discovered he had left of his own accord, traveling to Texas, and the case was closed. I think that's the way it should always be done, but I realize that different agencies have different resources available.

My former department always took missing persons reports on the theory that it was easier to clear them as unfounded if the person turned out not to be missing than it was to play catch-up if the case evolved into something else (like a homicide or kidnapping), and we investigated them without delay, too. But I discovered some jurisdictions, such as the Minnesota departments contacted by Brandon Swanson's parents when he went missing, resist filing reports.

Part of the resistance comes from their reluctance to complete what they consider unnecessary paperwork. It's true—the vast majority of missing persons turn up in a matter of hours, their disappearances a result of misunderstandings, miscommunications, or other domestic situations. Sometimes the responding officer doesn't believe the evidence is there, and that missed opportunity can leave families shaken and scrambling for answers when the missing loved one isn't late coming home but in trouble.

That is exactly what happened in Brandon's case in which a traffic mishap transformed an entire family. On May 14, 2008, when Brandon was nineteen, he was driving back to his Marshall, Minnesota, home through the flat agricultural area between his parents' house and a town called Canby.

According to Brandon's mother, Annette Swanson, "Brandon was living at home when he went missing. He had just completed his first year at Minnesota West Community and Technical College in Canby. He briefly visited friends in a nearby town before leaving for home—taking back roads rather than the highway. At approximately 1:50 a.m., Brandon called home asking his father and [me] to come help him. He had gone into the ditch and needed help getting his car out. Brandon told us he was near Lynd [Minnesota]."

The Swansons jumped into their truck and drove to the area where Brandon said he'd landed in the ditch but couldn't find him. They called Brandon and asked for help locating him. Despite much back and forth, they still couldn't connect, so Brandon decided to set off on foot and walk toward them. He remained on the phone the entire time—a forty-seven-minute call. Then, says Annette, Brandon said, "Oh, shit."

"The call ended abruptly. Several attempts to regain contact with Brandon failed. Brandon has not been seen or heard from since," she says.

"We encountered reluctance from law enforcement in accepting a missing persons report, searching, and investigating, but we are a stubborn, strong-minded, and determined family. Their reluctance and inadequacies would not prevent us from searching for our son," Annette says.

Like other families facing this type of situation, the Swansons channeled their energies in productive directions: they continued to scour the area for their son, even finding a search manager to coordinate the many wilderness searches they have conducted, and they made sure other families didn't face

Brandon Victor Swanson. Courtesy of Brian and Annette Swanson.

the same initial official disinterest as they did. Following a campaign by the Swanson family and their supporters, Minnesota Governor Tim Pawlenty signed Brandon's Law, which requires a faster and more proactive response from law enforcement when adults vanish, to give families a better shot at locating their loved ones and affords specialized training for law enforcement.

Law enforcement wastes no time when a young child is involved, but adults—even young adults like Brandon—are a different story. An eighteen-year-old is an adult in most states, although three—Alabama, Delaware, and Nebraska—consider nineteen the age of majority, and in Mississippi it is twenty-one. Some states also grant majority to those who have graduated from high school or joined the service.

Not all police take reports when an older child or young adult disappears under circumstances not considered suspicious. Many departments already operate on paper-thin resources and don't have the personnel to look for those old enough to leave on their own. Also, few agencies have dedicated missing persons units; in fact, the majority of officers have little or no specialized training in the field. I received none and believe my experience is typical of local police.

Because of this, older teens, including Jesse Ross, are often labeled as runaways, even when their families know better. Like Brandon, Jesse was nineteen and a college student at the time of his disappearance on November 21, 2006. The tall redhead, whom his family characterizes as "never dull," was attending a Model United Nations conference in Chicago and had called his

Jesse Ross. Courtesy of Don and Donna Ross.

mother, Donna, the day before to give her an update on the trip. It was the last time they would talk.

A good student with an internship at a local radio station, Jesse majored in communications and minored in politics at the University of Missouri–Kansas City. One of more than one thousand students attending the conference, Jesse and the other "delegates" were called to a mock emergency meeting at 2:00 a.m. at the Four Points Sheraton Hotel. Cameras on the premises caught the teen, dressed in a white T-shirt, jeans, and a green warm-up jacket, as he walked toward the hotel's exterior doors about half an hour later.

Jesse's hotel was a ten-minute walk from the Sheraton, where the conference was held. The Ross family says Chicago police claim no foul play is involved, yet they fear the worst: there has been no activity on their child's credit cards or telephone since he was last seen.

Jesse was missing for twelve hours before anyone "decided something was wrong" and contacted the Rosses, says Donna. Jesse's family has staged events and rallies, given interviews to many different media outlets, put up flyers, and visited the scene of his disappearance, looking for clues as to his whereabouts—all without success.

As for the police, says Donna, "No family is happy when their loved one is missing. We hoped police would ask for help . . . when they could find no clues. So far, they are keeping the case open, so our [private investigator] can't see the files, but they are not working a single lead."

I need to clarify that it's not the intention of this book to indict police and the way they operate—or to defend them, for that matter. I understand the difficult jobs they face, but some departments are better at working these cases than others. In law enforcement, like sports, there are differing levels of competence even though everyone is playing the same game. The good ones take the initial reports, are sympathetic to the families, and investigate and touch base with families so they don't feel forgotten. Agencies with excellent missing persons bureaus staffed with well-trained and competent officers are most often found in larger cities, but even a department without the resources for a missing persons unit can do a great job on these tough investigations.

One example of how efficient a well-trained missing persons unit can be is evident in an October 2009 case, when a transit police officer in New York City found Fernando Hernandez Jr. in a Coney Island subway station. The thirteen-year-old boy, who is diagnosed with Asperger syndrome, had been hiding out in the city's subway system unnoticed for eleven days. He rode the trains to avoid going home, where he was fearful he would get in trouble following an incident at school. His mother, a Mexican immigrant, was quoted in the *New York Times* as saying she believed her lack of English and legal status affected the response from police—a charge police denied.

In fact, the New York Police Department did launch a search for the boy. Officers took a report almost as soon as they were notified he was missing by his parents. They chased down leads and interviewed witnesses. After the child had been missing for six days, his case was transferred to the department's crack Missing Persons Squad. The squad focused its efforts on finding the child, and those efforts paid off.

His mother says her son's disability makes it more difficult for him to judge the appropriateness of his actions. When individuals with mental disorders disappear, police and families face a different type of investigation, and because current laws give the mentally disabled the right to terminate their medications, families often find themselves hamstrung in what they can do, even if police do find them.

Alicia Digna's mother, Pam Digna, says her missing daughter suffers from autism and a potpourri of physical ailments that range from a tumor to multiple sclerosis. Pam is worried about her sweet-faced daughter and her probable lack of medical treatment.

Alicia, who is twenty-six, disappeared from Romulus, Michigan, on August 27, 2008. Born with multiple birth defects, she has ongoing medical issues that combine to increase the likelihood of brain damage as her untreated conditions are exacerbated. Without Alicia's medication, Pam fears her daughter will not survive.

"We felt that there is a good possibility that Alicia has died and that we are now searching for a body," says her mother.

But my research shows that those with mental disorders aren't the only people who receive short shrift in the U.S. missing persons system. Substance abusers often receive little attention from authorities and little sympathy from the press or public.

Stacy White understands all too well because she and other family members have been searching for her husband Bobby's missing sister, Tabitha Franklin, since she disappeared on August 13, 2009.

The mother of three children and a resident of Cullman, Alabama, "Tabby" was twenty-eight years old when she vanished. Her family has put up posters and led several searches, but thus far they've found no sign of the bubbly blond who favors long, dangly earrings. While police have said they do not believe foul play was involved, Stacy says her sister-in-law has been the victim of domestic abuse in the past and the family suspects it might also be the case this time.

"Due to her addiction, she lives from one friend to another but is always trying to find work to make it better," says Stacy.

The family believes that Tabby's choices in life have made police less sympathetic toward her disappearance, but like all families of the missing, they have learned how to be her advocate—and they have some advice for those who find themselves in similar situations. "The first thing I would tell someone as the sister-in-law of a missing adult is to go with your gut feelings, and even if the police don't think something has [gone] terribly wrong, stay on it. If you have computer access, find a local search-and-rescue squad, talk to a [private investigator] . . . willing to work pro bono, print posters of your missing loved one [and] distribute them everywhere," she says.

Did Tabby Franklin decide to chuck it all and walk away from her life, as many do, or did something sinister befall her? Her family believes she fell victim to foul play. I have found that in some cases, though, the room for doubt narrows, and it soon becomes apparent that the missing person didn't leave on his or her own. But the daughter of pretty brunette Annita Maria Musto Price, a cocktail waitress from Moundsville, West Virginia, who vanished on May 30, 1974, doesn't believe her mother left on her own, and the evidence supports her theory.

Price was last seen after she dropped her boyfriend off at work and then headed for her own job at a local nightspot known as the Flamingo Club. Her daughter, Madonna Layne, says, "The car she was driving was found parked on the side of the road in the opposite direction from where she was headed. Her purse and all of its contents were found strewn on the front seat of the car."

Involved in a nasty custody battle at the time, Annita's disappearance was investigated for eighteen years. "A few years ago, a cold-case detective reopened the investigation after someone called in a tip. Nothing has been resolved and . . . the detective [has] been reassigned, and my mother's case is again just sitting on a shelf," Madonna says.

Cold cases like that of Annita Price often prove difficult to resolve. Evidence handling before the 1990s many times was casual and fairly low-tech: rape kits weren't always kept refrigerated, fingerprint analysis was a tedious procedure conducted by human technicians, and physical items were often improperly stored and subject to deterioration or loss. Evidence derived from human testimony or statements shifts and changes with time: witnesses move or die or their memories show the effects of age. Even physical features—roads and buildings and neighborhoods—change in the course of decades.

But thanks to scientific advances in evidence, like DNA and tighter media scrutiny, cold cases are being resurrected and reinvestigated all of the time. Some are matched with remains and even result in the occasional arrest, as in the recent case of a missing Alabama man named George Kevin Pody.

Pody, who disappeared from Mount Moriah on March 8, 1993, was a twenty-six-year-old working as an overseer for a large timber corporation at the time of his disappearance. Following a search in 2010, deputies say they found bones and some items belonging to the missing man. They made an arrest in connection to the slaying.

In rare instances where foul play was involved, as in the case of Utah resident Elizabeth Smart, who was kidnapped from the bedroom she shared with her younger sister, the missing person is found alive and well and is returned to his or her family. In Smart's case, her accused abductor—Brian David Mitchell—withstood numerous attempts by the prosecution to bring him to justice by claiming he was too mentally incapacitated to stand trial.

Not every case has an ending: Elizabeth Rivera says her daughter Elsha vanished from Fort Worth, Texas, in February 2004, leaving her with Elsha's four children. "She didn't just pick up and leave them because she was young and had so many children like the police and many have insinuated," Elizabeth told me.

Elsha had five kids (one is now deceased), and Elizabeth says she raises the surviving children on a small government stipend. Her days are long and she is weary, but she's also determined to find her daughter. She also says one of Elsha's children, Michael, suffers more than the other children from his mother's absence.

Elizabeth says Michael (who was eleven at the time I wrote this) has tried to interest the news media in his mom's disappearance, but no one responds. "I would like for Michael to be heard. He needs this. He needs someone to listen to him so he can heal in case she is never found and before he gives up completely," she says.

Elsha is a beautiful Latina woman, with long hair, full lips, and olive skin. So far, according to Elizabeth, the press has been uninterested in her story. She and Michael have begged newspapers and television news shows to feature their loved one, without any interest evinced in Elsha or the children she left behind.

Other minorities who have missing family members tell me they, too, find the media goes cold when their cases come up. Many claim it is due to something termed the "missing white woman syndrome" (also called "missing pretty girl syndrome") in which the press reportedly exhibits disproportionate interest in cases involving pretty, missing white girls, even when there are plenty of other missing persons out there who do not fit that description.

While Natalee Holloway, the teen who went missing in Aruba, did garner a lot of publicity, much of it emanated from the tireless efforts of her family, who devoted tremendous amounts of time generating newsworthy copy. Others work as hard but don't get anywhere near the press the Holloway case has generated. It's a disconnect that is hard to understand. Some cases click with the media, and some don't.

Those who manage to attract constant media interest work 24/7 at it. Hope Sprenger, whose fifteen-year-old daughter Kayla vanished after a friend dropped her off at another friend's house in Antigo, Wisconsin, on August 11, 2009, has kept her child's name in front of the media the entire time, but it's

Kayla May Berg. Courtesy of Hope Sprenger.

been exhausting, both physically and mentally. Newspapers, television news, and online resources including *America's Most Wanted*'s Web site have publicized Kayla's story—still, there has been no word on her daughter's whereabouts.

"This experience has been the absolute worst feeling in the world. It is like having your heart ripped out of your chest, someone coming and taking a part of your soul away without you even knowing what is happening, especially in the beginning," Hope says.

Hope says one of the hardest parts has been dealing with the inevitable rumors and gossip that go hand in hand with a disappearance like Kayla's.

"We have had to grow a very strong backbone," admits Hope.

She and the rest of her family have become pros at handling the media and have learned to ignore the creeps who come out of the woodwork—people who want to be involved in the case because they are attracted to the publicity angle, phonies who pretend to have information, so-called psychics, and others who want to snipe or gossip. What was once a normal, everyday life for the Berg family has turned into a struggle for normalcy ever since the pretty, brown-haired high school student vanished.

"There are some days I think that the only way I will ever see her again is in heaven," says Hope.

"I can't say that I can put things in perspective until I know what has happened to her. All I do is keep hoping and praying that something will break in her case and we will find out some answers. We will never give up on her. We try to remain sane, but sometimes that is easier said than done," she says.

Hope Berg's raw and ragged honesty has produced in me an unintended consequence: it makes me overprotective toward my own children, and I suspect every parent who reads or hears stories like Kayla's or Jesse's or Brandon's reacts with the same feelings. Some of the stories I've read or heard broke my heart. One example in particular stands out. Author Matt Birkbeck chronicled it in his book, *A Beautiful Child—The Story of Sharon Marshall*.

Marshall, who went by the name Suzanne Davis as a small child, was raised by a sexual predator and convicted felon named Franklin Delano Floyd. Floyd passed himself off as her father. Authorities don't know where Floyd obtained the child. Birkbeck says that during a jailhouse interview Floyd claimed a prostitute gave him the girl, but Floyd also told officials he rescued her after her biological parents abandoned her. One thing that's for sure—the little girl was not related to Floyd by blood.

Floyd moved around a lot, taking the child with him. When she entered high school, she was known as Sharon Marshall, a straight-A student who moved often, much like I did as a child. Upon graduation from a high school in Forest Park, Georgia, Sharon received a scholarship to Georgia Tech to study aerospace engineering. She never used it.

Sharon, a beautiful natural blond with a brilliant mind, next surfaced in the Tampa area, still in the company of Floyd, where she gave birth to a little boy. Although Floyd claimed the child was his, later tests proved he was not the father. Sharon was using the name Tonya Tadlock at that time and worked as an exotic dancer. After an exotic dancer with whom she was friends was found murdered, Suzanne/Sharon/Tonya and Floyd fled the area. Floyd then married her, but in 1990, she was killed in a hit-and-run accident that remains unsolved.

Her little boy, Michael Hughes, then in foster care, was abducted by Floyd and has never been found. Floyd refuses to tell investigators what he did with the child.

Although his book was published in 2004, Birkbeck continues to search for the boy, as well as the true identity of the child who went by the name Sharon Marshall. I understand his obsession. The stories of the lost, missing, and those found but still unidentified—and their families—will remain with me long after this book is finished.

In putting together this look at missing persons and those who search for them, I spoke with officials from many agencies, as well as the families and many individuals who feel the call to offer help and support to those who search for the lost. I have talked to parents whose children were abducted by noncustodial parents, families whose loved ones vanished while visiting foreign countries, and scientists trying to match the bodies of the unknown to their identities so they can be returned to their loved ones.

I learned a tremendous amount—searching for a missing person is not a simple endeavor. There are many who work to help guide families of the missing through the maze in which they've been thrust. Kelly Jolkowski, whose son Jason's story is told in chapter 11, has opened many doors for me and offered guidance born of her painful personal journey. It's something she does for many families of the missing, but there are others who are in it for a much different reason. For families working their way through this uncharted territory, there are many pitfalls to avoid and very few maps.

I tell many of the heartbreaking stories I encountered on the following pages, and I attempt as well to offer insight into the agencies that work these cases, including what they are doing right and where there is room for improvement. Some of the suggestions come from members of "the club no one wants to belong to," as Ed Smart puts it. And they speak, through me, with honesty and the hope that others never, ever have to walk in their shoes.

In the next chapter you will meet Bill Kruziki. I first encountered Bill's story when we corresponded about something I wrote for a law enforcement trade magazine at which I am a columnist. I later met him and his wife, Ellen, and was impressed with their ability to live their lives after suffering terrible tragedy. They have been kind enough to allow me to share their story with you.

Two Brothers: A Federal Marshal Confronts the Unthinkable

Don't expect anybody to do anything. You have to go on the
offensive big time. The police are not going to spend all of their
time working your case.—Bill Kruziki, retired U.S. marshal

*M*att Kruziki grew up in the upper-middle-class Milwaukee suburb of
Hartland. His dad, Bill, was a deputy sheriff, then sheriff, who had made the
transition from local to federal law enforcement with an appointment to the
U.S. Marshal's Service. In high school Matt and his older brother, Chris,
played sports, made decent grades, and had plenty of friends. As close as two
brothers could be, they were, nevertheless, individuals in their outlooks on
life. Matt, an outgoing liberal with a penchant for social causes, provided a
contrast to the more introspective Chris, who adopted a conservative stance
on politics and social issues.

Both boys attended college for a while, but neither was quite sure what
he wanted from life. Matt found his calling in the nonprofit realm. He started
as a volunteer, then parlayed one gig into a paying job. The gregarious young
man thrived in his position's travel, mission, and, most of all, opportunities to
make a difference.

"He was hooked on nonprofit work," says his dad, Bill.

During his nonprofit career, Matt encouraged inner-city voters, worked
with unionized health care, and made sure the less advantaged had a say in the
issues that affected them. He was passionate in his quest to represent the voice-
less and unabashed when it came to meeting new people and making friends.
Relationships were as necessary to Matt's existence as air.

"He wasn't afraid of anything," Bill says. "He could make friends with
a wall."

It was later, after Matt vanished in a tiny town hundreds of miles from home, that Bill would discover how many friends Matt had and how many other hearts he touched along the way. But the journey to finding out how much Matt meant to others was first complicated by the journey to find Matt—and to find out what happened to him.

⎯⎯⎯⎯ ⚭ ⎯⎯⎯⎯

On an icy-cold Christmas Eve in 2005, twenty-four-year-old Matt Kruziki disappeared while on a trip that led him to the city of East Dubuque, Illinois. With a couple thousand residents, the small river town once known as Dunleith flanks the muddy Mississippi and is connected by a bridge to the larger metropolitan area of Dubuque, Iowa, with its population of more than fifty thousand. Dubuque, perched at the juncture of three states—Illinois, Iowa, and Wisconsin—is a college town dominated by schools with religious affiliations, a place where the proverbial sidewalks roll up early. Many who hope to party late into the night slip across the Julien Dubuque Bridge to head for the strip of bars clustered along Sinsinawa Avenue in East Dubuque, where the fun continues until the wee hours of the morning.

It was one of the bars in this strip noted for Dubuque college kids, late hours, and a rough clientele that drew an unsuspecting Matt and his traveling companion. Matt's car had given out on him over Thanksgiving while he was on the road for his job. He left it behind on the interstate outside of Des Moines, Iowa, and flew home to Hartland, where he lived with his mother. He planned to return later and pick it up. Matt asked several people to drive with him to get his abandoned automobile, including his brother, Chris, but ended up with a neighborhood acquaintance when no one else could make the trip. The pair left on December 23 and later that day, exhausted by the drive, they checked into a hotel in Dubuque. After having a few drinks at the hotel bar, the two young men crossed the river and hit the bar scene in East Dubuque.

Some time during the predawn hours of December 24, Matt was relieved of his cash, coat, gloves, and hat by some of the questionable characters that frequented the bar. He'd been carrying $380 and, for reasons no one understands, had not brought along his cell phone. Intoxicated and alone, Matt was ejected from the establishment dressed in a shirt and jeans and wearing a pair of work boots. As he stumbled along in the numbing cold, he was stopped at about 1:10 Christmas Eve morning and questioned by a local police officer. The officer instructed Matt to go back to his hotel and then left the coatless and drunken young man to find his way alone back to that hotel room across the river in Dubuque in seventeen-degree weather.

He never made it.

At 9:30 a.m. on the same day, Bill Kruziki and his current wife, Ellen, who is also a law enforcement officer, received a call from his eldest son, Chris: Matt had not returned to his hotel room. Bill and Ellen went into cop mode.

"I knew what to do," Bill says. "I spent the first day on the phone talking to law enforcement agencies, even calling thrift stores to see if they'd sold Matt a coat."

The town and its law enforcement nearly ground to a halt on Christmas Day, but on December 26, Bill met with the police chief in East Dubuque.

Reflecting later on what happened to his son, Bill says he learned that the bar ran a scam that defrauded customers of their cash. He says the traveling companion, who later took a polygraph that came out inconclusive but deceptive, never answered to his satisfaction why he didn't leave the bar with Matt. But the one answer Bill would like to have is why the police officer that conducted the field interview with Matt after he left the bar did so little.

"That officer knew what happened in the bar, so why not go back and get him his coat?" Bill asks.

It is this question and others that prick at Bill Kruziki, who says of local police, "They could have done more, but that, of course, is a parent talking."

But Bill Kruziki is no ordinary parent. This one has juice. His connections in Wisconsin and federal law enforcement, as well as his experience on missing persons cases, makes him savvier than most parents whose adult child might be missing. Bill began summoning resources, calling in favors, working the system.

On December 26, the same day he met with the police chief, the Kruzikis began plastering the area with posters featuring Matt. The posters went on cars, college campuses, restaurants, bars, and hotels. The following day, Bill sought out the media. He didn't wait for them to come to him.

The family garnered newspaper, radio, and television coverage—every willing and interested media outlet they could find. A week later, the story went national. Back in Wisconsin, older son Chris worked the phones, calling all of Matt's friends, acquaintances, and coworkers, hoping they could shed some light on Matt's disappearance. There were no leads.

At the scene in East Dubuque and its sister city, Bill and Ellen continued to work their contacts. Not all attempts to drum up interest in Matt's case were successful. The Coast Guard, with its vast search capabilities, didn't respond to Bill's requests for search assistance.

"I knew by then if he wasn't somewhere alive, he was in the river. It was a recovery situation," he says.

Search dogs were brought into the area. Authorities dragged the river but couldn't search it without a special type of sonar. Bill found a team with that sonar capability. After several days exploring the area, all the team located were a few abandoned, submerged cars and a lot of trash.

Witnesses—about fifty of them—gave statements that Matt was tossed out on the street in the dead of winter without his coat or anything to keep him warm. More than one hundred volunteers completed a grid search, covering every square inch of ground they could in the two weeks following Matt's disappearance. Still, they could not find Matt.

The Kruzikis checked Matt's cell phone records and found 988 phone calls within a six-week period.

"It was then we realized just how many people he knew, how many friends he really had," Bill says.

Witnesses vanished, running rather than talking to investigators. A $25,000 reward was posted. The family and their friends put out the word everywhere they could. They contacted John Walsh's show, *America's Most Wanted*. Despite their efforts, nothing happened for a frustrating three months. The case went cold at the beginning of March.

Then, on March 18, the wait was over as abruptly as it began. Matt's body was found five miles downriver, spotted by an airplane flying over a spot with the ironic name of "Dead Man's Slough." Search-and-rescue teams had to break the ice to pull him out.

Bill and the rest of his family had to take what little comfort they could in the fact that they had Matt's body—they could at least put him to rest. But what they couldn't put to rest was what had happened to this bright, energetic, and popular kid, someone who was starting what would have been a good and productive life.

Matt's blood alcohol level of .11 (most states consider .08 too drunk to drive) revealed that he had indeed been intoxicated at the time he was thrown out onto the streets of East Dubuque to fend for himself. But his alcohol level, while indicating he was legally intoxicated, wasn't that alarming in a healthy young male who had been drinking all evening.

Matt's death is still an open investigation and that, says Bill, is a "double-edged sword," because as long as the case remains unresolved—neither a homicide nor an accident—the case file is closed to Bill. The police department is steadfast in its refusal to share any of the reports with the Kruzikis. Unless the case is inactivated, Bill will never know what, if anything, the police unearthed in their investigation.

———❦———

Gone was the boy who knew everything there was to know about sports. Matt could rattle off statistics about football players and games with the same ease as he could summon batting averages for baseball players. His father characterized Matt's mind as a "steel trap" and says his second love was music.

"He played guitar and sang, though [he didn't sing] very well," Bill remembers.

Chris, who was close to his brother, shared Matt's enthusiasm for sports. A high school wrestler, Chris also started college but did not graduate. He saw his friends move on with their lives while he tried to find his own path to adulthood. Matt's death hit Chris hard; he got a job in the mortgage industry that he liked and at which he excelled, but that was doomed when the industry collapsed. His job was downsized, and Chris was left with too much time to contemplate the loss of his brother and where he was in life.

Both boys had good social lives—the usual girlfriends, buddies, and coworkers. But the most telling relationship they had was with one another. Two years apart, Matt had long been Chris's shadow, as well as an individual in his own right. When people thought about Matt, their first thought was how kind and compassionate he was, how caring. And brother Chris, people said, was such a nice guy. Who didn't love them both?

Unemployed and down, Chris battled depression rooted in his self-perceived failure to go with his brother to pick up his car. He blamed himself for Matt's death, and it continued to eat at him, growing worse when he lost his job and had nothing but time on his hands. Right or not, Chris, his father says, "took full responsibility" for what happened to Matt.

On October 23, 2007, almost two years after Matt died, "Chris took his own life because he felt he let his brother and his family down," according to Bill.

Chris was twenty-seven and Bill's only living child.

———✸———

Having a loved one disappear brought Bill Kruziki full circle. He experienced a missing persons investigation from the viewpoint of both investigator and family member, and that mixture of professional and personal involvement did something else, too: it jolted him into recognizing the effect his cop approach to missing persons investigations had on the families of those who disappear.

"You have no idea how devastating this is to a family. Law enforcement is the first line of help. [Family members] have no place else to go," Bill says.

By tradition, law enforcement is trained to share little information with those involved in a case. It is a good tactic in most investigations because there is little to be gained by disclosing leads, suspects, or other investigational information. Additionally, what investigators learn and record in their notes can often be misleading. Police play their cards close to their chests for several reasons:

- Authorities don't want the general public learning information that could harm, impede, or prejudice an investigation. Premature release of information can have drastic consequences, particularly if it makes its way into the media. Suspects can flee or destroy evidence, alibis can be established, and the memories of witnesses can be tainted. One famous example of a case bungled in many ways, including information leaks that sparked sensationalism and provided a springboard for rampant speculation, is the still-unsolved murder of JonBenet Ramsey. JonBenet, the six-year-old daughter of a prosperous Boulder, Colorado, couple, was found dead in the basement of the family home on December 26, 1997. The child had been bound with duct tape and strangled with a garrote. Other evidence discovered at the scene, including a ransom note, and information that the family was the focus of the investigation was leaked along with many other critical crime scene details. As a result of the leaks (as well as the poor handling of the investigation), intimate facts surrounding the case were made public. There is no doubt that release of this information has impeded the progress of the case.
- Police want to avoid public speculation initiated by the news media. Press coverage played a significant role in guiding public opinion in the Ramsey case. Another example of viral press coverage took place in connection with the 2009 murder of Yale student Annie Le. In Le's case, some media outlets ran with unsubstantiated reports that the Yale employee accused of killing her tried to conceal her body by breaking her bones in order to force it into a very small enclosure. Although investigators who were working on the Le disappearance and murder denied those stories, the situation proved painful for her family and friends. In an ultra-competitive atmosphere, media outlets race to zero in on the most titillating details. Many officers consider the feelings of family members and won't relay those details to anyone—including the family.
- Police want to protect the family from the needless heartache and pain that certain types of information can induce. Disappearances and the facts surrounding them can often lead police into some horrifying and very dark places. Stranger abductions of children routinely involve the investigation of known and possible pedophiles: information police hesitate to share with families because the details are often so terrible. Most cops err on the side of caution when it comes to exposing families to such heinous possibilities.
- Police want to control the investigation. When sharing details, especially unsubstantiated leads, authorities run the risk of interested parties taking more active roles than perhaps they should. Police understand the frustrations of families wishing to see things happen in what can

often seem like an agonizing process, but they also don't want the investigation to grow out of control. There is always a chance information in the wrong hands could turn a bad situation into a tragedy.

• Police want to hold back certain information. It is standard procedure for police to withhold from release some details concerning the crime in order to help identify the perpetrator. A suspect with knowledge of the aspects of a case that only the guilty party or someone associated with the guilty party could know is that much closer to being convicted in court.

And that leads to this last point: police want to build a solid case in court. It is hard for families to understand that while officers are searching for their loved one, they must also control a case's trial integrity. Police have hard-and-fast rules they must play by, and the courts are mostly unforgiving when those rules are broken. Police are also often vilified in the press when they have bungled an investigation, so they're sensitive in most instances to the possibility of losing a case or key evidence. They have one chance to get it right. There are no do-overs in police work.

—❧—

Bill Kruziki knows all of this and he knows it well because he has handled plenty of missing persons cases himself. In his more than thirty-three years in law enforcement, he has had much experience with the investigation and coordination of investigations of missing children and adults. "As a former line officer and . . . law enforcement CEO, I have had to deal with the emotional stress from the families who frantically wanted their loved ones found safe and soon," Bill says. "As any experienced officer [who has been involved in] this kind of investigation, we have been trained to keep all information 'close to the vest' and share very little detail with the media and family. I followed this train of thought for many years until that early morning on Christmas Eve when Matt vanished."

Even though Bill understands that police still need to keep some details about the investigation to themselves, in the days since his son vanished and his disappearance turned to tragedy, Bill has become a passionate advocate for making as much information available to the families of the missing as is feasible. He says turning the tables changes the equation on every level.

"Family members must know that the police are going to be responsive, have empathy, and most importantly . . . not keep information from the family that may help them more readily understand where the investigation is going and what the police are going to do to find their loved one," he says.

He wants law enforcement to update the family regarding information gleaned from interviews with persons of interest.

"Even if the information is basic or of no use, the family needs to hear and know that the police are actively working to resolve this case," he says.

Bill points out that in most jurisdictions, missing persons cases receive low priority. An already-stretched-thin blue line must work homicides, robberies, rapes, assaults, and other crimes that count toward their annual Unified Crime Reporting (UCR) statistics, which is a federal accountability program that measures the national and local crime rates. In addition to working criminal cases, police also deal with traffic issues and crime prevention, subjects that resonate with their constituents.

Although the number of persons reported missing and entered into the system each year is staggering, most are found and the cases cleared. What changes that numbers game is the missing persons—adults and runaways for the most part—who are either not reported at all or for whom police refuse to take reports. No one knows how many people are missing and unaccounted for in an official capacity because no records are made or kept, but it is estimated that the numbers run into the thousands each year.

While missing children always bring out the neighborhood, missing adults, without clear-cut evidence of foul play, remain a low and sometimes nonexistent priority for police agencies.

"Unfortunately, many police are not trained properly or at all to deal with this type of incident," says Bill.

He calls on department heads—chiefs of police and sheriffs—to do some soul-searching and think about what time, resources, staff, and budget dollars they would expend if a family reported that their adult son or daughter had not been in contact with them for more than twenty-four hours.

"My bet is that most of you, depending on the circumstances, would tell the family that he or she is an adult and is free to do what they please and there is no current law against it," he says.

Families, as he points out, do not care about budgets and personnel, because they don't understand that point of view. They are about one thing: finding their lost loved one. And because of this, the former marshal says, "it is the duty of the department head to ensure that the family is aware of what level the agency is going to investigate this missing persons case."

Bill wants law enforcement agencies to take it personally. He says investigators owe it to families to be as forthcoming as possible with them, including sharing information whenever possible. "If searches are planned, no matter how small, the family should be notified and given the opportunity to be present. If media contact is going to be initiated by police, meet with the family first to discuss information that will be provided to them so [that the families] do not learn something new about the investigation by reading the paper or watching television," he says.

He touches on a sore subject among many families of the missing: it is not unusual for families to find out about the progress of an investigation—or even that a body has been found or an arrest made—through the media, either by hearing it on television or from a media inquiry. No parent wants to receive a telephone call that an adult child has been found deceased—but it becomes even worse when that call comes from some local news reporter trying to make a deadline.

Bill reaches into his deep law enforcement background as well as his role as a bereaved father to recommend that law enforcement agencies implement a two-pronged approach to missing persons investigations. He says departments should first appoint an officer to act as the contact liaison with the agency, while families should do the same by designating a family contact person. That way, both news and questions can be passed along without duplication and with reduced confusion.

Although the amount of time and manpower a department can dedicate to a missing persons investigation varies from agency to agency, Bill urges agency heads to keep families in the loop and make certain that liaisons stay in regular contact with them. If, for example, an agency decides to suspend its search for an individual or the investigation into his or her disappearance, Bill says the family has a right to know this.

"Nothing is worse than thinking that the police are actively trying to investigate the incident and then learn . . . the case is dormant," he says.

He believes that although police must walk a fine line in deciding what to share and what not to share, it is important to make families feel they are part of the effort to find their loved one.

"My son was found drowned in the Mississippi River almost three months after he went missing. As a family, we have some resolution to at least have him back. Think of the helpless and desperate people who are missing an adult family member [and] are still waiting for answers," he says.

The Kruziki family still has many questions about Matt's death. They want to know why the individual who was with Matt on the night he died didn't leave the bar with him. Why, Bill asks, did the East Dubuque police officer who stopped Matt at 1:10 in the morning on a freezing night not at least go into the bar and get Matt his coat? Why was Matt allowed to wander, intoxicated and alone without proper clothing, in a town where he knew no one and was staying in a hotel miles across the river?

What happened to Matt? Bill believes Matt's death was most likely an accident, but he would like to see what investigators turned up in his son's case. The only way he can do that is to allow the case to be closed, and that would mean the investigation would stop.

For Bill, it's a double-edged sword: neither option will bring him peace.

· 3 ·

The Police: A Report Card on Police and Missing Persons Cases

Any community's arm of force—military, police, security—
needs people in it who can do necessary evil, and yet not be
made evil by it.—Lois McMaster Bujold, *Barrayar*

$\mathscr{T}$ime chips away at promising leads and makes important information seem less significant. When too much time passes, witnesses no longer recall facts with the same clarity or detail. Notes get shuffled, lost, or misfiled. Old handwriting fades, pictures grow fuzzy and less defined, and people move on with their lives. Cases that remain unsolved grow cold.

Cold cases are difficult to work and even more difficult to crack. Resolving them requires skill, patience, and a big helping of luck. Some detectives don't have what it takes to work cold cases; others find they're good at digging up answers from the past.

In Rutherford County, Tennessee, Lieutenant Bill Sharp of the Rutherford Sheriff's Department Cold Case Squad and his partner, Sergeant Dan Goodwin, excel at cold case work. They thumb through the dusty, tattered files and boxes of evidence compiled in the twenty-odd cases assigned to their unit. Among those were the abductions of two small children: Bobby and Christi Baskin. The Baskin siblings were believed to have been taken by their grandparents, Marvin and Sandra Maple, when the kids were seven and eight years of age. Bobby and Christi disappeared on March 1, 1989, moments before a hearing ordered them returned to their natural parents.

The siblings were removed from their parents' home after the Maples accused them of sexually abusing the children. A subsequent investigation found the allegations to be false. Authorities say the Maples absconded with the two older kids, but left a third, younger child, Michael, behind with Mark and Debbie Baskin.

29

"You're saying they're doing terrible things to the kids, but why wouldn't you take the youngest kid, who was the most vulnerable? It makes no sense," notes Sharp.

Doctors and psychiatrists examined the children and found no signs of abuse. When the pair failed to show up in court, investigators launched an immediate search for them, but the trail withered and died. Soon the case was shelved for lack of viable leads.

Criminal investigators at the Rutherford County Sheriff's Office, like many law enforcement officers in rural areas, have impossible caseloads. It's not uncommon for a detective to carry 150 cases ranging from vandalism to homicide. Once the Baskin matter grew cold, the abductions were moved back in priority. Still, detectives would pull the file every once in a while and look for new leads, drum up a little press, and touch base with Mark and Debbie, who held out hope they would see their children again.

They had reason to hope. Occasional press coverage would yield a few tips, all of which were followed up by RCSO investigators. None brought home the gold, though.

Then the Baskin case was assigned to Bill Sharp and Dan Goodwin. Sharp has worked for the sheriff's office since 1993. With headquarters in the county seat of Murfreesboro, the RCSO is the fifth-largest jurisdiction in the Volunteer State. It lies southeast of Nashville.

The lieutenant's voice is soft and polite, laced with the distinctive twang of his home state. Sharp says he and Goodwin were transferred from criminal investigations and put into cold cases to work homicides, but his captain had investigated the Baskin abductions when they first occurred and asked them to take another look. They did.

They worked the case like it had just happened, interviewing the original detectives and following up on telephone numbers and leads. When a tip from a woman who recognized the children from age-progressed photos hit their desk, Sharp and Goodwin chased it and found the Baskin children, now grown, in San Jose, California. Sharp was overjoyed to tell Mark and Debbie that after two decades, their missing kids had been located safe and alive.

"They're fantastic people. I don't know that I could have handled the situation as well as they did," says Sharp.

But Bobby and Christi were no longer the same children raised by the Tennessee minister and his wife. They were grown-ups who called the Maples "mom" and "dad." And they no longer answered to Bobby and Christi; instead they went by the names Jennifer and Jonathan Bunting.

Debbie Baskin didn't care. She did what any mother who has not seen her children for twenty years would have done and hopped onto a plane for California. But this tale of two little kids taken from their parents was not resolved as well as Sharp and Goodwin had hoped: the kids—now adults—were shocked by the story told by investigators and—at least so far—have decided they want nothing to do with their biological parents. It was a tough blow for both investigators, who wanted so much for this story to have a happy ending, and for the Baskins, who spent a large part of their lives searching for their children.

"[Bobby and Christi] have access to the investigation; it's open records now, [so] they can look and see what was done. I can't believe intelligent young adults don't want to know," Sharp says.

As for Mark and Debbie, Sharp says it's been hard knowing their children are so close, yet still so far away.

"It's difficult on them. I just can't put it into words—the sorrow, the hurt, the anger—all the range of emotions they went through," he says.

Sharp says Marvin Maple exhibited no remorse when detectives interviewed him, telling them, "I raised the kids the way I wanted to. I won." Marvin Maple was charged in the case and is still awaiting trial as of this writing. Sandra Maple died before the children were found.

Despite this, the Baskins still have hope, Sharp says. They believe they'll be reunited with their children and although the family dynamics have changed, they will adjust to their new reality.

For the cop who has come to know the family and their heartache, it's a bittersweet ending at best. Solving the case is what a police officer does. Nourishing the hope it will end well is the human part of the equation.

———⟨∞⟩———

Drew Kesse's voice still retains a touch of Jersey edge. Kesse and his wife, Joyce, are longtime Florida residents now, but they maintain with pride their distinct Yankee attitudes. They also refuse to be pushed around. But as tough and uncompromising as he is, Drew's words sometimes falter as he talks about his lost daughter—blond, beautiful Jennifer—and what he sees as the failure of police to move forward on her case.

Jennifer Kesse disappeared on January 24, 2006. Smart and popular in high school, Jennifer moved without effort into college life at the University of Central Florida in Orlando, studying to be a doctor. She decided medicine wasn't her field and changed her mind, graduating with a degree in business.

Jennifer loved Orlando and wanted to stay there, so she found a good job as a financial analyst, bought a condo, and maintained a serious long-distance relationship with a young man in Fort Lauderdale.

"It was pretty much who was going to crack and give up their job [first]," says Drew.

Jennifer Kesse. Courtesy of the Kesse Family.

Jennifer was smart and happy—so happy her father says the family had a hard time finding a photo of her where she wasn't smiling. They needed it for the flyers they distributed when Jennifer vanished.

Jennifer had returned from a short Caribbean vacation with her boyfriend. The two spoke the night of January 23; they made a habit of talking every morning and again at night before they retired. She also telephoned her family every day. On the following morning, her boyfriend says they did not speak, and Jennifer failed to show up for work. It was so out of character for her to not call in that her employer contacted her family, who lives in Tampa. The family tried to reach Jennifer and, failing that, left for Orlando.

"Jennifer is very responsible. If she is going to be five minutes late, she will call," says Drew.

They first checked Jennifer's condominium and found that she had slept there and taken a shower earlier that morning. There were clothes laid out on the bed and other signs that she planned to go to work. Under normal circumstances Jennifer left for work between 7:30 and 7:45 in the morning, but no witnesses reported seeing her. They called the jails. They called the hospitals. They called the police.

The first contact they had with the police came in the form of the officer who took the initial report. Drew says, "He said she probably had a fight with her boyfriend; then he chuckled and walked out. He gave us a two-page incident report."

Their son, Logan, Jennifer's younger brother, "slammed on doors" at the condo complex, looking for clues as to what had happened to his sister. No one admitted to anything. By that afternoon, the family was putting flyers on cars.

Unhappy with the response of the first officer, Drew made some phone calls until two homicide investigators showed up at eight that night. He says the investigators did little to allay their unhappiness.

"We're pro law enforcement, but [police] need to be better at what they are supposed to be doing," Drew says. He adds that not all of the officers with whom they dealt were insensitive, but in the beginning some were.

On Thursday, January 26, Jennifer's car was found abandoned in a parking lot a little over a mile from her condominium complex. Old, grainy tapes showed a man parking the car and then walking away. Because the quality of the tape is poor and there is a barrier in front of the man, it has been impossible to identify him, even after using sophisticated enhancement techniques.

They searched surrounding fields using volunteers—something that Drew says he now regrets. Unprepared for the reality of dealing with their daughter's disappearance, the Kesses had no idea that using unqualified search-and-rescue personnel could destroy evidence.

"We've made the mistake of having fourteen hundred people trample a field. At the time that's what you think is needed: find the areas where she was, which you do, but you do it in the wrong way. And someone teaches you the right way and you think, 'Oh, God, what did we do?'" Drew says.

He says families depend on police to guide them. "The first two cops thought they'd find Jennifer in two or three days, dead, and it turned out to be a different situation," he says.

After her car was found, he says one investigator told him, "If you don't find her this hunting season, you'll find her by next year." The family engaged the media. They've appeared on *America's Most Wanted* and many other shows, always advocating for Jennifer. They believe it's essential to keep her before the public.

"We've been on every show known to mankind, except *Dr. Phil* and *Oprah*. When her story goes away, then that's it," Drew says.

Drew admits he is obsessed with finding his daughter and believes she was kidnapped and trafficked. He says no trace has ever been found of Jennifer—not even a rumor. And her bank account and credit cards remain untouched.

Her car was processed and one unidentified latent print was found. But finding a latent fingerprint is of no value unless there is another one on file somewhere for comparison. This one has not yet been matched.

Leads poured in—more than eleven hundred calls were received—and none panned out. The Kesses turned up the heat at the police department. They say they had been meeting with the police chief on a regular basis when one day she told them that the detective assigned to the case was being removed. The relationship with the Orlando Police ended on a sour note for the Kesses.

Drew is bitter. He says no one at the department would return his calls. He says the police made mistakes that "could not be undone," mistakes he believes could have cost both time and information.

He admits that many of the officers they met during this ordeal were good, hardworking police who did everything right. His bitterness is for the things that were not done well and his feeling that his daughter's case was kicked to the curb.

Drew Kesse is not an easy person to be around. He demands attention and is prepared to go to any length required to get it. When he's stymied in court by a prohibitive law, he presses his state legislature to change that law. He's been successful.

Some find it uncomfortable to be around Drew. Hurt flows from him like a river. He's drowning in it. He says, in fact, his whole family is drowning.

"We are a house of broken dreams," he says.

The FBI now has the case. Drew says they told him they would find his daughter. As for the police, he believes they were well intentioned and, "except for that first week, everybody has been on the same page for four years."

Drew says the biggest problem he sees with police and missing persons cases is the lack of training. "Homicide detectives should not be working missing persons cases," he says.

And he thinks the mistakes made in the case have cost them: Drew says Jennifer's dental records and other vital information have been misplaced, and she was not entered into all available databases at the beginning of the investigation.

Drew now works with families of the missing, helping them avoid the missteps that took place in his daughter's case. It's rewarding, but not a job he wishes on anyone.

"You're only as good as your first responder. Police really need sensitivity training," he says.

If anyone can empathize with Drew, it's Abby Potash, the program manager for Team Hope (www.teamhope.org), a volunteer arm of the National Center for Exploited and Missing Children (NCMEC): her ten-year-old son, Sam, was abducted by his father in July 1997.

Sam's father was supposed to drop the boy off at camp in New Jersey. Instead, the two lived for months on the run, and Sam would learn to call himself "Ben." They ended up in Texas.

Abby discovered Sam was missing when she went to pick him up at camp. "He wasn't there. The first thing I thought was that he'd had an accident," she says.

Soon it became apparent that Sam was still with his father, who relatives later told her had been acting strangely. Friends and family suggested she call the police, which she did. Soon she felt like a ping-pong ball.

"I called the police in the town where I lived and they couldn't take the report. They told me to call the town in which Sam's father lived. I did. They said it wasn't their jurisdiction and they couldn't take the report, either. Finally, the police in my town agreed to take it," says Abby.

Abby checked her ex-husband's apartment and found "everything gone but the garbage." And even though she knew her son had been abducted, she still had to battle the criminal justice system.

"The prosecutor thought it was okay because he was with his father. I had to convince him this was a crime," she says.

Victim's assistance had no idea how to help her, so Abby had to help herself. She had an old computer and searched the Web looking for help. And she set up her own site, www.findsam.com, which pulled in three hundred thousand hits.

"The computer felt like my umbilical cord," Abby says.

She says she ran into closed doors everywhere, even with the media. "They'd say, 'Write something up and we'll see what we can do.' They'd say, 'If I help you, I'll have to help everyone.'"

She was not sleeping or eating and her life was falling apart. "The walls kept coming down in front of me."

Abby was in need of some emotional assistance, but no one—least of all the law enforcement officers with whom she was dealing—knew how to give it to her.

Duane Bowers, a therapist, educator, and author, says what Abby needed was someone trained to deal with events like Sam's abduction.

"She's second-guessing herself all the way down the line. She needs to think the community is supporting her," Bowers says.

Bowers and Potash now team up to educate law enforcement and other first responders about how to approach families in crisis mode. They are interested in helping individuals deal with the discovery that a loved one is missing, as in Abby's case.

Bowers points out that police first responders most often deal with something that has already transpired. A homicide, while terrible, is over when they make contact with the victim's family. A missing persons case is active. "The trauma is still going on and you're still in it; it's still happening," he says.

Bowers says the victim's family is going to feel overwhelmed and sometimes without hope. It is up to the officer to be reassuring yet at the same time realistic.

Police need to build bridges with the families of the missing, and when that doesn't happen, sometimes the families need to be the ones who make the first move. Abby says she dropped by the police department one day and heard a couple of investigators talking about how everyone dumped on them.

"I started bringing them food. I wanted them to want me to come to the station," she says.

Abby and Sam's ordeal has a happy ending: he was found and returned to his mother on March 29, 1998, after a woman recognized his image from a picture postcard distributed around the country.

Abby knows that when it comes to the police, the street runs both ways. They are not often thanked for what they do. "I always call them on the anniversary of Sam's recovery each year," she says.

———❧———

Angela is one of those girls who attracts attention: the brunette stands a willowy five feet, seven inches tall, but it's her smoky hazel eyes that grab the viewer and make it hard to look away. Being sexy is a good thing if you live in Las Vegas.

Angela worked in Vegas as the head cage cashier at the Monte Carlo. She had a good work history with the club and a great relationship with her family. Then, without warning, things changed. Angela Marie Finger from Salem, Oregon, began dressing and acting like a stranger. It all started, her mom, Michelle Finger, says, when she met a man on the Internet who called himself Craig.

"She was dressing more seductively and acting rude to us. It was uncharacteristic," says Michelle.

But Angela's behavioral changes would become even more radical. She quit her job and moved in with Craig. Her parents didn't trust him, and the more they pushed Angela for answers, the more she in turn pushed them away. Michelle argued with her daughter and Angela either disconnected or changed her phone number. Now, Michelle could neither find nor reach her.

Michelle suffered a heart attack. After she recovered, she says, all she could think about was reconciling with her daughter. She began looking for Angela, but every lead turned cold, and by this point, Michelle had grown suspicious of Craig.

As it turned out, she had good reason to suspect Angela's new boyfriend. She says after she posted on classmates.com and made a MySpace page using Craig's assumed name, the real Craig contacted her. He told Michelle that the man impersonating him was William Matthew Smolich, a former classmate.

Researching Smolich on the Internet, Michelle found something that disturbed her even more: pornographic Web sites that appeared to be Smolich's, featuring nude photographs of Angela.

"My daughter was very modest and dressed very conservative before she met him," Michelle says.

But that wasn't the only thing giving Michelle pause. She also discovered that Smolich is a man with a dark and disturbing legal history: he is wanted by the Boulder, Colorado, sheriff's department on charges of attempted sexual assault on a child and nonconsensual sexual contact.

Michelle tracked Angela down through the Web sites. When she called Angela, she says Smolich answered and put her daughter on the phone. Michelle told her what she had found out about the man and within thirty seconds the phone went dead. She called back and the call went straight to voice mail. It was the last time she or anyone she knows had any contact with her daughter.

Michelle says one police officer told her that if she was going to pursue the case on her own, then he wasn't going to waste his own time. When police showed up at the residence Smolich was sharing with Angela, they found the place had been deserted: all of Angela's stuff was still there, even her kitten. A stakeout of the place revealed the couple was not coming back. Michelle is heartbroken that her daughter has disappeared from her life. She fears the worst.

"It is like she has fallen off the face of the earth. Another birthday, another Christmas, another New Year's without her. We are heartsick," she says.

The Finger family has been unhappy with law enforcement's response. They have dealt with several levels of bureaucracy, from local to federal, and with agencies from several different states. Many times it is this mix of agencies that frustrates families.

When David Potts of Florissant, Missouri, went missing, his parents also found themselves dealing with more than one police agency. The experience has left them perplexed, upset, and feeling as though they've been given the runaround.

Robin Potts says her family's nightmare started when a then twenty-one-year-old David went out with a friend on October 28, 2006. The two men had left a club and were traveling along Highway 70 in St. Ann, Missouri, when an officer spotted the car and ordered the driver to pull over. Instead, a high-speed pursuit ensued.

The Missouri State Highway Patrol joined the chase. When they hit a bridge, they say David jumped out of the car and ran. Officers chased him and one said he jumped over the railing. No one knows if he landed on the catwalk below or fell into the water.

His family had no idea that David had vanished until October 30, when he failed to show up for work. On October 31, they contacted St. Ann's police department and were told that David was considered a fugitive rather than a missing person. Robin asked that an officer contact her. No one did.

Frustrated, Robin called back the next day and was told that her son was "wanted," not missing, and that the officer involved in the pursuit would contact her.

"No one has ever called me," says Robin almost four years later.

Robin reported her son missing to the St. Louis County Police later that same day. On November 2, she says they asked the St. Ann police to launch a search for their son but never heard back. With assistance from the Shawn Hornbeck Foundation (www.shawnhornbeckfoundation.com), the Potts family and volunteers, along with the Missouri Water Patrol, searched the banks of the Missouri River, as well as the water. Robin says the river was dragged, but nothing—not even a footprint—was found.

Today, the Potts family worries and wonders what happened that night. They remain unimpressed by the efforts of law enforcement agencies.

For every family like the Potts or the Fingers who comes away from their experience with little faith in their police, there are those who report better rapport. Christy Davis says that although her son remains missing, she believes the police are sincere in their efforts to locate him.

Austin Davis was born on April 24, 1981, and disappeared on June 26, 2007, in Jacksonville, Florida. His dimpled smile, which gives him an almost cherubic appearance, did not reflect his frame of mind when he disappeared, according to his mom. Christy says that before he vanished Austin had suffered some personal difficulties that "left him depressed and looking for direction."

On the last day Austin was known to be in Jacksonville, he asked his boss for a day off and was approved for leave on June 25. But on June 26, his employer reported that he did not show up for work nor did he call in. All attempts to reach Austin proved unsuccessful.

His family was notified and they called the police. Christy says, "We were fortunate in that law enforcement was very responsive."

An investigation revealed that Austin had gone to a local Walmart, purchased shells for a shotgun, and then walked to a pawnshop, where he bought the shotgun itself. Austin was last seen walking down the street with the shotgun's muzzle protruding from a duffle bag he carried. An inspection of his apartment revealed that he left his backpack and laptop computer behind, something Christy says is out of character for her son.

"He didn't go anywhere without taking those things," she says.

Years have now passed and no sign of Austin has ever been found. Christy says his last paycheck was neither collected nor cashed. The family fears the worst, but also hopes for the best. They want Austin to come home and have tried to keep his name in the news. Christy says an encounter with someone who told her that Austin's story was "boring" made her realize that not all missing persons are equal.

"What about all those families that have a story to tell that may not be interesting to anyone but their family, the stories that don't get you on the edge of your seat . . . aren't these 'lost' stories just as important?" she asks.

Christy rates law enforcement as more responsive than the media in her son's case, although she believes they should have shared more of the investigative details with the family.

"Our law enforcement experience is so much better than many stories I've heard from other families of missing persons where sometimes the family couldn't even get [them] to take a report, but even so after an interview with the detective assigned to our case, he told me that their resources are limited and . . . the family would have to take up the slack," she says.

The Davis family has been searching for Austin since June 26, 2007. Christy says they won't stop looking until they find him.

———∞∞———

Two and a half decades ago, the Diaz family experienced the loss of their son and brother, Carlos. His disappearance has led them through a bitter lesson in the workings of bureaucracy.

Brooklyn born and raised, Carlos was thirty-two at the time he vanished. The beloved family dog had died in his arms. Carlos left the house with the dog's body, telling his family he would bury her. When he walked out the door, he also walked out of their lives. He has not been seen since.

Carlos was struck in the head some time before his disappearance and doctors warned he could suffer from memory loss at some point. He had no identification on him at the time he vanished, says his family, who worries that he could have become disoriented and not have known who he was or where he belonged.

His sister, Nancy Freneire, says when they tried to report him missing, the police told them that because Carlos was between sixteen and fifty-five, there was no crime involved; thus they would not take a report.

"My sister and mother were baffled upon learning that such a rule existed," says Nancy.

Nancy says that the lack of documentation has meant that the media has not taken them seriously. "Every attempt to search for my brother has been denied because we do not have a missing persons report," she says.

After years of battling the system, Nancy was able to get her own DNA into the national database so that it can be compared against unidentified remains. And the family continues its struggle to bring attention to their plight.

"I know there is a light at the end of this tunnel," she says. Until it shines on the Diaz family, they will keep searching for Carlos.

For many decades the plight of missing adults was shrugged off both by police and the legal system. In many cases, police refused to take reports because neither law nor internal police procedures compelled them to do so. Or they fell back on the old "forty-eight hour rule" (or twenty-four, depending on the jurisdiction), which, in essence, says that a person must be missing for the allotted amount of time before they'll take a report.

Although law enforcement acknowledges that there are problems in waiting two days to begin a missing persons investigation, many agencies still resist taking a report on a missing adult. Some of this resistance comes from tradition—there is no law preventing an adult from disappearing and not telling anyone. Other agencies have too few officers to work cases without definitive indications that the adult is either endangered or has been the victim of foul play; there is also the lack of agency policy or trained personnel to conduct these investigations.

Although his primary focus is juvenile justice, Ron Laney, associate administrator of the Child Protection Division of the Office of Juvenile Justice and Delinquency Prevention, could be speaking for all missing persons cases when he talks about how fast an agency should implement an investigation.

"What do you mean by immediate? Start right now," Laney said in an address during Fox Valley Technical College's annual conference, "Responding to Missing and Unidentified Persons" (see chapter 11).

Laney says when he hears an officer say, "Here in my jurisdiction, I don't have any missing kids," his response is that they're not looking hard enough. There are kids—and adults—who go missing all of the time. Many turn up, but for some families the agony seems never-ending.

Wayne Sheppard, associate director of training and outreach for the National Center for Missing and Exploited Children (NCMEC), says agencies and organizations must work together to improve police response. He points to the 2004 abduction and murder of eleven-year-old Carlie Bruscia as a good example of an investigation that could have gone better.

The judicial system was second-guessed when it came to light that the killer, Joseph P. Smith, had been cited back to court by his probation officer for a violation and freed by the courts a month prior to Carlie's kidnapping and slaying. In the beginning, the Manatee County Sheriff's Department decided not to issue an Amber Alert because there were no witnesses to her abduction. That move brought a thunderstorm of criticism both from the media and others who pointed out that the possible advantages of issuing an alert far outweigh the small amount of time it takes to issue one.

Detractors also said that the department's initial focus on the girl's stepfather led them to ignore other possible scenarios, including stranger abduction. But in following the girl's trail—she was walking home from a sleepover—officers spotted a motion-activated security camera along her most probable route and contacted the building's owner to view the video. They didn't look at the film until eighteen hours after Carlie vanished, by which time she had already been raped and strangled.

They found footage of the missing girl being approached by a strange man who grabbed her by the arm and led her offscreen. The Manatee County Sheriff's Department issued an Amber Alert.

Smith would be apprehended based on tips that came into the department following the release of the video to the media. He directed authorities to a church parking lot near the site where he had hidden Carlie's body. Smith is awaiting execution on Florida's death row.

NCMEC's Sheppard says police responses to incidents like Carlie's must be timely, organized, and systematic. He recommends that departments train dispatchers to ask the right questions, including, "Where was the last known location of your child?" By asking the correct questions, police can jump-start an investigation.

Police need to have a written protocol on handling cases involving missing children and that protocol should involve the police command system.

"Supervisors need to be on the scene," says Sheppard.

But the two most important factors in working a case involving a missing child—or any missing person—says Sheppard, are a combination of strong policy and procedures within the department combined with excellent training and education for the officers.

—◦◦◦—

On March 2, 2007, a woman named Jessica Lenahan, formerly Gonzales, addressed the Inter-American Commission on Human Rights. This is the story she told them.

Jessica, a former resident of Castle Rock, Colorado, was separated from her husband, Simon Gonzales. The couple had three little girls together—Rebecca who was nine, Katheryn who was eight, and six-year-old Leslie.

Simon had in the past exhibited "erratic and abusive" behavior toward Jessica and their daughters. Jessica described a time when she had to call for help; she found Simon trying to hang himself in front of the girls. He broke the kids' toys, threatened to kidnap and hurt them, and also threatened Jessica with both physical harm and sexual abuse. She says Simon took drugs and his behavior escalated until she separated from him.

In May 1999, Jessica obtained a temporary restraining order, or TRO, forbidding Simon from going near Jessica, the girls, or their home. During that time, Simon violated the order on multiple occasions. On June 4, 1999, a judge declared the TRO permanent and outlined specific visitation for Simon.

In the early evening hours of June 22, Simon abducted the three girls as they played in their front yard. That started the following chain of events:

- As soon as she discovered the girls were missing, Jessica called the Castle Rock Police. A dispatcher told her she would send an officer to her home. No one came.
- After two hours, Jessica contacted the police department again. This time two officers were dispatched. She shared the restraining order with them and told them that she believed Simon had the girls. Jessica says one of the officers told her, "Well, he's their father. It's okay for them to be with him." The officers left and told her to call them back if her daughters weren't home by 10 p.m.
- Simon's girlfriend contacted Jessica and told her Simon was threatening to harm himself.
- At 8:30 p.m. Simon answered his cell phone in response to a call from Jessica and said that he had the girls at a Denver amusement park. Jessica asked the Castle Rock Police to contact the Denver Police but says they refused and advised her to take the matter to divorce court.

• Jessica continued to call the police. At 10 p.m. she says, the dispatcher told her she was being "a little ridiculous, making us freak out and thinking the kids are gone."

• At midnight Jessica went to Simon's apartment. Jessica again called police. It had been seven hours since her children disappeared. The dispatcher agreed to send an officer. No officer ever showed up.

• Jessica went to the police station and spoke to an officer. She says the officer left and went to dinner after their conversation.

• At 3:25 in the morning Jessica received another call from Simon's girlfriend who said that she'd heard the sounds of shots being fired while she was on the phone talking with Simon. Jessica drove to the police department where she discovered that Simon had opened fire on the police with a semi-automatic handgun he had bought the day before. Police killed him. In the back of his truck they found the bodies of Jessica's three daughters, murdered by Simon earlier in the day.

• Jessica was held and questioned about the incident for more than twelve hours. She was not informed that her girls were dead until 8:00 that morning.

• Jessica filed suit against the Castle Rock Police Department, charging that they failed to enforce the court's restraining order. The case made its way through the state court system and was considered by the U.S. Supreme Court. The Supreme Court determined that enforcement of a restraining order is not mandatory under Colorado law, and the case was dismissed. Jessica now speaks as a voice for women and children victimized by domestic violence.

The Honorable Mark McGinnis, a circuit court judge in Outagamie County, Wisconsin, uses Jessica's case to demonstrate the sobering consequences of the police's failure to act. But he also uses the case to illustrate how one of the greatest fears of police—that of civil liability—should be secondary in these instances. Police fear being dragged into court in a civil case, so they often choose the path they perceive as the least litigious. McGinnis says officers shouldn't worry about the possibility of being sued.

"You can err on the side of finding the kid," he tells a room full of police officers from around the country at Fox Valley Technical College's annual missing persons conference.

McGinnis ticks off various scenarios for the officers. The first: a young child is missing and the guy across the street is a known sex offender who refuses the police entry into his home. McGinnis asks them, "What do you do?"

"Get a search warrant!" say several officers.

"Watch the house and call for a supervisor!" says another.

A few say they would go into the home anyway. "Bingo," says the judge. Right answer.

"You don't have to establish exigent circumstances," says McGinnis. He says officers should tell kidnapping suspects, "'If you don't let me in, I'm coming in.' This is different than a drug case, different than a forgery case," he asserts.

Although the judge says the age of the missing person is a factor officers must take into consideration when conducting a search, an officer's actions should be dictated by the totality of the circumstances. And, he says, missing adults should not be treated as afterthoughts by departments.

An Illinois-based officer says, "People want to report adult children missing and we take the stance that because they're adults—they can get up and walk away."

A New Berlin, Wisconsin, officer answers him, "If someone's reporting that person missing, then there is reason to put some time into [the case]. Just because your child's twenty-five doesn't mean we shouldn't take a report. I don't think you can operate like that anymore."

Judge McGinnis agrees with the second officer. "There are missing adults who need help," he says.

A police chief comments, "You take a report for a missing car right away. Why not take a report for a missing person?"

McGinnis says officers who shrug off missing persons reports show a "lack of interest, lack of honesty, and lack of professionalism." According to McGinnis, "It gives the perception the officer doesn't know what he is doing. If your kid was missing, would you want someone to be dishonest with you?"

And, says McGinnis, officers should stop returning to the liability issue. "If you act aboveboard, you can win."

Mary Wegner's twenty-one-year-old daughter, Laurie Depies, vanished on August 19, 1992. She has neither been seen nor heard from since. An employee of a shop at the local mall, Laurie lived in the town of Menasha, Wisconsin. Menasha, a small slice of Americana with a population of more than seventeen thousand, sits about one hundred miles north of Milwaukee, and south of Green Bay, on the northwest shore of Lake Winnebago.

The Town of Menasha Police Department has worked Laurie's case since she was discovered missing. As time passes and officers retire, are promoted, or move on, the investigators change, but the central mission remains: find Laurie.

Detective Lieutenant Michael Krueger and Special Agent Kimberly Skorlinski, Division of Criminal Investigation, Wisconsin Department of Justice, want Laurie's family to know one thing: their child has not been forgotten.

Laurie was last seen leaving the Fox River Valley Mall in Appleton. Wearing a black sleeveless T-shirt, shorts, and black shoes, Laurie drove to the apartment complex where her boyfriend lived. It was sometime after 10:00 at night. Her boyfriend and two other people were waiting for her at his apartment complex. He told police that they heard her car pull up because the car had a loud muffler. They waited for Laurie to arrive at the apartment, and when she didn't, the boyfriend went to check on her.

He found her older gray Volkswagen Rabbit parked in the lot with a cup sitting on top containing a drink she purchased earlier in the day. Laurie's purse and bag remained untouched in the car.

There were no signs of force, no signs of a struggle. No one heard anything out of the ordinary. Police theorize that someone she knew approached Laurie and she voluntarily walked away.

Police did most things right. Although they initially didn't take the complaint as seriously as they should have, they launched a search. In order to preserve any evidence that might have been on or in Laurie's car, they transported it to the agency on a flatbed and processed it in an open bay of a fire engine stall—the most secure place available at the time.

They dusted for prints and checked the position of the seat, concluding that it was consistent with a driver of Laurie's size. Additional officers were called in and they checked the parties that had taken place in the neighborhood and began interviewing everyone they could find who either knew Laurie or had seen her.

They canvassed the neighborhood, then went back and canvassed parts of it again. They gave her mother a packet of information and when the time was right brought in the media. The chief provided regular updates.

It seemed that everyone wanted to help: the department was flooded with calls, about five hundred tips a week in the beginning. Detectives sifted through leads and everyone worked overtime.

They drew blood from the family in case it was needed for comparison. The investigators looked at the clientele of the store where Laurie worked, then checked into her finances and personal life. She had money problems—her father was paying off her credit card as a birthday gift and she had asked her landlady about rent payment options. Detectives also read her journals and diaries.

"We learned a lot about her," Krueger says.

Police don't believe that Laurie planned to disappear. She had made a down payment on a ring for her boyfriend. She showed no inclination toward suicide or a desire to escape from her circumstances.

Krueger and Skorlinski have looked at suspected serial killers and other criminals who were believed to be in the area at the time Laurie disappeared. Says Skorlinski, "We don't have that home run, that DNA, that sample yet."

They compared her disappearance with that of Josie Huisentruit (see chapter 10), who vanished from the parking lot of her Iowa apartment while leaving for work one morning. Huisentruit also has never been found.

The detectives consulted with numerous agencies, including the FBI, and they polygraphed a number of individuals. Construction sites, ditches, and vacant fields were searched, and data on traffic stops in the surrounding areas were pulled and analyzed. They entered Laurie in every possible database and kept the district attorney's office in the loop as they went along.

Investigators dug even deeper and asked the hard questions. Did Laurie have a secret life? If so, then they needed to know. They checked the status of old boyfriends and kept tabs on everyone involved in the case.

Although there were few victims' services available in 1992, the officers kept in touch with Mary. They say that whenever a body was discovered, they would try and beat the media to let her know. The investigators say the media was "constantly working against us."

But the media did keep her name in front of the community. And despite what Skorlinski terms "tons and tons and tons of newspaper articles," Laurie's disappearance continues to remain an enigma.

Krueger and Skorlinski continue to look for Laurie. Every once in a while some new lead pops up. Human remains are recovered. They try to inform Mary before she hears it on the news but admit that she often "beats us to the punch."

These law enforcement officers share the polygraph results and evidence with Mary and try to keep her in the loop. And, they say, they have learned from the mistakes they have made in this case.

"The complaint was not treated as serious; they didn't take a lot of photos," says Skorlinski in retrospect. And what is most puzzling about the case is that there were lots of witnesses in the area, but no one saw anything.

"We turned over everything in that apartment complex, and it doesn't make sense for this woman to disappear," says Skorlinski.

Ed Smart, father of Elizabeth Smart, who was kidnapped at the age of fourteen as she slept in her bedroom and later recovered alive, says, "Everyone deserves to have their child back."

Donna Jean Glasgow reminds the world that families of missing adults also deserve to have their loved ones back. Her brother, John Glasgow, vanished at the age of forty-five. John was a hardworking, conscientious, straight-arrow kind of guy who would never fall off the face of the earth, according to his family. At the time he disappeared, he was in a good marriage, was established, and had plenty of money in the bank. When his car was discovered abandoned in another county, the Glasgow family found themselves dealing with two different law enforcement agencies. Donna says neither has made it easy for them.

"The laissez-faire attitude that the Little Rock Police Department has taken about the case has been very frustrating to the family. Since the car was found in Conway County, the sheriff there also shares jurisdiction over the case. We, the family, have taken charge in many ways because law enforcement just wasn't interested in what they regarded [as] a simple missing persons case," says Donna.

Donna and the rest of the members of the large and close Glasgow family believe John was murdered, but says, "Law enforcement never seemed to be very suspicious at all, and his case never rose above that of a missing person."

When does a missing persons case take on urgency for an agency? Mistakes in past cases have resulted in new laws, as well as the overhaul and establishment of departmental rules and regulations that require an immediate response when a child disappears.

Child abduction response teams (CARTs) are also gaining ground. These teams provide multiagency responses in emergencies. Much like the task forces set up to handle disasters, CARTs work with centralized communications and coordinated search and rescue. They drill to keep themselves sharp and ready.

But when it comes to adults who are missing, the reaction often can be different from agency to agency. Parents of young adults who have gone missing have been instrumental in changing individual state laws in order to require an immediate report and investigation. Still, many believe their police are both apathetic and unsympathetic to their concerns.

Not all departments fall into that category. Some have special missing persons units. Many agencies, and in particular the ones that have attained accreditation, have general procedures for dealing with missing persons cases.

Jacksonville, North Carolina, sits on the state's coast. With three large military installations located within Onslow County, Jacksonville's officers stay busy.

Michael Yaniero serves the city as chief of police. A transplant from Johnson City, Tennessee, Yaniero continued and refined the policies of his predecessors by establishing a formal protocol for missing persons cases.

Jacksonville's policy is simple and to the point: When an adult goes missing, they take a report. Period. There's no lapse in time, no officer who says, "Wait and see if he comes home," no one to suggest that maybe the individual left of his or her own accord so he or she is not technically missing, even when that's a possibility. They take a report and they do it at the moment the person is reported missing. The first paragraph of that general order states:

A missing person report will be completed for any person adult [*sic*], whose last known location was in the City of Jacksonville, or whose temporary or permanent residence is the City of Jacksonville, or when the person's last location is unknown, or whose parent's, spouse's, guardian's or legal custodian's temporary or permanent residence is in the City of Jacksonville. When in doubt, the officer will take a report.

The general order also outlines who will conduct the initial investigation, what steps the officer must take—from obtaining a photograph to notifying his supervisor when the person is mentally or physically challenged, elderly, or despondent. It also delineates the dissemination of information throughout the department to other agencies and to databases, outlines the responsibility for searches, and covers moving the case along to an investigator, if indicated.

Yaniero's general order also provides guidance for officers who come into contact with someone who might have been reported missing. All in all, it's a comprehensive policy and, so far at least, it's worked well for Jacksonville.

The chief says his department handles an average of between fifty and sixty missing persons cases a year. Of those, the majority are runaways—a statistic that is in line with the rest of the country. Most of missing persons cases, Yaniero says, are resolved within a few days.

The chief believes it's important to have a written policy for dealing with missing persons: it helps the officer secure critical information and cuts down on the chance that something will be missed. But he also stresses that taking the initial report and following up are the right things to do.

"It doesn't matter [if the person has only been gone for] two hours," Yaniero says, adding that the old forty-eight hour rule would violate North Carolina's present statutes regarding adding a missing person to the national database.

"If someone's missing, that's a void that's in their life forever. If you're talking about moral obligations, I think our obligation as police officers to police the community is to focus on improving the quality of life, not just to arrest, not just to serve," he says.

Yaniero says simple compassion should guide officers. "People won't care about you unless we care about them."

One problem that holds back police investigations is when a missing persons case moves into another jurisdiction. Often the originating agency doesn't have the resources to pursue a missing person in other areas—particularly when a case that originates in one state moves to another. Under those circumstances, agencies must rely on the police in the other jurisdiction to follow up for them.

Another major challenge is financial. In the movies, DNA is tested and the results come back within hours. In real life, the process is expensive and it takes months to get an answer.

As for more training, Yaniero says he'd take it if it was available, but in most cases, it's not. "The resources just aren't there," he says.

In the meantime, his officers work under guidelines that dictate they take every missing persons case seriously. The best way to do that is for the officers to treat every family in a missing persons case the same way they'd want their own families treated.

"A lot of the time departments are judged by one person. While we do our best to select the best people for the [job], obviously we're still dealing with humans, and sometimes humans make bad decisions," Yaniero says.

• 4 •

Yesterday and Today: DNA, Dental Records, and Other Forensic Tools

Science is the search for truth—it is not a game in which one tries to beat his opponent, to do harm to others.—Nobel Prize winner Linus Pauling

YESTERDAY

This is what is known about the child without a name: he was somewhere between four and six years old, a little guy who weighed about thirty pounds—as much as any healthy two and a half year old. Found on a frigid, fading February day in 1957 on the trash-strewn side of Susquehanna Road in the Fox Chase section of Philadelphia, the child's body was stuffed in an old J. C. Penney bassinet box.

Bruised and malnourished, the little boy was naked, the nails on his fingers and toes clipped to the quick. His brownish blond hair was shaven to the scalp in places, gashed and uneven, as if the makeshift barber was in a hurry. Traces of the shorn hair still clung to his body. Investigators theorized that whoever cut it did so after the child's death, possibly to help conceal his identity. Seven scars, some consistent with medical treatment, were found on the body. His eyes were blue.

Stuffed into the box with the boy was the remnant of an old plaid blanket. The unrelenting cold weather helped preserve the boy's remains but made it tougher to pinpoint the hour—or day—he took his last breath. Estimates were that he died anywhere from two days to two weeks before his discovery.

Police photographed the child, who came to be known as the "Boy in the Box," and blanketed the Philadelphia area with flyers and posters. They checked bassinet sales and accounted for all but one purchased in the area.

They tracked the blanket and searched medical records in their quest to solve the riddle of the anonymous dead child.

Although detectives played out every lead, interviewing thousands in the decades since his body was found, the little boy remains without an identity. Many years after burial, authorities disinterred his body to extract material for DNA comparison, but decomposition made it impossible to obtain nuclear DNA. Instead, they settled for a sample of mitochondrial DNA, known as mtDNA.

And that microscopic bit of genetic material may one day be the key that unlocks this mystery.

TODAY

While the Boy in the Box waits patiently for a name, a second child—also abused, also abandoned—sleeps forever under another Philadelphia headstone.

Of African American descent, this child was believed to be about four years old. Wrapped in old bed sheets and a towel, then stuffed in a pastel green, pink, and blue nylon duffel bag, his nude, decomposed remains were tossed into a vacant lot under the Ben Franklin Bridge in Philadelphia.

The tiny boy's face was so beaten and decayed it was nearly impossible to make out his features. His remains weighed forty-one pounds, and at thirty-eight inches, he would have stood slightly over three feet tall.

The boy's body, abandoned in January 1994, remained under the bridge in his makeshift shroud until discovered by a passerby on May 27 of that year. By that time, snowstorms and the biting cold had yielded to spring thaws and waves of presummer heat.

An autopsy revealed the child was no stranger to frequent and vicious beatings. Old broken bones and healed wounds covered his body. The little boy's head and face told the story of his terrible, final moments: he had been beaten and killed with a blunt object.

The medical examiner preserved bits of tissue and other biological material from the tiny corpse. And from those bits, DNA was extracted.

DNA that helped unlock the mystery of the "Boy in the Bag."

———

To understand how DNA works in matching missing persons to unidentified remains, it is necessary to first understand a little about the nature of DNA or, as it's known by its full name, deoxyribonucleic acid. All DNA is not created equal. Normal human cells contain both the nuclear and mitochondrial DNA (mtDNA); however, each individual cell holds only one copy of the nuclear DNA, compared with up to one thousand copies of mtDNA.

Nuclear DNA is both much more fragile than mtDNA and also more useful because both biological parents pass along identifiable genetic material to the child through nuclear DNA. Mitochondrial DNA is different. The father's DNA is not present in a child's mtDNA. Children receive mtDNA only through their mothers; thus this type of DNA links only maternal relatives. Nuclear DNA can establish paternity, but mtDNA cannot; however, both types can establish maternity.

Like a fingerprint, though, DNA is only useful if there is something with which to compare it. That's a concept many misunderstand. Simply finding blood evidence or fingerprints at a scene isn't enough to solve a case, although their presence enhances the chances of a case's solvability. If a fingerprint is discovered at the scene of a crime, one must either have access to the person who made that fingerprint to compare those prints to the latent evidence, or one must have a fingerprint already on file in a searchable database, such as the Integrated Automated Fingerprint Identification System (IAFIS) maintained by the FBI.

As in fingerprint evidence, there also must be a record with which to compare DNA samples. In the case of a missing person, authorities often evaluate recovered DNA with that of a blood relative if a sample of the missing loved one's DNA is not available. To identify the Boy in the Box, authorities would need a maternal relative or sibling who shares the same mother, since only mtDNA was recovered. The father would not work.

In the United States, the DNA profiles of convicted offenders are stored in a large computer database accessible to law enforcement agencies. The database, which also contains DNA profiles obtained from crime scenes, is called the Combined DNA Index System, or CODIS, also maintained by the FBI. Thousands of matches, or "hits," have resulted from CODIS, enabling police to solve many crimes. Conversely, CODIS also exonerates the innocent.

In addition to CODIS and IAFIS, the FBI has a missing persons DNA database. This database is used to compare submitted DNA profiles (such as DNA taken from a body) against the DNA of missing persons whose DNA profiles are already in the system.

Once only possible in the imaginative realms of movies and television, DNA works real-world magic. First isolated in 1869 by a Swiss physician, the genetic material didn't receive much public attention until the 1950s, when its study launched the science of molecular biology. Back in the 1950s when the Boy in the Box was found, DNA was as mysterious as a black hole. But in 1993, just one year before the Boy in the Bag was found, DNA had become the impetus for novels and movie plots, like the late Michael Crichton's *Jurassic Park*. Today, DNA pops up all over the small screen, both from Jerry

Springer–type reality television shows to crime dramas, like *CSI: Crime Scene Investigation* and *NCIS*.

But investigators who work with the nameless dead know that reality and fiction rarely intersect. Death investigators know there is nothing noble, nice, or comforting about coming to a violent and lonely end. Since they can't stop what has already taken place, they instead do their jobs.

They start by putting a name to the victim. Sometimes that's easy: the victim is known, has identification, is recognizable, or matches a poster or an APB (all points bulletin). Other times, as in the case of the Boy in the Box, the body has been deliberately disguised, stripped of anything that identifies it, decomposed or skeletonized like the Boy in the Bag, is far, far from home, or has been dead for many years, leaving the trail cold and close to impossible to track.

Lou Eliopulos understands cases of unresolved identities. Throughout his more than thirty-year career, which has taken him from the Florida Medical Examiner's Office to his present position as chief of the Forensic Consultant Unit of the Naval Criminal Investigative Service (NCIS), Eliopulos has dealt with hundreds—maybe thousands—of unidentified bodies. He remembers well those unmatched to names, buried in lonely graves in strange places far from the people who loved them.

Author of *The Death Investigator's Handbook*, a well-regarded publication used by countless homicide investigators, Eliopulos says the longer a body goes unidentified, the greater the chances of the deceased being from another area—one reason it took so long to identify the Boy in the Bag, who, as it turned out, was not from Philadelphia.

"You can imagine the problems [we face] of people coming [to this country] as illegal immigrants and working on farms as seasonal labor," Eliopulos says. Add to that mix the runaways, the homeless, the mentally ill, and drifters, and our highly mobile population presents a real challenge for law enforcement.

But sometimes investigators get lucky, a family member's persistence pays off, or there's simply a break in a case. Then the unknown body becomes someone's missing sister or son or mother or husband.

And, in the case of the Boy in the Bag, he becomes a missing four-year-old named Jerell Willis.

Prior to DNA turning into the gold standard for identification, investigators often relied on the science of forensic odontology, also known as forensic dentistry. This is not to imply forensic dentistry is outdated or no longer effective. Quite the contrary: forensic dentistry continues to be one of the most important tools for matching the missing to their identities. Until DNA matching became practical for criminal justice purposes, forensic dentistry was an investigator's best chance of identifying unknown recovered remains. That's because teeth, like fingerprints, are unique. No one shares the exact same pattern of dental work, wear, growth, decay, and distribution. Since the United States has a large and comprehensive system of dental records, they are often used to identify unknown bodies.

It isn't really a modern science, though. Forensic dentistry has roots based in Roman legend. Proving that the apple doesn't fall far from the tree, Nero's murderous mother, Agrippina, reportedly ordered the slaying of another woman. When the head was brought to Agrippina as proof of her demise, the emperor's mother didn't at first recognize her, but by looking in the dead woman's mouth, she found a bad tooth she knew belonged to the unlucky victim.

To identify bodies, forensic dentists have worked on mass disasters such as tsunamis, airplane crashes, fires, and acts of terrorism. Of course, the dead victims must have dental records on file somewhere in order to make comparisons. Like DNA, there must be something with which to compare the evidence for the evidence to have value. Most of the Indian Ocean tsunami victims in 2004 were identified through DNA extracted through the molars.

Historically, forensic dentists or odontologists have not only identified crime victims, but also villains: Adolf Hitler and his mistress, Eva Braun, were matched to their dental records following their 1945 deaths in a German bunker. Forensic dentists can also use teeth to determine the gender of a victim, and since teeth are one of the hardest and most indestructible substances in the human body, they are likely to survive trauma that destroys flesh and blood. And, as mentioned before, they are also a good source of DNA.

"The purpose of the teeth is to locate STR or nuclear DNA, usually in the molars if there [have] been no dental fillings, root canals, etcetera. If the collection method is done carefully there is a chance that STR can be found in the pulp of the tooth," says Gerald Nance, a case manager with the National Center for Missing and Exploited Children and retired criminal investigator.

For small children, like the Boy in the Bag, forensic dentistry can provide clues about age and level of dental care. He had a chipped front tooth, but the damage could have come from the beating that killed him. The other Philadelphia child, the Boy in the Box, was bucktoothed and had a full set of baby teeth, but in the 1950s dental care for young children was not as common as it is today. Many never saw a dentist, and for kids raised in poverty, the odds were even greater that there were no dentists in their lives. Sadly, the same holds true today.

Still, for one unfortunate missing woman, frequent and extensive dental care eventually paid off in reuniting her—albeit postmortem—with her family. Eliopulos, who spent fifteen years working as an investigator for the Florida Medical Examiner's office, says it took a quarter of a century before the girl he knew as "Angel" was reunited with her family.

The seventeen-year-old derived her nickname from an angel tattoo she wore. Struck and killed by a van on a major highway, Angel's extensive dental work made her unique. Although investigators were able to track the girl to a waitressing job in a nearby state, Angel had worked under an alias and the lead grew cold. The medical examiner's office considered her a runaway, but despite their efforts she remained a Jane Doe.

Six months after Eliopulos left the medical examiner's office and began work with NCIS, the mystery was solved. Angel's sister started looking for her again and, although investigators had checked all available databases in the United States at that time, she wasn't on any of them. The reason? Angel was from Canada. A forensic odontologist matched the remains to her dental records.

Another case where dental records helped bring home a missing loved one involved a young sailor not seen alive in twenty-three years. In the military, when someone disappears, he is declared absent without leave, or AWOL. After thirty days, he is labeled a deserter. Because of this classification, many who fall victim to foul play are never considered missing persons in the legal sense—only absconders. It is a problem that often leads to a lack of information when identifying found bodies.

"They may very well escape any type of inquiry from medical examiners or coroners looking for a missing person who's in the military," says Eliopulos. "We need to change that."

When his sister reinstituted a search for the missing sailor, investigators found an unidentified body that matched his basic description at the time of his disappearance.

"The body was long gone and buried," Eliopulos says. But the medical examiner's office had pulled the jaw and saved it, just in case. It was a match.

"The fortunate thing is his sister still obviously cared, but his parents had died without knowing their son wasn't a deserter," he says.

The sailor was exhumed and reburied with his mother.

While that case did not have a textbook happy ending, it was at least resolved so the family could claim and bury their relative. However, not everyone gets that chance.

Many thousands of bodies remain unclaimed, identified only by a medical examiner's case number. The public's expectations are often skewed by the media, and television in particular, which make it seem remarkably simple to track down identities using science. These expectations result from a phenomenon known as the "CSI effect," an imaginary knowledge of scientific techniques gained from watching fictional television shows including *CSI* and *NCIS*. It imbues families of the missing with false hope and drives investigators crazy.

Here is a real case that demonstrates how strong an impact the CSI effect has had on the American criminal justice system. The victim in this case was a tiny woman who managed a small store. A robber entered the empty store as another man left. Once inside, he viciously beat the woman and left her for dead, took the store's cash, and fled the scene.

The robber was identified in several ways: the man he passed on the way out of the store was a friend of the perpetrator's family and had known the robber since he was a child. The victim looked at more than two hundred mug shots and picked the same perpetrator named by the witness as her assailant. And when police attempted to arrest the robber, he fled the city, returning months later when he thought things had cooled off. It should have been an open-and-shut case, but it wasn't. In fact, the case ended with a hung jury and a mistrial.

After court adjourned, police spoke with the jury's foreman, a construction supervisor who wanted to be a police detective, and, as it turned out, someone who was clearly in the grips of the CSI effect. He said that if the suspect had been in the store, he would have left fingerprints. Since the crime scene technicians didn't find his fingerprints, he must not have been there.

He learned this from watching cop shows on television and convinced the other jurors he knew best. That jury turned loose a criminal based on an erroneous premise.

But inaccurate portrayals of evidence and how it's collected make for colorful reading and viewing, so fiction prevails over fact most of the time. In one recent crime drama in which a body was exhumed, the coffin was dug up and opened right in the cemetery by the side of the opened grave. Even worse, a crime scene technician rummaged around inside—no medical examiner, no removal to the medical examiner's office, no other witnesses, and probably no exhumation order.

Although it's great to see science get its due on television and many have been inspired to seek scientific careers based on the interest these shows kick up, they do tend to distort reality. For example, the real-life NCIS has more than one lab person, and real labs specialize. One person cannot testify as an expert in firearms and ballistics, chemical analysis, DNA, explosive devices, tool marks, computer forensics, and so on. But much of the public believes one person can do it all.

So science, which now offers so many good and useful tools to convict the guilty and exonerate the innocent, also presents valuable approaches to help trace missing persons and link a body to its identity. But there are a multitude of variables when it comes to what it is possible to do and what happens in the make-believe world of fiction, television, and movies.

Because DNA matches take seconds on a television program, viewers confronted with real-life cases expect DNA verification to be instantaneous and always possible. It is not. In fact, even though great strides are made daily to refine and speed up the evidentiary processes, it takes time to do them right. While the wait can be agonizing for families, making a positive identification is more important than making a speedy one.

When an investigator on a television show hacks into a secure federal computer system to search for a missing person, the public gets the message this is not only doable, but accomplished with ease. It's a shame because it stokes their hopes to an unrealistic level.

But then, there is always this: for now it's entertainment, but who back in 1957 would have thought something called DNA could prove a person innocent of murder, put a name to the Boy in the Bag, or lead to the identification of bones found in a forest as those of a long-missing young man? Even though the application of forensic science through the filter of entertainment often results in unrealistic expectations, those shows do give the hardworking and often underappreciated forensic experts a well-deserved tip of the hat. Because of these individuals and their relentless dedication to reuniting the missing with their families, many have been brought home.

All made possible courtesy of real-life crime scene investigation professionals.

———

In a picture taken many years ago, a little boy is dressed in a pair of pants and a long-sleeved, white shirt. A dark vest covers the shirt, and his feet are clad in shoes and socks. He is propped up in a chair covered with white cloth, most likely a sheet, and photographed in both right and left profiles. Bruises are visible in both photos. In one, the boy looks like a young version of actor Macaulay Culkin, who starred in the *Home Alone* movies. But he's not. The picture is of the Boy in the Box.

In an effort to make the child appear more natural and lead to his identification, investigators dressed and photographed him as if he were alive. The photos generated leads, but nothing came of them. The child remains unidentified today.

In the past, it has not been uncommon for police and medical examiners to release photos of the dead in the hopes someone might place a name to their faces. Often, though, damage or decay renders the person unrecognizable. In the case of skeletonized remains, skulls cannot be identified without dental records or recorded past trauma.

Forensic artists were called in to bring the dead to life again by drawing a "living" version of the deceased or by creating a bust based on the skull and other recovered evidence, like hair. Now, science and art have met the computer and the outcome is faster and more lifelike.

Glenn Miller's cubicle at the National Center for Missing and Exploited Children (NCMEC) in Alexandria, Virginia, is littered with computer screens bigger than most plasma televisions. Lining the windows in neat single file stand sculpted clay busts, much like the one made of the Boy in the Bag. That bust, created without charge by Philadelphia artist Frank Bender, was key in helping to identify the child. Those that line Miller's windows today were also used to identify the dead in cases past.

Miller is a retired cop, but he is also an artist. He teaches other forensic artists the delicate specialties of facial reconstruction and age progression—the first critical to identifying recovered remains, the second a vital tool for investigators seeking a missing person.

Miller "draws" not with a pen or pencil or paint. Instead, the secret to his skillful, lifelike images can be found in computer software: Adobe Photoshop, to be precise. "Photoshop is the Holy Grail, a universal language," Miller says.

In the beginning, Miller used a program designed to age progress a child. When the ability to digitize photos became possible, the process was revolutionized by Adobe's software. Unlike a word processing program, not everyone can be successfully trained to use it. Miller says departments that send officers who are not artists to the classes he gives are disappointed because success in his discipline rests with a knowledge and background in art. But, in Miller's words, "you don't have to be a Rembrandt to get a good likeness."

The results of Miller's labors surround him and the others who work in the NCMEC's forensic art unit. One bust, depicting the face of an adolescent or young man, is compelling. The face, Miller says, is a re-creation of a skull found by a dog.

"The family dog . . . brought home the mandible [and] femur bones. [Police] put a GPS on the dog but never found where the dog was collecting the bones," Miller says.

A forensic anthropologist analyzed the recovered bones and determined the individual both suffered from a severe deformity and used a wheelchair. Because the skull was thicker in one area and other conditions were present, the forensic anthropologist also believed the person was mentally retarded. The bust was created using the recovered mandible.

"Years later, a woman looking for a missing loved one went to the Garden of Missing Children [a now defunct Web site] and saw a photo of a missing boy," Miller says. Because the boy's photo reminded her of her own sister, who was retarded, it stuck in her mind.

At the NCMEC Web site she saw the bust of the boy created from the bones the dog had recovered. The woman thought the bust resembled the boy's photo. She was right.

"It was a match. [The boy] was blind, and his father had burned to death in a house fire," Miller says. Authorities now believe the boy's death was the result of a "mercy killing."

Instead of busts, which take much longer to craft, Miller now uses Photoshop to re-create human faces in NCMEC's quest to match names to as many recovered remains as possible. And Miller is also able to turn a corpse into someone recognizable.

In the case of a young African American woman found murdered, Miller took a photograph of the dead woman's face and erased the trauma, then added a spark of life to her face, computer-enhancing her eyes and expression. When the photo circulated, her sister stepped forward to identify her. The likeness Miller achieved is remarkable when viewed side by side with the woman's driver's license.

"What I love about doing this is we can be the link that solved it," Miller says. "The family searching for its loved one will at last know what happened. Now they can stop living in a time capsule."

Miller leans back in his chair and thinks for a moment. When he speaks again, his voice is soft and low. "I show as best I can what that person looked like on the day he or she died. I re-create that face," he says.

In addition to bringing the dead "back to life" in his art, Miller also moves time forward, as if thumbing the pages of a book ahead to another chapter, revealing the story midplot.

Age progression is where art meets science. By taking an individual and approximating what that person might look like two or ten or twenty years after last being photographed, forensic artists can arm both police and the public with a tool that has worked to bring victims back home and put on-the-run suspects behind bars. It is an art form that requires time, patience, and a particular set of tools.

When looking at a photo that has been age progressed, particularly of a child, it is often assumed that the artist "makes the person look older." It is not quite that easy.

Good age progression relies on an artist having knowledge of how the human face changes as it grows older: what sags, what expands, and what differences are common in the course of human development. Between the ages two and seven, children experience rapid growth in the bottom two-thirds of their faces. Adult teeth grow in. Baby fat fades away, their noses lengthen, and their necks fill out. But some types of change depend on heredity. That's why family photos prove essential.

"You have to get reference pictures of biological parents to age progress a missing child," Miller says.

In one well-known case, Miller age progressed young Madeleine McCann, the British four-year-old who was abducted on May 7, 2007, during a family holiday in Portugal. The progression, like all progressions, relied on photographs of the child's parents.

Miller says, "I had a great picture of [mother] Kate and a great picture of [father] Gerry, and I could see Kate's mouth and Gerry's nose in [Madeleine]. In my opinion, [the age progression] is in the ballpark."

His images of little Madeleine McCann were released on the *Oprah Winfrey Show* but haven't yet resulted in her recovery. The British child, believed abducted from the hotel where her family was staying, has been the subject of an international search effort.

Miller uses his altered photographs to predict how children will change as they age. If the father has a long, thin nose that widened as he grew older and the son has the same nose, then Miller will approximate that nose in the progression. He doesn't guess what the child could look like; he bases his estimates on the child's genetics.

It is almost impossible to age progress an infant, although it has been done in a few instances. Under normal circumstances, a child must be one to eighteen months old and missing for at least two years before he or she can be progressed. As a child ages, Miller requires photos of the parents when they were close to the same age as the missing child. He says the ears are important because they are "as individual as a fingerprint."

Many times when kids are identified from age-progressed photos, the public looks at the picture that led to the child's recovery and thinks, "That doesn't look at all like that kid." They are both right and wrong.

"The progression is going to have subtle differences," Miller says. The actual person may have a different hair color or length, eyebrows can be bushier or grow in a different pattern or be plucked and shaped, and the nose could be somewhat thinner or thicker. But Miller knows the trick is finding that certain special something that will trigger a spark of recognition in someone who knows or has seen the child. Perhaps it's the shape of the eyes or ears that stick out; maybe it's the smile or shape of the jaw. What may not resemble the actual person to a stranger will, it is hoped, be as unique and identifiable as a fingerprint to an acquaintance or friend.

Miller has had striking successes with this technique. A woman watching an old television show, *Unsolved Mysteries*, saw an age-progressed photograph that resembled her half sister. She called to her to come look, saying, "This is about you." "I sure hope I look better than that," responded the sister. As it turned out, she *was* the child in the photo, missing since her noncustodial mother ran away with her from their home in Hawaii and established a new life in California. The photo had been age progressed from seven years old to age forty-five, using a photograph of the woman's biological brother at age thirty-five to help create the face later recognized by her half sister.

Another success story for Miller and NCMEC was the case of Alexander Hillman, who was abducted from West Tisbury, Massachusetts, at age eight. Hillman, along with eight other abducted children, was featured in a piece about Miller and age progression that appeared in a 2002 issue of *People* magazine. Someone recognized Hillman, ten years old at the time, from the photo, leading to the little boy's recovery.

It doesn't matter to Miller how much the photo he doctors looks like the person being sought, as long as it's good enough to lead to his or her recovery. For him, his job is not about being good at what he does; it's about connecting with a witness, because that's what brings children home.

When the Boy in the Box was autopsied by Philadelphia Medical Examiner Dr. Joseph Spelman, he discovered the child had been beaten. Dark bruises covered his head, chest, arms, and legs. Moreover, the person who committed this crime has managed to conceal the boy's identity for more than five decades.

Thirty-one years later, when the Boy in the Bag was found, an autopsy revealed that human beings had not outgrown their enormous capacity for cruelty: he, too, had been beaten. The autopsy reported the child died from wounds inflicted by a blunt object on his neck and head, but it was obvious from the proliferation of old, fractured ribs that the preschooler lived with nightmarish violence.

Across the country, medical examiners and coroners' offices hold thousands of cases of unidentified, recovered remains. Historically they stand little chance of positive identification. For the families of these silent, missing dead, each new sunrise brings fresh anguish.

Until recently, no national protocol existed for handling the dissemination of information in regard to recovered bodies. Instead, each jurisdiction dictates its own rules, which translates into a general dearth of information in the national pipeline and reduces the number of people outside a jurisdiction with access to that information. The fewer people who know about a case, the less likely the chance of resolving it and bringing the deceased back home.

According to the National Crime Information Center (NCIC), about one hundred thousand open and active missing persons cases are on the books in this country each day. Many of them are resolved, but as old cases are cleared, new ones spring up to take their places, so the numbers remain nearly constant.

Medical examiners and coroners' offices hold more than forty thousand sets of unidentified remains. To put this in perspective, that number is large enough to represent a small city.

In the last century alone, thousands of other recovered bodies were buried, cremated, or otherwise destroyed—a tragedy that cannot be rectified. This forever leaves some grieving families without the tools to identify or recover their lost loved ones' remains. Part of the problem is that states don't all use the same medical examiner system.

A 2004 Bureau of Justice report showed that there are about two thousand medical examiners or coroners' offices in the United States, but the staffing levels, qualifications, duties, and budgets vary, from elected coroners with no medical training covering large rural areas with miniscule budgets, to large, modern facilities with statewide jurisdiction, manned by forensic pathologists with staffs of investigators and budgets sufficient to do the job.

Considering that these offices receive almost a million cases annually (and accept about half of them), it's easy to see that the system is overworked and understaffed. What falls through the cracks here are the nameless dead.

For decades, medical examiners and coroners were not allowed to place unidentified remains on NCIC, the national database accessible to police across the nation. As a result, positive identifications were mostly the result of dogged determination or luck.

Enter the National Institute of Justice (NIJ). In 2005, the NIJ sponsored a conference convened to look at this issue. Organizers pulled together a vast sampling of individuals involved in missing persons investigations. Medical examiners, coroners, detectives, and family members of the missing and the found joined with scientists, criminologists, and others to hash out a plan to bridge the critical gap that would link unidentified remains to reported missing persons.

They made many recommendations. Out of those came a system that has already helped resolve at least three cases. And what is so revolutionary is that the mail carrier and the store clerk, the lawyer and the cab driver, the student and the readers of this book all have access to a lot of information once only available to law enforcement agencies. It can be viewed now on one central Web site, www.namus.gov.

Had the National Missing and Unidentified Persons System (NamUs) existed back when the Boy in the Box was found, his story might have had a different outcome. But that child's body was found more than fifty years ago, a month after the inauguration of President Dwight D. Eisenhower and six months before state and federal troops faced off in Little Rock, Arkansas, over racial integration.

On February 25, 1957, there was no DNA database available to detectives, nor much in the way of communication between agencies. As a result, missing persons were identified most often because they were local, because someone in their family had reason to believe they were in the area, or because the case received massive publicity that paid off.

The Boy in the Box received massive publicity, but it was fruitless. Over the years, investigators continued to follow up, engendering new leads through shows like *America's Most Wanted* and by asking the Vidoq Society, a distinguished national crime-solving group, to investigate. But the fact remains that if two things had been possible in the days before President Richard Nixon betrayed his office and pilot John Glenn flew fighter jets instead of spaceships, the child might now have a name. Those two things are the extraction and use of DNA for genetic comparison and the creation of NamUs.

To explain the thinking behind NamUs, consider the history behind the first fast-food chain, McDonald's. The restaurant started as a drive-in, quite traditional for that era, with carhops serving customers in their cars. But when the brothers who opened the first restaurant took a closer look at their business, they saw a way to maximize profits by simplifying the menu and speeding up service. They dumped the carhops and broke the menu down to hamburgers, fries, and drinks.

NamUs does something similar: it creates a simpler, faster, and more efficient way to conduct the business of connecting human remains to their identities. To speed things up, NamUs allows direct access to its database.

Rather than wait for all components of NamUs to go online, its developers smartly went active on an incremental basis, says Kristina Rose, acting director of the National Institute of Justice. It's sort of like McDonald's perfecting its hamburgers and selling them before they have the fries down pat.

As a result, cops, medical examiners, coroners, families, and those with an interest in the plight of missing persons can now access the database. Here is how Rose describes the problem and solution.

"Victims' families, members of the public who had missing loved ones . . . had to go to all kinds of offices: law enforcement, medical examiners, coroners' offices. The need was identified to create a central repository of those missing persons and unidentified dead and coming up with a technical solution to make those databases speak to each other so that matches could be [made] when data was entered into the database."

Medical examiners, police, and civilians can all enter information into NamUs. The information is quality controlled by NamUs supervisors. In addition, families of the missing can submit DNA profiles, as can medical examiners and coroners.

The DNA profiles are created at no cost to the DNA donor by the Center for Human Identification (CHI) at the University of North Texas Health Science Center in Fort Worth.

All the information goes into the huge, searchable database. The system itself looks for matches, but like any system, it is fallible.

Consider the case of a sixteen-year-old boy who was thought to have disappeared in 1995. Missing persons posters were created, DNA samples were taken, and law enforcement conducted massive searches for the youth.

"There were no good leads, no good hits," says Rose.

In March 2008, the Virginia Medical Examiner uploaded a case into the NamUs database. The description of the deceased was a man between the ages of eighteen and twenty-two. He had been found on June 6, 1995, prior to the date the young man had been reported as missing.

Then the Doe Network got involved. Members of this private organization that seeks to reunite the missing with their families search online for matches. A Doe Network member was scrolling through NamUs and saw the boy's case.

"Even though the information showed that the unidentified decedent's case actually came before the missing person report, there was so much . . . that was similar, they went ahead and contacted the National Center for Missing and Exploited Children," Rose says.

It was a match—a match based on a hunch, persistence, and a unique public-private partnership. And although the fledgling agency's efforts are still evolving, the program had three matches in the first full month of its operation.

"There are three families that we were able to bring some information and give them—I don't want to call it 'closure,' because closure doesn't really exist in these types of cases—but it certainly helped them to understand what happened; now they know where their loved one is," Rose says.

———∞∞———

As the Boy in the Box rests nameless under a tombstone etched with the words "America's Unknown Child," another Philadelphia grave holds the other little boy who suffered such a similar fate. But more than time separates the two slain children—one has a name, one still does not.

In the case of the Boy in the Bag, despite investigators' efforts and widespread media coverage, it took eleven years before the sweet-faced child was identified. The year was 2005; that's when an uncle who had been out of town for many years began to ask questions about the boy's whereabouts.

Looking through online databases, the uncle found the Boy in the Bag case and told officials the child was Jerell Willis, a Camden, New Jersey, resident who lived with his mother and her boyfriend.

The brutalized four-year-old died after undergoing terrible beatings, and even more disturbing, not one person, official or otherwise, appeared to notice when he disappeared. If not for his uncle and the online database, the boy might have remained a John Doe forever.

Later, the child was linked to his mother through his mitochondrial DNA. The mother, Alicia Robinson, pleaded guilty in connection with his murder, but she received a light punishment. The other individual charged in connection with the child's death was scheduled for trial in 2009.

Little Jerell's story is poignant because it also proves that even in the face of the worst that humanity has to offer, there are also many good and caring people. The child's body remained unidentified and housed in the morgue until 2001, when an elderly Philadelphia woman, the late Mary Peck, concerned that he continued to be unclaimed, paid for a funeral and headstone. When he was identified, a new headstone carved with his name replaced the first one.

The Boy in the Bag and the Boy in the Box lived and died about forty years apart. One case was solved, but the other continues to challenge investigators and scientists today. The difference between the two cases can be found in the time frame in which they took place.

Yesterday's science fiction has become today's reality.

• 5 •

Running Away from It All: Missing by Design

He's not missing. He knows exactly where he is.—an old police expression

$\mathcal{O}$n the day John Stonehouse, British Labour Party member of Parliament, folded his clothes and placed them into a neat little pile on a beach in Miami and then walked away, he was doing more than reacting to a troubled life: he was trading it in, much the same way one would swap an old car for a new one. To the rest of the world, including his wife and political allies, Stonehouse drowned in the Atlantic Ocean. To police, who nurtured a suspicion based on past experience, he was missing. To Stonehouse, however, the act of disappearing represented the key to a new start as a different person, unencumbered by the detritus of his previous life.

The British politician chose drowning because it is difficult to produce a suitable corpse while the "dead" person still inhabits it, as evidenced by many fake suicides before and since. The convenient thing about large bodies of water is that they are unpredictable: they either surrender remains or conceal them forever. The nature of a watery grave helps those who stage their own deaths get around that pesky question of what happened to the body.

A former postmaster general and the son of a mayor of Southampton, Stonehouse appeared to possess a brilliant future. He studied at the prestigious London School of Economics and served as the secretary to the minister of aviation; however, the young man whose rise to prominence under Prime Minister Harold Wilson had been steady as a drumbeat planned to climb even higher, aspiring to Wilson's office. Every move Stonehouse made in his early days supported that trajectory, but when problems in his personal and political life arose, his real agenda played out. Instead of making history as Britain's prime minister, Stonehouse would be remembered as one of the world's most infamous missing persons.

The circumstances of that disappearance would rival the plots of one of Stonehouse's favorite authors, Frederick Forsythe. In fact, Stonehouse drew inspiration and more than a little practical help in leaving behind his former life from Forsythe's novel, *The Day of the Jackal.*

In the book, the main character, an international assassin, creates a new identity by stealing that of a dead child. Stonehouse copied the technique Forsythe described when he created his own alternate identity: A. J. Markham. Later, the Parliament member masqueraded as Markham, trying out his new persona before slipping into it on a permanent basis. Stonehouse planned to evolve into Markham after staging his death by pretending to drown.

Trapped in an unhappy marriage and longing to join his lover and secretary, Sheila Buckley, Stonehouse obtained a passport under the new, false identity and opened foreign bank accounts to channel hidden funds. Then, on a trip to Florida in November 1974, he staged his disappearance, leaving those stacked clothes on the fine white sand.

Everyone bought it at first. His wife, Barbara, and other family members were inconsolable. Police searched the ocean but found nothing. Although some expressed early doubts, the public and members of Parliament believed him dead. However, police both in the United States and Great Britain were more suspicious. Rumors floated that Stonehouse might have been involved in espionage.

Meanwhile, near the same time Stonehouse staged his disappearance, another prominent Brit, Richard John Bingham, the wealthy and troubled seventh Earl of Lucan, also vanished. Descended from the third Earl of Lucan (held responsible for the deaths of six hundred cavalry during the Crimean War's infamous Charge of the Light Brigade), Lord Lucan attended Eton College and lived a life of privilege. He married and settled into the tony Mayfair area of London with his wife, Veronica.

Veronica, who had given birth three times, suffered from postpartum depression and had difficulty adjusting after each of the births. Lucan, however, was more concerned with feeding his growing gambling habit—a habit that became both his obsession and profession.

Lady Lucan sought treatment for her depression, but the couple grew apart, as Lord Lucan's gambling drew them deeper in debt. In 1972 they separated, prompting Lord Lucan to attempt to obtain custody of the couple's children. Despite his efforts, the children remained with their mother, in the care of their nanny, a woman named Sandra Rivett.

According to British newspaper reports, Rivett was similar in build and height to Lady Lucan, which police believe may be the reason the nanny was beaten to death in the basement of Lady Lucan's residence on the night of November 7, 1974. Reports say Rivett was struck multiple times with a blunt object (later determined to be a length of pipe covered in tape). Lady Lucan told police that she, too, had been attacked that night and identified her attacker as her husband, Lord Lucan.

The not-so-noble lord didn't help his case. He claimed he stepped in a pool of Rivett's blood while aiding Lady Lucan. Several individuals received calls from Lord Lucan the night of Rivett's slaying, and investigators, following Lucan's known trail, found bloodstains. The lord himself vanished.

Not long after Lord Lucan disappeared, a teller at an Australian bank became suspicious when a new customer made a sizable deposit. The police were brought in, and soon the suspicious man, John Stonehouse, was under surveillance. Police noted that he read English newspapers and suspected he might be the missing fugitive, Lord Lucan. When they requested photographs of Lucan, they also requested a photo of John Stonehouse, just in case.

Stonehouse was identified and arrested on Christmas Eve, a little over a month after he faked his disappearance, and all because another Englishman chose the same time to vanish in a blaze of worldwide publicity.

As for Lord Lucan, at the time this was written, he remains a fugitive from justice.

<hr />

Thousands of people disappear each day, most of them by choice. Although juvenile runaways are by far more prevalent, plenty of adults also decide to vanish. Most do so without national attention, but some, like the American Jennifer Wilbanks, attract the white-hot glare of the public spotlight as infallibly as a cobra responds to a snake charmer's tune.

Wilbanks, who became known as the "runaway bride," disappeared five days before her April 30, 2005, wedding. The young woman vanished while out jogging, triggering a massive media response. As reporters tripped over themselves questioning her husband-to-be, her parents, and her bridesmaids in her home state of Georgia, Wilbanks traveled by bus through Las Vegas and other western cities, leaving in her wake plans for a lavish nuptial ceremony that included a wedding party of twenty-eight bridesmaids and groomsmen and a guest list of more than five hundred.

Police say her escape was well planned: she purchased a bus ticket from her Duluth, Georgia, home to Austin, Texas, cut her hair, and instructed a cab to pick her up from a random location to take her to the bus station. Wilbanks covered her tracks like a pro.

She called Georgia on the day of her wedding and claimed she'd been abducted—a story concocted to make it easier to return home. Wilbanks admitted she lied, but the search-and-rescue bill for the city was calculated at a cost of more than $40,000. She and her fiancé, John Mason, initially reconciled, but parted after selling their story for a reported $500,000.

Many who "disappear on purpose" do so because they're trying to avoid detection of criminal activity or arrest. One of the most famous and successful intentional disappearances in the United States is that of James J. "Whitey" Bulger, who has been on the run for more than a decade.

Bulger, a Boston-based gangster who goes by numerous aliases, disappeared in connection to an investigation that revealed he had an FBI agent on his payroll. In addition to nineteen counts of murder, Bulger is wanted today for drug trafficking, extortion, and numerous conspiracy charges. He vanished on December 23, 1994, after being tipped off about federal indictments by John Connelly, an FBI agent and Bulger's man on the inside. Sources say Bulger planned for his future disappearance well: he established safe deposit boxes containing alternate identification, money, and other valuables in numerous places.

Despite being featured on the FBI's ten most wanted list, becoming the subject of numerous books and articles, and having his story appear on television episodes of *America's Most Wanted*, as far as anyone knows, Bulger remains alive and on the run. A $2 million reward has been offered for information leading to his arrest.

Bulger was notorious before he went on the lam, but he certainly is not the only well-known individual to intentionally vanish over the years. Although she did resurface, many questions about the disappearance of mystery writer Agatha Christie were never resolved. Christie vanished in 1926. Her car was later found abandoned while police continued to search for the authoress, one of England's biggest celebrities. She later turned up at an inn, registered under another name. The British writer never fully explained or discussed her disappearance, although for decades her fans have speculated about her reasons. Personal problems, not legal ones, were the most plausible impetus.

Another literary luminary, Ambrose Bierce, did his disappearing a little earlier than Agatha Christie. Born in 1842 in Horse Cave, Ohio, Bierce was a respected Civil War veteran who became a well-known San Francisco columnist and writer. After being posted in Washington, D.C., Bierce revisited the Civil War battlegrounds in Virginia, dined with presidents, and developed a caustic but respected outlook on war and politics. In 1913, Bierce departed the nation's capital on his way to El Paso, Texas. From there he crossed the border into Mexico. The celebrated writer's final communication to the world was a letter he wrote on December 26, 1913. No trace of Bierce, then seventy-one years of age, has ever been found. While some believe he met with foul play, others think he vanished intentionally—theories that may never be debunked or proven.

Another well-known writer who took a hike was Ken Kesey, hippie author of *One Flew over the Cuckoo's Nest.* Kesey faked his death by suicide during the 1960s in order to avoid drug charges but was revealed as a sham after only a few months in hiding.

Kesey and John Stonehouse's preferred method of vanishing, by faking one's demise, is a popular vehicle for escaping an unhappy life—or the consequences of that life. In a case that grabbed headlines in 2008, disgraced hedge fund manager Samuel Israel III, son of a wealthy and well-known New Orleans family, pretended to have jumped to his death from a New York bridge rather than go to prison in connection with a plot to defraud thousands of investors. Authorities put little stock in Israel's staged death, unmasking his plan after Israel turned himself in at the urging of relatives.

Celebrities and criminal masterminds aren't alone in occasionally walking away from their lives. News reports are full of ordinary people who disappear and then resurface, sometimes many decades after they were last seen.

The relatives of an Indiana man missing for fifteen years ended their ordeal when a determined Indiana State Police investigator reopened the old case of his disappearance, using his driver's license to track him down.

Monty Stutzman, who vanished in 1993 at the age of twenty-three, was reunited with his family at his Mississippi home after Indiana State Police Detective Scott Jarvis played a hunch and tracked Stutzman through a driver's license check. He was found living with his new family in Mississippi and reportedly told investigators he fled the area because he faced a probation violation.

Fear that he was the target of law enforcement also allegedly drove a Florida man to emulate John Stonehouse and stage his own drowning. Bennie Harden Wint failed to return from a dip in the ocean, leaving his fiancée frantic and the beach patrol on a fruitless search—fruitless because investigators say Wint swam down the beach, walked out of the water, and hitchhiked to a new life in North Carolina.

Wint, who went by the name of William Sweet, was unmasked in January 2009 when police pulled him over for a minor traffic violation in the Tar Heel State. Booked into jail because he couldn't produce any official identification, Wint was identified by authorities as the man who "drowned" off the Florida coast on September 24, 1989.

For those who manufacture elaborate alter-identities, the point of vanishing is to close forever the previous chapters of their lives. They intend to live as someone else—a moderately difficult feat in 1974. Today, in this high-tech, information-driven society, to establish a new identity and live without detection is a much more complicated proposition.

Wired magazine writer Evan Ratliff chronicled the pitfalls of disappearing and avoiding detection after he wrote a story about people who do so (*Wired,* issue 17.12, December 2009). Ratliff went "on the run" in August 2009; his story appeared in the magazine the following November. Ratliff and *Wired* then turned the article into a real-life reader's challenge: Ratliff would disappear for a month, and the reader who found him before the month's end would win $5,000.

In the piece he wrote for the magazine after his unmasking, Ratliff documented the preparations that went into turning himself into James Donald Gatz (a name based on a character in F. Scott Fitzgerald's *The Great Gatsby*). Ratliff created his new identity and established misleading clues to spark reward hunters to look in all the wrong places. He succeeded in remaining "missing" for twenty-five days before a couple of guys combined their information and found him. But Ratliff's experiment, while interesting, was made more complicated by virtue of its high profile. *Wired* provoked readers to try and find him, the kind of attention people like Stonehouse eschew. Most who disappear—with the exception of celebrities and well-known criminals—try to do so with as little fanfare as possible.

Frank Ahearn reigns as the sultan of intentional disappearances, an enterprise he knows and understands from both sides. After years of working as a skiptracer (a term for people who find others), Ahearn decided to put his considerable knowledge of the skills it takes to vanish into practice, and now he not only looks for people who've skipped out, but also advises others on the proper way to disappear. Ahearn and his partner, Eileen Horan, have authored a book, *How to Disappear*, which presents advice on the ramifications and pitfalls of vanishing. The upshot: it takes a lot to complete a convincing vanishing act, and it's not as easy as movies and books make it appear.

Most who make up their minds to leave make critical mistakes. Among the most common errors: not severing ties with individuals from their past; using traceable cell phone numbers, credit cards, and ATMs; requesting the transfer of medical or educational records; forwarding mail or magazines to a new address; using accounts tied to a previous (real) identity; having a traceable Internet account; incorporating a real name (or something associated with a previous identity) into a new one; or leaving behind clues to an eventual destination.

Experts say aliases can trip up those on the run. Often they will choose names that prove easy for them to remember: "Douglas Alan Martin" might become "Alan Douglas" or Mona Sims, who once lived on Johnson Boulevard, may choose Monica Johnson or even Monica Simmons—both names that she can recall with ease.

Skiptracers like Ahearn once relied on paper trails but now depend on electronic ones. What makes electronic "crumbs" so compelling are that they are difficult, if not impossible, to erase: once in a database, almost always in a database.

Unique characteristics can also hurt. From hobbies to food preferences, the devil is in the details. *Wired* writer Ratliff, who says he suffers from celiac disease and eats gluten free, blew his cover by going to a restaurant that offered gluten-free pizza. He also risked detection to attend a soccer game.

Being a vegetarian, having salon-applied fingernails, drinking Turkish coffee, or following a favorite NFL team can all lead to discovery. Ahearn and other experts like him agree that the details that make you an individual also make you easier to find, and the people doing the searching are going to know as much about a person as possible.

Those most successful at disappearing walk away from everything. These people take nothing from their former lives and leave no hint that they planned to vanish. They stash clothes, new identification, and money against the day they leave. They do their research.

Ahearn says he believes each of us nurses the fantasy of walking away from it all, but the numbers who follow through are miniscule. "I look at my Web stats, and I get 200 to 250 hits a day. And 99 percent of those hits typed in 'how to disappear'—from Finland to Germany to Russia, from all over," he says.

Ahearn says the Internet encourages people to explore the idea by providing ways to test the waters and the tools to plan exits from real lives. "I think having the Internet at our fingertips lets us dream. It's kind of therapeutic," he says.

While a potential runaway can use the Web to plan an escape, using technology to abandon one life and start another also carries its own price tag: it leaves a trail that professionals like Ahearn have no trouble following.

"I'm the person who can locate the guy with $2 million in the Caribbean," Ahearn says. He explains that as a skiptracer he is more prone to pursue a fake drowning victim like Samuel Israel than a missing high school kid.

Ahearn says people usually leave for two main reasons: money or danger. Those reasons are divided along gender lines: men leave for money, and women for danger. Men tend to come into some cash and decide to live out their fantasy, or they get into financial hot water and want out. Women can react to stalking situations or violent and abusive relationships by running. And while the bulk of intentional disappearances were once men, Ahearn says more and more women now choose to bail out. As for numbers, there is no real way to know how many people disappear by choice each year and how many are abducted because not every case is solved.

"We're seeing more professional women coming to us or contacting us, women who are married and need an exit plan," Ahearn explains.

When it comes to finding someone, Ahearn says it all depends on the sophistication of the hunter. "If it's somebody who is searching you out, like a cop or a skiptracer, and they are pretty savvy with technology, it's a question of who is better. It's like a duel," he says.

Law enforcement officers who track white-collar criminals do so by learning to think like them, much as those who specialize in violent crimes delve into the habits and psyches of killers and rapists. Tracking a man who has embezzled a large sum of money and run off with his secretary takes a different skill set than tracking a pedophile and child abductor.

"If law enforcement is looking for you, they know at any time you [could] pop up on the radar; how many criminals are caught because a headlight is out?" Ahearn points out.

Criminals often fall into the hands of their pursuers because little things go wrong, or they do something stupid (from their point of view, not so much from the cop's vantage point), like run their mouths. Often intentional disappearances are resolved the same way—the perpetrator does something unplanned or without thinking—getting back into the same line of work, providing skiptracers with a juicy lead.

"You can't be Joe the bus driver in Chicago and then disappear and be Joe the bus driver in Wisconsin," Ahearn says. "The two facts [to take into consideration] are who you are and who is looking for you."

If there's a common thread running through those who intentionally skip out, it is that they are seeking freedom of some sort: freedom from somebody or something, says Ahearn. "I don't think that disappearing itself is that hard; what it always comes back to is that the grass is always greener. Once you get there you have to rebuild your life. Some people are good at it; some aren't," he says.

As for the process itself, Ahearn claims that a successful disappearance is more about preparation and follow-through than walking out. He says someone who wants to disappear the right way—perhaps a woman trying to get away from an abusive partner—should prepare for her new life by leaving nothing to trace. She should obtain a mail drop and use it for all mail in connection with her future life. He recommends prepaid phones and monetary resources that can't be traced (like a new bank account or a stash of cash). For research, Ahearn counsels avoiding Internet cafes, since most have keystroke loggers in place, which remember passwords and personally identifying data, which in turn allows others to trace that information, and instead use a laptop. Connect on random wireless locations around a town or city.

For those searching for a loved one who is missing, he advises them to pursue every lead: credit cards, cell phone bills, trips, and so on.

"Most likely there will be a clue there somewhere," Ahearn says. "Everybody makes mistakes—that's the bottom line." Ahearn urges answering questions for clues: Does the missing person have relatives? Is he in contact with them? What does he do for a living? Look at the whole picture, especially the data, and that could lead to the next step.

"You still have to be who you are," says Ahearn. But the difference with those who are intentionally missing is in the amount of discretion they use. Some have no problem adapting to a new identity and life; others do.

"Some just want this new life because the old life is so bad," Ahearn says. On the other hand, he believes that in many cases the passing of time can make the individual feel less threatened and lead him or her to return. As far as how many leave with the intention of never coming back, Ahearn thinks statistics are wrong and many more people disappear on purpose than is believed.

Being trapped and feeling hopeless are what Dr. Geraldine Merola Barton, a New York–based psychologist, says spark some to abandon their lives. Bad home situations where there are few, if any, alternatives create desperation in both adults and juveniles. Barton recalls a young woman in a situation where the violence continued to escalate. Knowing she could not rely on her parents to help her, the young woman planned her getaway. During her lunch break at work, she boarded an airplane and flew across the country, where she began a new life as someone else.

"She felt she had nobody who could protect her, no resources. So she turned to herself," Barton says.

Medication issues also can provide an ignition point for impetuous and often spontaneous flight. For some classes of mental illness, the individual feels better when he's on his medication, so he thinks he can do without them and stops taking them. This is especially true for individuals with bipolar disorder, who often thrive on the manic episodes and may miss the high they bring. Once off medication, leaving home may seem as if it is a reasonable move, but many who need drugs to function in a normal environment and stop taking them without medical clearance or supervision end up on the streets as part of the homeless population.

Others may experience neurotic behavior, angry overreactions to situations, and the inability to properly evaluate their problems. There is little that can be done about such behavior.

"We don't have a Big Brother society; we can't force someone [to take their medications] unless it's an extreme emergency," Barton says.

For those who don't suffer from mental illnesses like bipolar disorder or schizophrenia, though, Barton believes there still may be other less obvious psychological disorders in play.

She recalls a case where a patient who was also a gambler claimed he went into a fugue state (defined as an altered state of consciousness in which a person moves around, talks, and otherwise functions, but is not aware of what he or she is doing) for two weeks, during which time he left his home, his wife, and his kids, and ended up in Las Vegas. When the man "came to," he did not know how he got to Vegas and found money and clothes he didn't remember acquiring. Barton says that although the case is extreme, it's a good example of someone suffering from an underlying dissociative disorder.

"He had two very distinct sides to him: One was very conscientious, and the other was sociopathic with no conscience. One was very impulsive; the other was restrained and restricted and full of guilt, shame, and denial," Barton says. "One side of him was highly devoted, the other deceitful. One side was passive, the other [full of] rage."

Barton says many who make big commitments without enough fore-thought end up feeling trapped. She cites Jennifer Wilbanks, the runaway bride from Georgia, who was profiled earlier in this chapter.

"People who are trying to meet other people's expectations and demands on them feel more and more like they're being buried alive, and they don't know how to get out of it," Barton says.

But, Barton adds, there is also sometimes a failure to attach emotionally and connect to the other people in their lives. As a result, these individuals often find it easier to walk out and leave behind obligations and commitments. They form no real bond with others and opt to cut already tenuous ties with their previous lives, Barton says.

Narcissists also sometimes walk away from their lives because they view others merely in relation to themselves and the others' ability to provide the narcissists with the things they need. "So the other person doesn't have rights and feelings as far as the narcissist is concerned," she says.

Disappointment—either in the other person or directed at the narcissist—can ignite flight. Once this happens, the other person ceases to exist as far as the narcissist is concerned, and it's not difficult to walk away. When most people leave, says Barton, they generally either have an underlying mental disorder or are leaving behind something they perceive as threatening.

"I think a lot of people who run away have a tendency to think in terms of, 'You can't fire me because I quit,'" says Barton. She categorizes them as the types of individuals who change jobs on a frequent basis and are impulsive. "They're always leaving relationships, jobs, homes, always thinking, 'There will be something better for me there.'"

She says it's called the geographic cure—what Ahearn referred to as "the grass is greener"—and adults are not the only ones who seek it; juveniles often also look for something better than what they have. But when a child leaves home, they're not seeking greener pastures, just different ones. Barton says no matter why a child runs, for parents, the idea of not knowing where he is can be "almost worse than knowing he's dead."

— ∞ —

Kelly Hawkins knows what Barton means. Hawkins has been through the wringer with her foster daughter so often that she feels flattened. A therapeutic foster parent trained to deal with high-risk kids, Hawkins's foster daughter, Maggie (not her real name), takes off with the same casualness that other teenage girls employ when they change clothes. Hawkins says Maggie is both promiscuous and a habitual drug user. She also has assaulted her foster mother.

"[Maggie] went into foster care when she was five. Her mother was a meth addict, and they actually busted a meth lab in the basement of her house," Hawkins says. Authorities removed two infants who tested positive for drugs at birth from the home but left behind the older children, including Maggie.

"That was the big number-one failure there," says Hawkins.

Maggie eventually ended up joining the others in foster care, where the siblings were broken apart for adoptive purposes. The children were placed into pre-adoptive homes: Maggie's was with Kelly. Hawkins herself has not formally adopted Maggie because if she does, she will lose access to many crucial services, including intensive mental health treatment, but she did petition for guardianship of Maggie and received the appointment.

Maggie spent some time in a respite home. Since most foster care programs do not allow kids to stay in unlicensed homes, some states provide respite care in the form of homes that take foster kids on a temporary basis. It gives both the foster parents and the children a chance to experience time away from one another. Hawkins says Maggie began hanging around with the wrong kids and doing drugs.

"The first two times she ran away at age thirteen, she was only gone overnight," Hawkins says. But then Maggie upped the ante: she disappeared for two weeks.

"No one cared or even comforted me. I was beside myself doing the things other parents of missing kids do, and no one even asked how I was or if they could help. When I confronted one close friend about it, her response was, 'It's not like you didn't know something like this might happen.' Another said, 'It's her own fault,' as if that made me feel better," Hawkins says.

The entire missing persons reporting system is stacked against the parents of runaways. Most police agencies have few resources to dedicate to finding kids who have left home. Once they turn sixteen, many states consider them adults and won't look for them without a strong indication of foul play. If a child who is old enough to be on his own is found, often the department has no legal right to tell the parent where the child is or give any details other than to ask the child to contact the parent. It's even worse when the runaway has crossed jurisdictions.

Police will do courtesy checks for officers in other jurisdictions—that is, if an officer has a lead on a child's whereabouts in another city, that jurisdiction will send an officer to try and locate the child. But unless there is something more to the case that's as much as the other jurisdiction is going to do. Runaways form a huge national problem. Many times they turn into homeless street kids or support themselves by becoming involved in drugs, prostitution, and other crimes. The Office of Juvenile Justice and Delinquency Prevention concurs with the National Runaway Switchboard's (NRS) lower-end estimate that about 1.6 million American kids run away from their homes each year, but of that number, the Center for Problem-Oriented Policing (POP) says about a third are technically missing. Of the remaining two-thirds, either the parents know where the kids are or the child is a "throwaway"—a kid whose parents or guardians don't want him or her in the home. Other sources lean toward the high end of the NRS's estimate—2.8 million—and believe the number of runaways is much higher than official statistics indicate, since some parents and guardians avoid police involvement and don't report the child as missing. Although law enforcement officially works with parents to locate these kids, many agencies find themselves constrained by a lack of money and manpower from doing much follow-up.

Even though Hawkins's daughter was a child who had no business on the streets, she discovered her foster-parent status made her even less likely than other parents to engender support from criminal justice agencies or other authorities. On the runaway ladder, foster parents occupy the bottom rung.

"There are no supports, no help for parents like me. There is no Amber Alert, no donations to pay for posters and ads, no all-night vigils, no articles. No one gets worried about a foster kid who runs away, no one thinks I should care, no one wants to hear what I'm doing to find her, [and] no one thinks I should even let her back into my life. My friends and family mean well when they say they are worried for my safety and that I should turn my back on her, but this is my daughter," Hawkins says.

According to a report authored by Kelly Dedel (a criminal justice consultant with a doctorate in clinical psychology) for the nonprofit POP, which works with criminal justice agencies to find solutions to issues confronting police agencies, "Juveniles in substitute care (e.g., foster care, group homes) are more likely to run away than juveniles who live at home with a parent or guardian. The chances of juveniles in care running away are highest in the first few months after placement, and older juveniles are more likely to run away than younger juveniles. Juveniles who run away from substitute care are more likely to run away repeatedly than juveniles who run away from home. Although they are only a small proportion of the total number of runaways, those who run away from care also tend to stay away longer and travel farther away than those who run away from home."

Overwhelmed and underfunded police agencies tend to see foster kids a lot—many times as troublemakers and runaways. Most are not as lucky as Hawkins's daughter Maggie; without anyone to advocate or search for them, they often slip into a statistical dead zone.

Maggie, who is seventeen as of this writing, has spent time in jail and is predisposed to return there in the future, if she doesn't meet a more sinister end on the streets—a potential that Hawkins realizes and fears.

"She is my child and I love her, but the constant emotional turmoil brought on by wondering where she is and what she's doing is wearing me out," Hawkins admits.

Hawkins knows her situation with Maggie is not the norm. Although many kids who run away have substance abuse issues or harbor mental illnesses, others who take to the streets see it as an escape hatch from difficult situations. Dr. Peter Ferber, a Massachusetts-based child psychiatrist, says he believes that children who are mentally whole do not abandon relationships with parents in a family that is healthy and has good relationships. Sure, the occasional rebellious moment or blowup may produce a momentary fracture, and the child might threaten to leave or go to a friend's house for a day or two. But in the long run, the kids who end up on the streets with no intention of ever coming home are, in Ferber's opinion, the products of homes with severe issues.

Broken homes, sexual abuse, parental substance use, and violence—all contribute to the growing problem of runaways in this country, according to Ferber. "In many cases, there is a selfish, self-centered parent who is unable to see the kids as separate sentient humans with a separate viewpoint and a separate set of needs."

At other times, outside pressures can cause a child to make a poor decision.

"I've seen any number of kids just before or just after college entrance who seem to have been functioning well until that point. They are away for a couple of months and find themselves unable to study or make friends and can't tolerate the separation from their home or parents," says Ferber.

Ferber adds that a lot of runaways leave when they are angry or when they are restrained from activities their parents see as harmful. He, like Barton, points to specific pathologies as leading indicators of children who might be more inclined to run away from home.

Children who have attention deficit disorder are impulsive, as are children with bipolar disorder and conduct disorders. "Unrecognized learning disorders can lead kids to fight with their parents and run away," says Ferber, who adds that "impulsive kids are much more likely to become involved with drug cultures."

Living on the streets isn't glamorous or exciting, but many kids who end up there get caught up in the drugs or fall into the hands of those who exploit children. When the economy is in a downturn, experts say, the number of runaways increases, which is unfortunate because a down economy often translates to less money allocated for youth services that deal with runaways.

The NRS, which fields calls from kids who have left home or are considering leaving home, says that among their crisis callers, increasing numbers are turning to panhandling, the sex industry, and selling drugs. In 2008, they reported that the majority of their crisis callers were ages fifteen to seventeen, and, as Ferber affirms, the most commonly reported crisis involved family issues and abuse.

Youth shelters, youth crises centers, and other private and public initiatives to return runaways to their homes have been established in every state and major city in the nation. And cities are where most of the kids end up—not in crisis centers, but on the streets of New York or Los Angeles, Miami or Minneapolis, Dallas or Seattle. Runaway hotlines offer kids a chance to contact their parents or talk to an adult who can give them advice or the opportunity to connect with a sympathetic ear. Greyhound Lines offers a free bus ticket home to runaways, and there are other organizations that help reunite kids with their families, but the truth is that the runaway has to want to come home for any of this to work.

For parents looking for their runaways, the best advice is to grab a page from Ahearn's book and take what they know about their kids and use it to map their most probable paths. Where do they have ties or where have they expressed a desire to visit? What are their habits, likes and dislikes, passions and needs? Looking for them the way Ahearn traces a skip—the precept of thinking like the enemy in order to defeat him—might elicit success.

As for the children nobody's looking for, the throwaways, the unreported missing and foster kids who aren't lucky enough to have someone like Kelly Hawkins in their corners, the future holds little but a short life on the streets and the eventual victimization that comes with that lifestyle.

———

"I wish I could just run away." It's a sentiment almost everyone has experienced. Even the most privileged of the privileged, Princess Grace of Monaco, once expressed wistful envy of the lifestyle of those with no ties to responsibility. For adults crushed under the weight of modern demands, the idea of a life that starts at ground zero, ready to be reconstituted in a fresh new form, has merit. But few make the move, and of the ones who do, their families are often left to search and wonder what happened.

For the teens that take off, the reality of living outside the family unit is often tragic. Many panhandle, commit petty crimes, or sell their bodies in order to stay alive. Kids who get caught up in drug and alcohol abuse or turn to prostitution begin a downhill slide—crime and homelessness send many to the morgue, used up at much too early an age.

With the exception of those who flee abusive situations, adults who walk away from it all leave behind pockets of victims: parents, spouses, children, and the others who love them. When a kid runs away, he or she also often *becomes* a victim. Either way, those who disappear on purpose add to this country's expanding missing persons population.

· 6 ·

Parental Abduction:
Stories of the Parents Left Behind

Children who are victims of family abduction are uprooted from
their homes and deprived of their other parent. Often they are
told the other parent no longer loves them or is dead. Too often
abducted children live a life of deception, sometimes under a false
name, moving frequently and lacking the stability needed for
healthy, emotional development.—*Family Abduction Prevention*

To the best of Stephen Watkins's knowledge, his former wife, Edyta
Ustaszewski, is in Poland with their two sons, Christopher and Alexander.
Stephen has not seen the boys since March 2009. He discovered they were
missing when they did not show up for school. Their disappearance, however,
did not come as a surprise.

"The threat [of abduction] was there initially; there were a lot of little
clues," says Stephen, who lives outside of Toronto.

Stephen did not sit and wait for the boys to vanish. Because he had anticipated their possible abduction, he worked to minimize the damage, documenting details about the boys' mother, trying to anticipate when she might make her
move. He says Edyta, born in Poland, holds joint Canadian-Polish citizenship
and, in addition to the main languages of both countries, also speaks French and
German. Prior to allegedly taking the boys, Stephen says Edyta enrolled them in
a Polish school where they learned the language. She also enrolled them in the
Boy Scouts—the Polish Boy Scouts. When Stephen and the courts asked her for
the boys' passports, he says she claimed she did not have them.

There were other indicators that Edyta was planning to run with the children, says Stephen. She threw him off-balance by leveling criminal allegations
at him, each of which, he says, were investigated by police and the Children's
Aid Society and unsubstantiated.

From left, Christopher and Alexander Watkins. Courtesy of Stephen Watkins.

"Every single type of allegation was [brought] against me. They were so far-fetched," Stephen says.

Stephen, who had sole, court-ordered custody of the boys, says his attorneys warned him that his ex-wife might do such a thing. Now he worries about what she might be telling his children about him.

"I just want my kids found," he says.

The regional agency that is handling the Watkins boys' kidnapping is conducting an ongoing investigation into the abduction. They have gathered banking, credit card, and flight data in connection with the case, but Stephen says he knows little about the information they've gathered because they refuse to share it with him or his attorneys. Police tell him that releasing it could impede both their investigation and eventual prosecution.

"I feel there is more emphasis in making sure you have a very solid court case than in trying to find the kids," Stephen says.

According to Stephen, no one knew where Edyta was living prior to her disappearance. She paid no child support and, Stephen claims, she was "playing games" with both him and the court. Stephen last saw his children on March 6, 2009, when they went to spend the weekend with their mother. Edyta's elderly father, who is Polish but lives in Canada, picked up the boys. Stephen discovered something was wrong at 9:30 a.m. the following Monday when the children's school called to say they were absent.

Stephen called Edyta but received no answer. He then contacted his attorney and the police, and the search was under way.

Stephen and the authorities theorize that Edyta's father drove them over the Canadian border into Rochester, New York, where they boarded a plane to Germany. His father-in-law was charged criminally in connection with their kidnapping. Thus far none of the leads generated by Stephen's contacts there have produced any solid evidence as to their whereabouts.

Stephen is both angry and confounded that Edyta and the boys could have escaped by crossing the border and boarding a plane out of the country, especially because Edyta's Canadian passport had been revoked by the Canadian government. She should not have been legally able to fly. Stephen also had court orders preventing the boys from using their passports, but none of that mattered once the airplane in which they were passengers took off.

"No Amber Alert was ever issued as law enforcement authorities told me it was too late for that. They were already gone," Stephen observes.

Because Stephen suspected Edyta might flee with the children, he prepared in advance by completing the paperwork required to file under the Hague Convention, an international treaty that, among other things, governs the return of children illegally abducted by a parent and taken to another country. He says so far the convention has not been much help.

Although Stephen had the paperwork ready, the Polish authorities did not accept it because it was written in English. They required that it be translated into Polish. "By that time we had lost two to three months [due to paperwork delays]," Stephen says.

Stephen has hired a private investigator to look for the kids and says he does not have any leads. Although he has not yet traveled to Poland to look for his children, Interpol—the International Criminal Police Organization—has become involved in the case.

Stephen has done everything he can think of to keep his case in front of the public, including building a Web site devoted to the boys' abduction, creating videos in multiple languages, and staying in touch with the news media. Most of his coverage, he says, has been local. While he doesn't disparage the local Toronto coverage, he also points out that it isn't terribly beneficial since his case involves international child abduction.

"The kids' pictures are at every single airport here and in the United States and also at border crossings, because when I go [to the United States] I can see them on the wall," he says.

"But the kids aren't here. We know where they are—they're in Europe."

Photographs of Christopher and Alexander stare out at shoppers in Canadian Walmarts, and they've been featured in bank statements and cable bills—in total, twenty-one million envelopes mailed out in Canada. Again, says Stephen, while all publicity is good, he is having a more difficult time getting coverage where he needs it: internationally.

"My story tends to get lost in the mix," he says.

Stephen's professional background is in computers, so he's savvy about getting his kids' names out in front in search engines. "If you type my kids' name in, they're pretty much going to be on page number one," he says. Stephen spends much of his spare time maintaining the Web site devoted to recovering the boys, www.Watkins-Missing-Children.com.

Searching for the boys isn't cheap, either. So far he has committed both a massive amount of time and money to finding them. He says it has cost him and his family about $200,000 thus far, and he knows there will be more expenses ahead.

"We're going at a snail's pace," he says, summing up his frustration.

When Stephen looks back at what has happened, he says he has one piece of advice for other parents facing similar situations: don't let it happen to you.

"Don't lose your kids. Don't have them abducted in the first place. Make sure you have everything in order. There were so many times the court system, the police, the borders, the passports . . . so many times this could have been stopped. We fell through the cracks and the judicial system failed here," he says.

Since 2004, New Jersey resident David Goldman nourished a single-minded goal: to bring his little boy back home. His son, Sean, had been taken to Brazil by his mother, David's former wife. Once there, she remarried—this time to a Brazilian attorney—but she died giving birth to another child. Despite the fact that David is Sean's birth father and his mother's family had no legal claim to Sean in U.S. courts, the family members managed to block his return to his father for five years. During those five years, David spent thousands of dollars and worked around the clock for his son's return, using a dedicated network of friends and strangers who recognized the injustice of Sean remaining in Brazil with his maternal grandparents rather than being returned to his New Jersey home.

David kept up the publicity, appearing on news shows, building a Web site, and fighting for his son through the Brazilian court system. On Christmas Eve 2009, due in large part to the support he received from his publicity campaign, which attracted the sympathy of many Brazilian people as well as the personal intervention of U.S. Congressman Christopher Smith (R–NJ), David was allowed to take his son home. Since then, he and his supporters have continued to tackle the issue of parental abductions to other countries. They also have supported Smith's bill, HR 3240. If enacted, the bill would improve the chances of victims of international child abductions being repatriated and reunited with their U.S. parents both in countries that are signatories of the Hague Convention, as well as countries that are not signatories to Hague.

The Bring Sean Home Foundation (www.bringseanhome.org), which advocated for Sean's return, says, "Sean Goldman was the first child ever to be returned from Brazil, [and] not one child has ever been returned from Japan, not in fifty years."

Japan has proved one of the most difficult countries with which to deal in matters of parental abduction. Under present Japanese law, the noncustodial parent has no rights—not even for visitation. Furthermore, the Japanese legal system allows the parents of biracial children brought into Japan to retain custody because to do otherwise would, as Japanese courts have stated in the past, remove the child from a stable home environment, even when the parent who kidnapped the child did so in violation of a U.S. court order.

Recently the United States urged Japan to sign a treaty that would allow for more equitable treatment of both parties in cases involving the children of Japanese citizens and foreign spouses. Joining with France, Canada, and Great Britain to urge Japanese cooperation in connection with these abductions, the United States cited a report that charged Japan with the seventh-highest rate of international parental abductions involving U.S. children. Mexico ranks first on that list. Countries that have also proved uncooperative in returning abducted children to their U.S. parents include India, Slovakia, Honduras, Russia, and Switzerland.

Parents of children who are the victims of international parental kidnappings often don't know where to turn or even how to begin the process of locating and recovering their kids.

Stephen Watkins recognized the signs that his former wife might flee and take their boys, so he attacked the problem before it grew. Although his efforts proved ineffective in preventing their abduction, they gave Stephen many of the tools he needed to launch a thorough search for the children.

Since Stephen is Canadian, he worked within the framework of Canadian law in preparing for the anticipated abduction of his sons. In the United States, when there is a possibility of an international abduction, experts say it is important to retain an attorney to ensure that custody and visitation rights are spelled out in any court documents. It is also essential that a court order contain a "statement of the basis of the court's jurisdiction and the manner in which notice and opportunity to be heard were given," according to the Office of Juvenile Justice and Delinquency Prevention (OJJDP). That provision helps clarify jurisdictional issues that will arise down the road.

The OJJDP also suggests asking the U.S. State Department to flag the child's passport (although, in Stephen Watkins's case, his children were transported over the Canadian border into the United States and allowed to travel to Europe even though the kids' passports were no longer valid). The OJJDP's publication, *A Family Resource Guide on International Parental Kidnapping*, is a free government publication that offers information and advice to parents who believe their children may become victims or whose children have already been abducted. Much of the advice offered also applies to any parental abduction, including the steps one should take if a parental abduction attempt is anticipated. Much of it is good, old-fashioned common sense and contains steps parents should implement anyway, even if they do not suspect their child could be targeted for kidnapping. The OJJDP, the National Center for Missing and Exploited Children, and other experts say these include the following preventative measures:

- Have current, high-quality color photos of your child. Take both front and profile views.
- Make a video of your child. Keep both the video and photos current.
- Determine that the child knows his or her name, address, and telephone number.
- Record your child's description: in addition to the obvious traits like height, weight, and coloring, also record other identifying data, such as whether the child uses corrective lenses, and any birthmarks he or she may have. Remember: missing persons can sometimes be located because of quirks or habits they have. When describing your children, also record favorites, including music, television shows, and toys they may favor; any medical conditions they may have or medications they may take; allergies; food preferences or dislikes—anything that might make a child stand out in someone's mind.
- Fingerprint your child and keep both the fingerprints and the child's Social Security number in a safe, accessible place.
- Teach your child how to call you. Have him or her memorize phone numbers where you can be reached, if the child is old enough. Explain collect calls and let the child know how to make one.
- Make sure your child's dentist maintains up-to-date dental records and keep track of where his or her medical records are located.
- Make certain all schools, day care centers, babysitters, and anyone else who might have care and control of the child are aware of outstanding custody orders. If you have reason to believe abduction is a possibility, put the other caretakers on alert. Provide them with a photograph of the noncustodial parent so they can better identify him or her, and give orders to be notified if the noncustodial parent shows up unscheduled or if the child fails to arrive when expected.

- Establish rules about where your children can go, including whose car they can ride in and whose homes they can enter. Make sure your children understand these rules.
- Listen to what your child says. Sometimes there are clues that a non-custodial parent may be planning a kidnapping and they may not seem significant until viewed in hindsight.
- Keep a DNA sample. One way to do this is to take a swab of the inside of your child's mouth with a clean, dry cotton swab or a used toothbrush kept in a brown paper envelope stored in a cool, dry place.
- Reinforce with anyone who has possession or control of your child—even a friend's mom or the soccer coach—that the child is not allowed to leave or deviate from a preapproved schedule without your permission.
- Assess possible abduction factors and ask the court to consider ordering supervised visitation and other provisions that will help circumvent kidnapping attempts.
- Retain three certified copies of the court order granting you custody.
- Keep records on the other parent, including address, phone number, physical description, photograph, any identifying numbers (like a driver's license), birth date, background information including prior places of residence, relatives, friends, hobbies, habits, vehicles, and access to other resources such as bank accounts and cash.
- Talk to your lawyer about flagging airlines and speaking with police or the prosecutor's office if the threat seems imminent.
- Know the proper authorities and resources available to you if an abduction attempt occurs or is successful.

The Hague Convention, mentioned earlier, is an important component for remedying international parental abductions. The convention was put in place in part to reduce the harmful effects of international abductions and to promote the rapid and lawful return of children kidnapped and taken abroad. It doesn't always work that way, though: not all countries have signed the convention and of those that have signed not every one is always in compliance.

The Philippines is not a Hague Convention signatory, nor does the United States have a treaty governing child abduction with that nation. A child who falls victim to a parental kidnapping and is taken from the United States to the Philippines, therefore, would be subject to Philippine laws and the way their courts interpret them.

Furthermore, parental abduction is not a crime in the Philippines, as it is in the United States; instead, it is considered a civil matter. It is traditional in that country for children under the age of seven to be placed with their mothers unless authorities deem them unfit. And, although the United States and the

Philippines have a standing extradition treaty, parental abduction is not extraditable. Laws that vary so much from nation to nation make an already-difficult situation even more frustrating, especially when a parental kidnapping involves multiple foreign countries.

A nation that is a signatory of the Hague Convention, like the United Kingdom, would in theory offer more assistance to the aggrieved parent than one that is not. However, even convention signatories are not always cooperative, resulting in what can turn into years of haggling in court over the return of a child. In all fairness, other countries have complained that the United States is also slow in righting wrongs in cases of parental abduction when a child has been removed to the United States. When viewed under the lens of world opinion, Americans don't always practice what they preach.

According to KlaasKids Foundation (www.klaaskids.org, established in honor of twelve-year-old Polly Klaas, who was abducted by a stranger from the bedroom of her California home and slain), "family kidnapping is committed primarily by parents, involves a larger percentage of female perpetrators than other types of kidnapping offenses, occurs more frequently to children under six, equally victimizes juveniles of both sexes, and most often originates in the home."

Some believe because the kidnapped child is with a parent, he or she is safe; however, these abductions deprive the remaining parent of the child's company and can lead to a much more sinister conclusion.

According to the OJJDP, parental kidnappings have the potential for many negative effects on the targeted child. Abducted children can be

- exposed to psychological harm;
- forced to live a fugitive existence;
- subjected to having their names and appearances altered;
- prevented from attending school;
- coerced into believing their left-behind parent does not love them, was abusive, or is deceased;
- coached to fear authority figures such as police;
- neglected or mistreated; and
- killed.

Parents run with their kids for a variety of reasons, but the most common motivators are power, control, and revenge: they want to hurt the other parent, deprive him or her of the child's companionship, and show that parent "who is boss." And every so often, the parental abductor does the unthinkable, as in the case of Lindsey and Sam Porter, ages eight and seven, whose father, Daniel, picked them up for a weekend visit on June 5, 2004.

At the time, Daniel and his wife, Tina, both of Independence, Missouri, were going through an acrimonious divorce. Tina Porter later told investigators that the kids were excited about spending time with their dad. A judge had granted Daniel weekend visitations with his children despite his history of substance abuse and threats toward Tina. When her husband collected the kids, Tina reminded him to have them back by six o'clock on Sunday night. Later that day, Tina told investigators, Daniel began to send her a series of strange, menacing messages.

Tina said the text messages led her on a bizarre search for her children, a kind of macabre scavenger hunt in which Daniel would direct Tina to different places where he claimed to have hidden either clues to Lindsey and Sam's location or had stashed the children themselves. He also called with repeated suicide threats. Tina later told reporters she appealed to police, who pointed out that because the couple was still married, Daniel had as much right to the kids as she did—the equivalent of an official shoulder shrug.

The time to return the kids came and went. A frantic Tina again contacted police and begged for help. She said she was told to give Daniel a little more time. The next morning officers launched a search. Monday night, Daniel was arrested and charged with driving under the influence of an impairing substance in a nearby jurisdiction, but because there was no hold put on him, he bonded out of jail. Two days later, authorities located Daniel again, and after a bizarre confrontation in which they shot out the tires on his truck, he was apprehended and questioned as to the whereabouts of his children.

Daniel told anyone who would listen that the kids were "in a better place." Charged with both parental abduction and kidnapping, he was tried and sentenced to eight years imprisonment because the children had not yet been found.

Three years after their father picked them up for a weekend outing, the skeletal remains of Lindsey and Sam were found in a wooded area near Independence, a place where Daniel once liked to hunt. Daniel murdered them a few hours after he picked them up from their mother.

"Daniel had actually taken them, put them face down, shot them in the back of the head, and buried them in a grave that was less than three feet deep," says one individual involved in the case who asked not to be named. "It was horrible."

Authorities say Daniel told them that after taking his kids to a fast-food restaurant for breakfast, he drove them to the wooded area, where he spread out a blanket, blindfolded them, and had them lie on the blanket. He then shot them both at the same time, a gun in each hand.

—∞∞∞—

Not every case of parental abduction ends in such a terrible way. Jake Schmidt, a private investigator who works out of Beverly Hills, California, takes on a few pro bono parental abduction cases each year. He once heard of a situation involving a little boy believed to have been abducted by his noncustodial father and taken to Mexico.

Schmidt says that Colton O'Neal's mother and his stepmother, frustrated by the inability of local police to track the missing child, approached the feds for assistance. The women claimed they got the brush-off, so they launched their own initiative, establishing a Web site, giving interviews critical of law enforcement, and snagging Schmidt's attention.

In one month, Schmidt was able to find the boy and bring him home. The child had been missing for a year and a half before being reunited with his family.

The California private operative has a long list of cases of children he has located who were taken by noncustodial parents. He found little Everett and Celestia Langille (who were ages one and two, respectively, when they were abducted) in Los Angeles after their father, Michael, was discovered working there—far from their kids' home in Pennsylvania. The children were reunited with their mother, Nicole, after evaporating for five months—a long, agonizing time for the young mother who, as Schmidt remarked when he found them, was robbed of seeing her young son take his first step.

"The first thing I tell any client is to have reasonable expectations about what can be done, and don't base [those expectations] on movies and television," Schmidt says, adding, "Most people don't have reasonable expectations."

Family abductions are the most common type of child abduction, and child abductions are more common than most realize: according to the National Incidence Studies of Missing, Abducted, Runaway and Thrownaway Children (NISMART-2), which was released in 2002, more than 200,000 children are reported as abducted by family members each year. Another 58,000 kids are taken each year by nonfamily members, and about 115 of what are referred to as "stereotypical" kidnappings occur in which ransom demands are made, the kidnapper plans to keep the child permanently, or the victim is killed.

The NISMART report broke down the statistics on family-abducted children even further: of a total of 203,900 abductions classified as family abductions for the purposes of the report, 117,200 are classified as "caretaker missing," a subcategory that the report's authors defined as "the caretaker did not know where the child was, became alarmed for at least an hour, and looked for the child." In 56,500 of the family abductions studied, the child was reported as missing to authorities.

That's another number that bears closer scrutiny: not all children who are abducted by a parent are reported missing. In fact, the majority are not reported because many times the custodial parent is aware of the child's whereabouts. One example of this takes place when a child is on a visitation with the other parent and is not returned at the appropriate time.

Family abduction ranks second to running away as the most common reason a child goes missing. Of family-abducted children, the fathers took 53 percent, while mothers are responsible for 25 percent. Grandparents, aunts, uncles, and other family members abducted the remainder of those children.

The good news is that 46 percent are returned within a week; 21 percent are returned within a month of their abductions. The majority of kids taken by a family member are recovered in a short amount of time, but other custodial parents, like Stephen Watkins and David Goldman, must launch complicated and expensive searches for their children.

In the excellent government resource, *Family Abduction Prevention*, author Patricia M. Hoff outlines the following steps a parent should take when searching for a child:

- File a missing persons report with the appropriate law enforcement agency.
- Request that the agency enter your child into National Crime Information Center Missing Person File with a child abduction flag.
- Request the issuance of an Amber Alert.
- Contact the National Center for Missing and Exploited Children.
- Search for information under any aliases the abductor may be using (think maiden, middle, and former names, and so forth).
- Keep a record of every person and agency with whom you come in contact, and stay in touch with them.
- When your child is located, follow up with the agencies and individuals who assisted you with your search.

In addition to the above suggestions, it also helps to network with missing persons organizations, including the clearinghouses in each state (a full list of these clearinghouses can be found in *Family Abduction Prevention* or at www .klaaskids.org). Another exceptional resource can be the organizations that belong to the Association of Missing and Exploited Children's Organizations (AMECO), whose member organizations offer various levels of support and advice for families whose children are missing. One of those sites belongs to Kelly Jolkowski, founder of Project Jason (www.projectjason.org).

Many of the people Kelly helps through her Web site and work have children who were the targets of parental abductions. But there are others who advocate for children kidnapped by a parent for a very different reason. They are members of an underground network that helps women who claim to be fleeing abusive partners for the sake of the children.

The most visible of these is an Atlanta woman who has admitted to operating an underground network that assists women who claim the fathers of their children present a danger to those kids—the most common being molestation. The underground network reportedly helps the women prepare to leave, assists them in establishing new identities for themselves and their kids, and then helps them relocate.

The woman from the underground network has told the press that she stopped relocating families in the United States and now helps them escape abroad, most often to countries where the inclination to enforce the Hague Convention is lax. She also has claimed in interviews that over the years she has received unofficial support from law enforcement officials, including the FBI and prosecutors. Whether certain officials give her a wink and a nod is not known, but the fact remains that she been very successful, even withstanding threat of both civil and criminal actions. And she is not alone: evidence suggests a large underground network dedicated to the same cause.

In 2007, a man who went by the name of Clark Rockefeller was charged with kidnapping his seven-year-old daughter, Reigh, from her mother's custody. Although he claimed to be a scion of the famous New York Rockefellers, he was exposed after his arrest as a German whose real name is Christian Karl Gerhartsreiter. He stayed on the run for six days until authorities apprehended him in Baltimore. Reigh was recovered and returned to her mother.

Extensive press coverage helped nail Gerhartsreiter and led to the little girl's return, but even media coverage doesn't always result in a quick and happy resolution.

In 1979, a Harvard Law School Legal Clinic supervisor took his two daughters—five-year-old Rachael and two-year-old Wendy—and fled with them to Florida. The girls would be raised under an alias. His former wife, Barbara Kurth, spent eighteen years looking for her children.

Arrested in 1998, Stephen Fagan, now known as Bill Martin, served no active time. He claimed in court and to the media that he ran with the children because his ex-wife was violent and a substance abuser—two unproven charges that Barbara and her family have denied. No concrete evidence supports his claim, but as far as anyone knows, the girls—both now grown—have failed to re-establish a relationship with their mother.

Although both matters were resolved, as in all instances of family abduction, no "happily ever after" exists. In Reigh's case, her father was exposed as a fraud, and the story will follow her wherever she goes in life. In the Fagan abductions, the family was broken apart and the probability is that it will never heal.

While these cases may seem extraordinary, family abduction itself is not. NISMART's figures indicate that in the United States alone enough children are abducted by family members on an average day to fill a school bus every other hour, twenty-four hours a day, seven days a week, 365 days a year.

The Mentally Ill and Substance Abuse:
The Forgotten Missing

The main symptom of a psychiatric case is that the person is per-
fectly unaware that he is a psychiatric case.—attributed to Oleg
Shchepin, Russian health official

*T*om Zinza had not contacted his family or anyone else as far as they know
for more than two years. They were mystified as to what could have happened
to him, but what they did know was this: the Fairbanks, Alaska, resident and
would-be writer climbed aboard a commercial airline flight on February 17,
2008, and landed in Cleveland. It was the first leg of a planned trip to Boston,
but for some reason no one understands, Tom chose not to make the connection. Instead, he slept in a Cleveland hotel room that night. The next day he
drove by rental car through a place called Wooster to Emlenton, Pennsylvania,
where he checked into the Emlenton Motor Inn.

Two days later, the cleaning lady at the motor inn called the Pennsylvania
State Police and told them that the man who rented Tom Zinza's room never
slept there. His rental car also sat unused, where he parked it when he first
signed the motel's guestbook.

Other circumstances flagged Tom's disappearance as out of the ordinary.
For one thing, Ohio law enforcement officers found Tom's luggage, including
his laptop and a collection of his writings, along a highway near the town of
Wooster. And, prior to the former U.S. Marine's departure from Fairbanks,
he told his father and older brother, John, that he was sure someone was trying to kill him.

That someone might be out to kill Tom is a theory most would dismiss
out of hand, but he had a long history of mental problems, and those claims
were in sync with his illness. Tom suffered from post-traumatic stress disorder,
bipolar disorder, and psychosis. He also experienced constant pain due to

repeated right ankle fractures, chronic knee problems, and a herniated disk. But Tom had been doing well over the past few years, living independently on his disability checks in a cabin with his two cats, writing poetry and stories, and pursuing his dream of being published.

Tom was the type of nice guy that people remembered. With an extensive network of buddies from his hitch in the service, he had stayed in touch with many of his old friends, although in recent years he led a more secluded life. When he was on his medication, he did fine. When he went off his meds, the world tilted.

Although Tom experienced downward slides before, his brother John helped him overcome his demons time and time again. John says that the last big breakdown started in late 2003, but by spring, Tom was back on track. The experience brought the two brothers—one disabled and fighting for an identity, the other a successful civil engineer—much closer than they ever had been.

John kept in constant contact with Tom, following up with Tom's mental health clinic, making sure he was taking his medications, putting out the little fires before they became bigger ones. Both John and his father sensed something was afoot about ten days before Tom boarded that plane. John says Tom made some financial changes, was preparing to deal with his debts, and placed at least one phone call to a number in Mt. Pocono, Pennsylvania.

Then Tom told his brother he was going to leave Alaska as soon as possible to visit Tom's former wife, her three daughters, and some friends from his Marine Corps years. The next day, February 15, Tom dumped his medications in the trash and asked his mental health provider to prescribe some new ones. Tom boarded a plane the day after that and vanished somewhere along I-80 in Pennsylvania.

John Zinza grows so emotional when he talks about his gentle younger brother that he chokes out the words. John knew that because Tom was diagnosed with a mental illness some agencies would not give his disappearance the weight it deserved. Tom could have been anywhere, without the ability to contact his family or to do something as simple as telling someone his own name.

After Tom disappeared, John retrieved his brother's car from the airport and visited his Fairbanks home. The cabin looked as if Tom had just walked out the door for a moment. There were no signs he planned to be away for any length of time. John found Tom's cats and took them to a shelter, cleaned up the garbage Tom left behind, and read through the stack of unopened mail for clues as to what might have happened to his brother. The bank would later foreclose on the simple cabin.

Then John started bumping heads with the system. Tom flew out of Fairbanks, landed in Ohio, and drove to Pennsylvania. John dealt with both state police and local law enforcement in all three states. Alaska said from their viewpoint, Tom was not missing because he left the state of his own volition. Ohio pointed to the fact that Tom landed in Ohio but checked into a Pennsylvania motel. Pennsylvania referred John back to Alaska.

In early 2010 John said, "I don't think he's in good law enforcement hands. I don't know if Ohio followed up on any of the leads on his case. Alaska says Pennsylvania is the lead agency. Pennsylvania says the same thing about Alaska."

In fairness, Pennsylvania authorities did search the wooded areas near the motor inn where Tom was last seen, but the searches were not for Tom—they were for his corpse. That was in the summer following his winter disappearance. In the spring of 2009, John managed to spark another search using trained cadaver dogs and multiple search-and-rescue groups as well as law enforcement agencies.

With his voice breaking, John said afterward, "I think they will find bones in the area five, ten, or maybe even twenty years from now. I cry every day for my brother."

But Tom was not the only brother for whom John shed tears. In a family of five boys, two have vanished without a trace. James Zinza, one of John and Tom's two older brothers, has not been seen nor heard from since February 28, 1992, when he disappeared from his Mesa, Arizona, home.

John says his older brother, whom he called Jimmy, was not diagnosed with mental illness, but there were signs all was not right with him prior to his disappearance. Jimmy is intelligent and spiritual, according to John, who says Jimmy attended community college, rode his bike everywhere, loved cats and pizza, and led a quiet but fulfilling life. Still, in retrospect, John says he sees many of the same characteristics in Jimmy that Tom later exhibited.

Jimmy moved around a lot, traveling across the country before settling in Mesa. "That is where we started seeing the cracks," says John.

The very last time John saw Jimmy—a thirty-year-old with an easy smile and receding hairline—was right before he went missing. John and his wife were moving and had a pile of magazines they thought Jimmy would like, so they drove over to his place to drop them off. Their last meeting was awkward for reasons John didn't understand at the time. Jimmy told him he didn't want the magazines, didn't invite them to sit down, and seemed anxious for them to leave.

"He didn't want anything to do with me," John says.

Then Jimmy was gone. By the time the Zinza family discovered he had vanished, no one had seen Jimmy for days. The oldest Zinza brother (John is the middle child of the five boys) hired a private investigator to look for Jimmy, but he failed to turn up any clues pointing to Jimmy's fate.

It was as if Jimmy Zinza never existed.

"If he's dead, he's not been found. Is he in a landfill underneath some vegetation, or in some sheriff's office, cremated, or maybe in an unmarked grave somewhere?" John asks. His voice quavers when he talks about Jimmy.

For years, the four remaining Zinza brothers and their parents looked for Jimmy, trying to break through the limbo of not knowing where their loved one is or what happened to him. Then, almost fifteen years later, Tom followed Jimmy into the void. It is almost more than one family can handle.

John says there is a distinct difference in how his two brothers' cases were handled. He believes everything possible was done to locate Jimmy, while help came too little and too late for Tom. He thinks both men disappeared as the result of mental disorders but at one point he didn't know whether either—or both—ended up as part of the homeless population or dead. Time is the enemy in these cases, and the law makes it hard for families to exercise any control over their situations.

"I'm burnt out mentally on all of this stuff. I cry. This is the last three years of my life," says John.

But he never gave up on Tom, and he hasn't abandoned his decade-and-a-half search for Jimmy, either. "I don't want to go through the rest of my life feeling like I didn't do everything I can do to find them," John says. And so he plugged on, talking to law enforcement, putting up flyers, chasing down each and every lead, no matter how vague or pointless it seemed. But each night, when John climbed into his bed, he did so with a little less hope, a little less determination, a little less spirit than he had when he first arose.

"You can't begin to imagine what it's like," he says.

On October 3, 2010, the skeletonized remains of Tom Zinza were found in the woods not far from the Pennsylvania motel where he had been staying. An autopsy concluded no foul play was involved in his death.

———&oxo&———

They huddle on the sidewalks, holding cups and begging coins. They push grocery carts loaded with items fished from trash bins and picked up from the side of the road. They crowd shelters when they can find them, curl up in cardboard boxes when they can't. Many times they end up frozen and dead in some morgue, as nameless and anonymous in death as they were in the last days of their lives. They are the chronically homeless—people who remain on the streets, not the ones who find themselves without a place to live for a day or two—and many are mentally ill.

Sherrill Britton believes her missing son, Adam Kellner, once joined the homeless ranks that haunt nearby Los Angeles. Britton and her other son have combed the area's homeless district, known as Skid Row, looking for Adam, putting up flyers, talking to everyone they meet, with no success. The widow and former Miami resident knows Adam is out there somewhere, but he remains out of reach.

Adam, who at the time of this writing was thirty-seven, couldn't make it through the day without his pack and half of cigarettes and the hat he always wore to cover his bald spot; yet a couple of weeks before Thanksgiving 2007, he walked out the door of the beautiful upscale home he shared with his mother and stepfather thirty miles north of Los Angeles and left his pack of Benson and Hedges behind. Adam took with him no clothes and no money, not even his ever-present hat. The one item Britton couldn't find was the note pad Adam used to write down the names of his imaginary girlfriends.

Adam has schizophrenia. He hears voices, but he's a kind, sweet man who cared for his ailing stepfather and preferred the insulation of his mother's home to the uncertainty of the outside world. Adam didn't drive—his license was revoked following his diagnosis—instead he took buses. When he disappeared, Britton talked to the bus drivers with routes through Stevenson Ranch, where she and Adam lived. None had seen him.

Adam's medication played a key role in keeping him on keel. Britton put his meds into one of those plastic Sunday through Saturday containers—one for day and one for night—and Adam knew how to administer his medications

Adam Kellner with his late stepfather and his mother, Leonard and Sherrill Britton. Courtesy of Sherrill Britton.

without assistance. On the date he vanished, it appeared Adam had taken his daytime pills.

Britton was on a brief overnight business trip, the first one she'd taken in years. Her husband, Adam's stepfather, was recovering from surgery and Adam had taken an active role in his care.

From Miami before moving to California, Adam was a standout athlete and a good student who showed no signs of mental issues until he started college. That's when things began to slide downhill. When his illness began to affect his birth father's new marriage, Adam moved to California to live with his mother and her new husband, establishing himself in a happy, though somewhat isolated, life.

When Adam first vanished, Britton and her family went into overdrive. They filed a missing persons report with local authorities, made and distributed flyers, searched the surrounding area, and even had a spot on a local news program. Based on a tip that came in, Britton believes Adam may have ended up on L.A.'s Skid Row.

Skid Row, which extends several square blocks in Central City East, is home to an estimated eight thousand "residents." No one knows the exact population of Skid Row, and no one ever will because it changes daily as the pool of homeless circulate in and out of the district. It's a tough area, and a hard place to look for someone since a lot the residents don't want to be found.

Britton discovered how difficult that natural resistance could be when she started looking for Adam there. A security guard she encountered told her that he had given her son a pair of shoes—but the size was wrong. Others swore they had seen him and were convincing enough that Britton felt a small spark of hope from their stories. But her search yielded nothing, not a single substantial lead.

"Even the missions down there tell you. 'We can't tell you if he's down here or not,'" she says. In the eyes of the law, Adam has certain rights, even though his mother says he isn't competent to make life-altering decisions.

Not giving up, Britton put a video about Adam on YouTube and created a Facebook page for him. She offered a reward, hired a private detective, and collected both his dental records and DNA evidence in case the news, when it comes, isn't good.

And despite her efforts, Britton fears it won't be. Her home backs up to a large stretch of wilderness and she wonders if Adam could have wandered into it. "There was no argument, no compelling reason for him to leave," she says. "The police didn't suspect foul play and neither did I, and we couldn't get search and rescue to go into the woods."

Officials, as a rule, resist mounting large search-and-rescue efforts when there's no compelling evidence the individual might be in a particular area. It's frustrating for the families of the missing but understandable from a cold, hard numbers point of view. Most jurisdictions don't have the money to pursue theories.

But there are other issues at play when the missing person is mentally ill. Britton says she sees it all the time: mentally ill individuals are less valued as persons and many people fear them.

"There is an absolute prejudice against the mentally ill," she says. "If he were a beautiful blond or a five-year-old, his case would get tons of publicity. A thirty-five-year-old (Adam's age at the time of his disappearance), mentally ill man is not a sexy case; it just isn't."

Looking for Adam has occupied almost all of Britton's spare time. She returned to Skid Row on the first anniversary of Adam's disappearance with a fistful of flyers and saw the ones she posted the previous year, tattered, but still there. The experience has been an education.

"I had no idea how many missing people are out there," Britton says.

Of the thousands who go missing each year, many have been diagnosed with mental illness. Andrew Sperling, director of legislative advocacy for the National Alliance on Mental Illness (NAMI), echoes Britton's thoughts. "Sure," he says while pecking away at his computer keyboard, "there's a stigma associated with mental illness." But Sperling adds that compelling the mentally ill to take medication is a complex issue with two distinct camps of thought and no clear-cut moral right or wrong.

One side believes the mentally ill should have the right to accept or decline medication, while the other says that without the medication the mentally ill cannot make informed or healthy choices. Both have merit, but what is not open for debate is that the presence of mental illness makes it much more likely that an individual will end up missing or on the streets. Mental illness also often leads to addiction of one sort or another. The drunk or the druggie who sleeps on the heat vent or crowds into the local shelter many times suffers mental illness of one sort or another. Treatment is an imprecise science, a slapdash thing, almost like throwing mud at a wall and seeing what sticks. Some drugs work, some don't, and their effects vary from individual to individual. Sometimes, those drugs also have side effects that make patients feel strange, dull their cognitive abilities, pack on the pounds, or cause them to be unsteady and lumbering. Most psych drugs are prescribed in combinations known as cocktails, and they can have deadly, life-altering side effects, resulting in disorders like tardive dyskinesia, which manifests as involuntary movement (somewhat akin to Tourette syndrome), usually of the face, and is permanent and nonreversible.

Still, there are few viable alternatives to drugs. And when an individual who requires drug therapy to remain on an even keel goes off the drugs, tragedy can result, as in the case of Kendra Webdale and Andrew Goldstein.

Webdale, a thirty-two-year-old New York resident, stood on one of that city's subway platforms on January 3, 1999, shivering against the cold, when a schizophrenic named Andrew Goldstein approached her and asked the time, then shoved her into the path of the oncoming train, killing her. Goldstein was off his medication and out of control when the incident took place. Following that incident, New York instituted Kendra's Law, which allows individuals to seek court-ordered assistance in forcing the mentally ill to remain on their medications. But, even with some legislation in place (and not every state has this type of provision, and when they do, they are not always permanent codifications, but often temporary), some diagnosed with mental illnesses quit taking their meds.

For those affected by diagnoses such as bipolar disorder and schizophrenia, the fallout from abandoning drug therapy as prescribed can be inestimable: crime sprees, substance abuse, and the disruption of a life that might have been under control. And it can get worse; for some, stopping the meds that keep them on an even keel can increase their vulnerability, lead them to wander off, or make them more susceptible to foul play. Some, like Tom Zinza and Adam Kellner, vanish like wisps of smoke, leaving behind few clues and a family who wonders what happened—did their loved one walk away or was it something more sinister that took them from the safe and familiar? Is he or she living on the streets or huddled in a homeless shelter somewhere, or was that person a victim of crime? These are recurring, always cycling questions for the families of the missing mentally ill, and often no real answer ever presents itself.

And these are the same questions Randa Jawhari's large and loving family is forced to confront every day. They want to know whether the petite and vivacious Michigan woman entered the nameless, faceless sea of the displaced and homeless, and if not, what happened? They don't believe the devoted mother would choose to walk away from her life. It wasn't like her. The Jawharis, a large, close-knit group, search for Randa in every crowd and every face they see.

Naheda Jawhari, one of Randa's seven siblings, says her sister disappeared from her Fenton, Michigan, apartment on February 11, 2009, and hasn't been seen since. Randa, who was diagnosed with bipolar disorder, lived an independent life, but sometimes had difficulty understanding the importance of her medication.

"She was not good about taking her medications," Naheda concedes. "She'd gotten off of them in the past and in trouble with her driving. It seems everybody can see something's wrong except the person who is ill."

Naheda's point is one that is recognized as an ongoing problem with many who suffer from mental illness. It is probable Randa suffered from a condition known as anosognosia, which the Treatment Advocacy Center (TAC) defines as an "impaired awareness of illness." The TAC also says anosognosia is "the single largest reason why individuals with schizophrenia and bipolar disorder do not take their medications."

In other words, the person who is sick does not recognize that he or she has an illness and doesn't feel the need to take the medication. In many cases, he or she resents being medicated.

Although Randa strayed from her prescriptions now and then, the family had a routine structured for her and she was doing well following it. Naheda says she is sure Randa was taking her medication the way she was supposed to at the time she disappeared. "She was fine; she was fine. If I knew that she wasn't medicated, part of me would think she did walk away," Naheda says.

Randa's mom, who has custody of her young daughter, visited Randa every day. Mrs. Jawhari set out Randa's meds and clothes and looked after her. Randa, a tiny woman who stands five feet, one inch and weighs in at around one hundred pounds, thrived on her family's attention and was addicted to telephone calls. Naheda says her sister stayed in constant phone contact with her and other family members.

"Her form of communication is the phone. She calls every day, several times a day; there is constant communication with her. She's a family gal," Naheda says.

And that is why her persistent silence is like a wound that won't heal.

Randa was on disability but living on her own at the time of her disappearance. The day she vanished, Randa did not call her little girl—something Naheda says she did without fail every morning. When her mom went to Randa's apartment to check on her daughter, she found the clothes she had set out for Randa the night before still there, untouched, unworn. The only item of clothing missing was Randa's blue robe, which she had been wearing the night before. They canvassed family and friends, and no one had seen or talked to her since about 11:30 the previous night.

Randa, like Sherrill Britton's missing son, Adam, is addicted to cigarettes. Naheda remembers Randa once panhandled at a McDonald's for enough money to buy a pack. The local police called her mother, who picked her up and brought her home.

"Randa has no conception of money," says Naheda, who says no one who knows Randa believes her sister abandoned her daughter and family. "We believe something serious happened to her, but we hope we're wrong."

She says the police theorize Randa's illness prompted her to leave. Her apartment was not treated as a crime scene, nor was it processed, according to

Naheda, who believes an opportunity was missed. Five days after Randa vanished, Naheda says officials searched the surrounding area using a helicopter, but still no sign of the effervescent, attractive young mother surfaced.

"It's not being investigated as a crime—she's a missing adult unless someone sees her or she comes home on her own," Naheda says.

The Jawhari family raised a reward, distributed posters throughout the area with a concentration on homeless shelters and missions, and sought news coverage. They've also pestered local law enforcement to revisit Randa's disappearance. The Jawharis drive cars decorated with posters bearing Randa's image. They've sent Randa's information as far south as Florida, hoping that if someone has seen her, they'll contact the police or the Jawharis. They've tried to get their congressman involved, contacted the state attorney general's office, written letters, and made calls to anyone and everyone who will listen, but thus far their sister and daughter stays missing, and they remain frustrated.

"We know it's like looking for a needle in a haystack, but it just takes one person," Naheda says, her voice colored by her ever-present but dwindling hope.

Does she believe Randa's case has warranted different treatment due to her mental illness? Without a doubt. "They're not listening," says Naheda, with a palpable bitterness. "If my sister was a politician's daughter or the daughter of a police chief, it would be a whole different thing, but she's not important to them."

Law enforcement does look at the mentally ill in a different context than other individuals since their illness can lead them to vanish without warning. But because in many cases there is no evidence to support the premise that the individual left for any reason other than mental problems, they are also perfect victims. Randa Jawhari could disappear, and due to her mental illness, no one in the world of officialdom would find it compelling enough to engage in a full-court press to find her.

Says her sister, "Nobody cares. Nobody. It's like screaming and screaming at the top of your lungs with no voice coming out. If my sister is not living, I still want her soul to rest. I want to know what she went through."

As for law enforcement's response to her troubled sister's vanishing, Naheda believes that overall, they're not trained to deal with cases like Randa's.

"If they were better trained, then maybe we could have found Randa and not be where we are today: wondering where she is, wondering what happened to her. Always, always wondering," says Naheda.

Libba Phillips, founder of Outpost for Hope (www.outpostforhope.org), sympathizes with the Jawharis and their frustration. Phillips has undergone her own odyssey through the maze of missing persons while trying to bring home her sister, Ashley, who suffers from both bipolar disorder and drug addiction.

Ashley's story began in 1999, when the young woman first disappeared from Tampa, Florida. According to Libba, police told the Phillips family Ashley was not missing because, under Florida law, she was considered an adult who left of her own will. Tracing Ashley to Georgia, where they found she had served time in jail on a drug offense, the family hoped Ashley would be arrested and jailed so they could get her back into treatment. Instead, Libba believes, Ashley was dismissed out of hand as a prostitute.

"My experience with [filing a report as a missing person] boils down to stigma," says Libba. "Ashley was described as a drug-addicted, mentally ill prostitute. When a person hears that term, they put her in the category of subhuman."

Ashley has never been arrested and charged with prostitution as far as the Phillips family knows, but Libba believes that her status on the street marred any chance the family had of getting their daughter and sister back and that police, as well as society in general, were predisposed to dismiss Ashley as someone not worth bothering about. Libba and Ashley's mom, Michelle, tried on many occasions to file a missing persons report, but they were always denied that right. In the meantime, what the Phillips family learned of Ashley's life left them bruised and shaken. Ashley had been hit by a car, beaten, and locked up—and her family remained one step behind her.

The family also applied to have Ashley committed under Florida's Baker Act. The Baker Act provides for voluntary or involuntary commitment to a psychiatric facility for observation, diagnosis, and, if warranted, treatment. It is often invoked when the individual is engaging in behavior that could lead to serious harm. Libba says the judge agreed their case had merit, but in order to proceed under Baker, they needed Ashley's location, which the family could not provide. Like all of the streets the Phillips family traveled in its quest to help Ashley, this was one more dead end.

Libba decided that if she could not save Ashley, at least she could draw attention to the thousands of individuals she terms the "missing missing," or the unreported missing. Among those she includes are persons who are estranged from family and friends and thus no one realizes they are missing; individuals who disappear and do not qualify for one reason or another for official missing persons reports, like Ashley Phillips; undocumented or illegal aliens; and unknown dependent children of unreported missing persons—like babies born to street people or prostitutes.

Outpost for Hope, the organization Libba founded to champion the rights of the thousands of unacknowledged missing in the United States, claims there are approximately one million unreported missing persons in this country alone, and that is a conservative estimate. Libba believes that many of these unreported missing are victims of human trafficking and other exploitative situations. Others are shunted aside as mentally ill, homeless, street people, or kids in foster care—people who fall through the cracks of the social system.

Many times the "missing missing" Libba Phillips refers to are those whose lives play out on a different stage than the one the average American sees: in back alleys, slums, and the wrong sides of the tracks. She notes that the prime modus operandi for Gary Leon Ridgeway, a serial murderer known as the Green River Killer who preyed on women in Washington State, was to pick victims who would not be noticed and reported as missing. He did a good job: among the forty-eight dead women and teenagers whose demises are attributed to Ridgeway, several still remain unidentified years after their slayings.

Without a doubt, the mentally ill, and in particular those with concurrent substance abuse problems like Libba Phillips's sister, Ashley, form the single greatest component of the missing and unreported population. According to Outpost for Hope, individuals with mental illness are more than twice as likely to become victims of violent crime than the general population, and about half of mentally ill homeless adults also suffer from substance abuse and dependency, which makes them even more difficult to track.

Because each jurisdiction sets its own standards for reporting a person missing, the playing field is uneven where the mentally ill are concerned. Some jurisdictions take all missing persons reports seriously and err on the side of documenting a person missing erroneously rather than failing to file a report, while others will not take a report on a missing adult without suspicion of foul play. For those families with adults suffering from mental disorders, being unable to report their mentally ill kin as missing makes it hard to search for them. Many official avenues are closed to those who don't have an official missing persons report. And that often leads to incredible heartbreak, as in the case of Susan McDonough of Reading, Pennsylvania.

In December 2008, forty-two-year-old Susan, a victim of schizophrenia, disappeared. It was bitter cold that winter and her relatives, including her half brother Mark, were worried about her safety. Mark says he tried to report his sister missing, but in the beginning no one would take the report.

"It would have been very simple to fill out the report; it would have taken no time at all," Mark says. "But the officer spent more time [than a report would have taken] convincing me that he couldn't take a report because she was an adult. [Another officer] told me his brother was a drug addict [who was] missing over ten years and said they couldn't go looking for every adult, because [missing adults] had a right to do what they wanted."

Susan had a long, torturous history of going off the medication that kept her illness under control. After she and her mother were evicted as a result of Susan's inability to get along with neighbors, Susan lived for a time with the man she believed to be her father (although he never acknowledged paternity) in a house on Linden Street in nearby Reading. When the home in which they lived was sold to satisfy a tax lien, Susan drifted from one living arrangement to another, but she kept returning to the Linden Street home. On December 4, 2008, she tried to camp out in the lobby of a hotel and the police were called. Police asked where she lived and she provided the Linden Street address—the place where she had once lived for so long. Her official identification corroborated her story, so the officer gave her a ride there and dropped her off. It was the last time she was seen alive.

When Susan failed to contact family members, Mark, his mother, Barbara, and other friends and family began to search for her.

"We knew something was wrong," Mark says. Calls to the police yielded no help at first, although a later visit to the Muhlenberg Police Department resulted in an offer to file a report if the Reading Police continued to refuse to do so. At last, the Muhlenberg Police did take a report on Susan's disappearance.

Prior to her disappearance, the McDonough family battled for years to compel Susan to take her medications and get treatment but found themselves stymied by Pennsylvania law, which, Mark says, required "a clear and present danger—like the equivalent of holding a gun to someone's head—before they'd do anything.

"We knew she was headed for disaster but [because of the laws concerning mentally ill persons] our hands were tied. It was so, so frustrating," Mark says.

The McDonoughs were in constant contact with local law enforcement as a result of Susan's tendency to wander. Mark says the system made it difficult for them to help Susan. She would be institutionalized on occasion for a week to ten days and then released. "They would let her go with no follow-up," Mark says. "Obviously, she wouldn't take her meds; she'd be sleepy and feel horrible. She wasn't in anywhere long enough to have a proper transition. They let them go when the side effects are full-blown."

When Susan refused her meds, her family could do nothing legally to compel her to take them. Then December came and Susan vanished. The family couldn't get help when she was wandering and couldn't get anyone to care that she was nowhere to be found. It was the ultimate bureaucratic catch-22: no one seemed willing to help Susan or her family.

"They 'can't do anything.' It's the same mantra everywhere. I don't know how much of it is the law, but I know that putting the mentally ill on the streets causes more problems, and ultimately costs more," Mark says.

But Susan didn't stay on the streets for very long that frigid December. Instead, investigators later theorized, the night she got the ride from the police officer or not long afterward, she broke into the little house where she had lived on Linden Street. The home stood empty and deserted, having been sold for unpaid taxes, but to Susan McDonough, the freezing little place was still her home. So she curled up on the floor of the kitchen and went to sleep. It was a sleep from which she would never awaken.

On May 30, 2009, a man contracted to renovate the Linden Street home for the new owner found Susan's body. She had been missing for almost six months. Mark remains angry about the circumstances that led to her death and his family's inability to access help for her.

"She had a great smile and was very generous. She took care of our grandma. Whenever anyone was sick, Susan always wanted to help. People loved her and wanted to be with her. This disease [schizophrenia] made her into someone we didn't know," Mark says.

Mark admits to frustration with the system, which he believes failed his sister in many ways. "The Reading Police said because she was homeless she wasn't really missing from anywhere," he says.

The McDonough family has lobbied for changes in the way their state handles the mentally ill who enter crisis mode, but no amount of legislation will restore Susan to their lives or assuage their grief. "She was such a beautiful person when she was doing okay," he says. "We are tormented and very angry about it."

Emma Carroll raised eleven children before her mind began to suffer the ravages of age-related dementia. Carroll, whose husband perished in a car accident in 1975, brought her children up with lots of love, the good cooking for which she was famous, and an unwavering faith in her God.

But at age eighty-three, Emma was losing her sharpness: she couldn't remember recent events and, to the sorrow of her extended family, was becoming more and more socially withdrawn. On July 18, 2009, the elderly African American woman who also suffered from hypertension walked away from her Pembroke, Georgia, home. She has not been seen since.

Unlike many who suffer from mental disorders, Carroll's granddaughter says there was an immediate, massive ground and air search for her grandmother.

"Over two hundred volunteers, air patrol, four-wheelers, canine patrol, and law enforcement from eighteen state and local agencies searched from sun up to sundown for eight straight days," says Dawn Williams. In the end there was no sign of Emma, no evidence of where she'd gone.

The family hopes that someone saw Emma and picked her up. They've hired a private investigator, held candlelight vigils, and distributed flyers emblazoned with her likeness. Based on the theory that Emma could have left the state with help, they're expanding their search into nearby areas of Alabama, South Carolina, and Florida.

"We will continue to look for her until we have a reason not to," Williams says.

NAMI says African Americans are less likely to receive proper diagnosis and treatment for mental illness. However, when it comes to dementia, there seems to be no racial lines and few differences in the rate at which individuals seek treatment.

Perhaps the reason the missing who suffer from dementia now grab more attention is because over the past few decades, awareness of mind-robbing diseases, including Alzheimer's and vascular dementia, has gravitated from the backs of medical journals to the front pages of newspapers. Ronald Reagan, one of this country's most iconic presidents and world leaders, suffered from Alzheimer's in his last years, a fact both he and his family acknowledged.

When an elderly individual with a diagnosis of dementia wanders off, most law enforcement agencies begin an immediate search. In many states, this is done under the auspices of a "Silver Alert" program.

Suggested by Oklahoma State Representative Fred Perry (R–Tulsa) and modeled on the Amber Alert program, which initiates a widespread public notification when a child goes missing, the Silver Alert was adopted by the Oklahoma Department of Public Safety and signed into law in April 2009. It is used to inform the public, news media, and various agencies when a qualifying individual goes missing.

Various forms of the Silver Alert exist from state to state, but almost all of them are aimed at elderly persons with dementia or other mental impairment. They aim to find the missing senior as fast as possible, and in many cases they succeed. Georgia has a successful program known as "Mattie's Call," named after a sixty-eight-year-old woman who wandered away from her Atlanta home. Her body was found eight months later a few hundred yards from her home.

While not all states employ an alert system for seniors, many experts believe they should because these systems work. In Georgia the Mattie's Call system helped return seventy of seventy-one missing seniors during a three-year period. Federal legislation to create a national Silver Alert system was stalled at the time of this writing, but supporters hope to push it through Congress.

For some, though, there is no bright and shiny piece of legislation to bring their families help and hope. Like Libba Phillips's sister, Ashley, their situations don't spark an immediate response by searchers. Instead, reactions tend to fall into the "he got what he deserved" category, and that adds more pain into the mix.

It took one word for the responding officer to stop taking notes on Troy Spencer Marks's disappearance: addict. Ashley Marks, Troy's wife and the mother of his two boys, admits her missing husband has demons, but she says he is trying to get straight and that no matter what substances he chose to abuse, he deserves to have someone out there looking for him.

Troy Spencer Marks. Courtesy of Ashley Y. Marks.

"I was interviewed for less than five minutes by a motorcycle officer from Ascension Parish [Louisiana]. I told him that [Troy] was an addict. Once I did this, the report was ended," Ashley says. "He even told me that I was better off."

Ashley says the officer also said an investigating detective would touch base with her the next day. "It's been three-and-one-half years, and I am still waiting for that detective to interview me," she says.

Like the mentally ill, those addicted to drugs and alcohol are more often than not given short shrift by an overburdened criminal justice system. For many officers, looking for individuals who disappear under circumstances involving drug abuse is an endless chore and one they have neither the resources nor the time to pursue.

But Ashley insists her husband is a good man, despite his chemical dependencies, and it is true that many addicts suffer from concurring, but often undiagnosed, mental disorders. While Troy has not been diagnosed with mental illness, Ashley says he fought to remain sober and never came home to his children when he was under the influence.

A handsome man with a shaved head and a goatee, Troy has blue eyes that sparkle with wit and a couple of distinctive tattoos, including one of Yosemite Sam holding a gun and a football. When he disappeared, Troy lived in New Orleans, where he worked concrete in the rebuilding efforts following Hurricane Katrina. On June 6, 2006, a friend dropped him off near North Dourgenois Street. Later that day, Troy failed to show up for work. He has not been heard from since. Some time later, his abandoned truck was located in the parking lot of a Baton Rouge apartment complex under suspicious circumstances.

Ashley says she knows deep in her heart of hearts that her Troy met with foul play. She understands better than anyone that his drug habits often led him to go to dark places where he should not have been. But she also believes that Troy's bad choices in life shouldn't result in his marginalization as a human being; nor, says Ashley, should it affect his status as a missing person.

She thinks law enforcement responds faster to missing persons who are mentally ill than to missing addicts and alcoholics—that they are society's last priority.

"I believe people look at drug addicts as low[lives]," Ashley says. "I want the world to know that regardless of what a person is, an addict or a mental patient, these are people. These are sons, daughters, mothers, fathers, wives, husbands. They do not deserve to be dismissed because they are not perfect members of society."

Ashley did get someone to listen to her—the police in Baton Rouge, where her missing husband's truck was found. Ashley believes the detective assigned to her husband's case (Detective Larry Maples of the Baton Rouge Police Department) wants to find Troy—or find out what happened to him. "He keeps the communication lines open and respects my opinion," Ashley says of Detective Maples. "I believe that is how we even the playing field: take the defects of character out of the [missing person] and focus on the fact that they are a person who happens to be missing."

Ashley is not naive enough to believe Troy is going to walk in her door any minute, alive, well, and sober. But she is hopeful that she will someday have answers. She wants her boys to know their father didn't desert them, that he loved them, wanted them, was proud of them.

"My sons need to know that Daddy did not leave them, because I do not believe he would ever just walk away," Ashley says.

Lisa Hodanish is another who doesn't believe a loving father would walk out on his children, even though her dad was approaching seventy when he disappeared and his children were grown.

David Neily, a slight man with a gray beard and piecing green eyes, has a history of mental illness, but his family had years of experience dealing with his disorder and his tendency to go off his medicine. Lisa says her father would cycle off his prescriptions, suffer an episode, get picked up by the local sheriff's department (Neily lived in Westport, California), and be confined to a mental hospital. "They would put him on lithium until he was stable and then release him to a relative," Lisa says.

David, diagnosed with bipolar disorder after years of shifting diagnoses, disappeared under circumstances that his children—five of them from two marriages—believe are suspicious. But because their father suffered from mental illness and had a history of disappearing, Lisa says law enforcement has also been slow to investigate their dad's situation.

"I think this case isn't important to authorities . . . because of his age," says Lisa. She adds that, despite his condition, he charmed those who met him. "He was at my wedding and no one could tell he had a mental illness. Everyone loved him and he loved to dance and dance," Lisa remembers.

Like Susan McDonough, David Neily also traveled through that revolving door of treatment and release that those with more serious psychiatric disorders often experience. After stabilizing as an inpatient, he'd go home. Lisa says, "They simply release the patient after about a week on meds just to be put back into the world and be responsible for taking their meds on their own."

Lisa says this didn't work for her father. And she, along with many families with adults who face mental disorders, believes that the current philosophy supported by law and adopted by the mental health system in this country does little but add to the population of missing persons—especially older ones.

"I think . . . not much is done for missing persons who are elderly. The cases that are more highlighted are missing children and pregnant women. I

David Neily. Courtesy of Lisa Hodanish.

believe all missing persons deserve to be found, no matter what their age or mental stability," Lisa says.

———∞———

The child snatched from a playground, the young housewife who vanishes leaving her kids behind, the college student who never returns from an evening out with friends—these are the kinds of cases that grab the headlines. When people suffering from mental illness or substance abuse disappear, they often attract little interest, either from the media or officials, although their numbers are thought to be in the hundreds of thousands. Advocates such as Outpost for Hope's Libba Phillips and Oklahoma politician Fred Perry work to give these missing individuals parity with the rest of the missing, but for now the sidewalks of this nation's cities are crowded with people someone, somewhere loves and misses but has no way of ever finding.

Far and Away: Disappearances Abroad

Traveling is a brutality. It forces you to trust strangers and to lose
sight of all that familiar comfort of home and friends. You are
constantly off balance.—Italian writer Cesare Pavese

On March 13, 2006, a couple of months shy of his twenty-fifth birthday,
Ryan Chicovsky disappeared from the guesthouse where he had been staying
in rural Xieng Kok, a port on the Mekong River in northwestern Laos, within
sight of the Laotian border with Burma (officially the Union of Myanmar).

Ryan grew up on Lopez Island in Washington State, attending a close-
knit high school with a graduating class of fewer than twenty. Raised as part
of a small, rural community, he led a secure, outdoor-oriented life. He snow-
boarded, sailed, backpacked, and played soccer. After high school he attended
Western Washington University in Bellingham, but his mother, Judy Frane,
says it wasn't until he began studying Chinese that something clicked for him.
He had a natural facility for the language and a deep, abiding interest in both
the people and their country.

"He was supposed to graduate in 2005, but he postponed his graduation
so he could do a study abroad in China," Judy says.

Once there, Ryan took on tai chi and other martial arts in addition to
his studies in Chinese. Those experiences inspired him to remain in China
and teach English. When he announced his plans to his family, they were
delighted for him.

Ryan returned to China and settled into a teaching position about fifty
miles west of Beijing. He changed schools and then, at the end of February
2006, his work permit ran out. He had to exit the country to obtain a new one.

"He had all sorts of plans to travel. He decided to go to Laos for three
weeks, then meet us in Hong Kong, and then the three of us—my husband

Ryan Chicovsky. Courtesy of Judy Frane and David Chicovsky.

and I and Ryan—would spend a month going around China to the different places he wanted to show us," she says.

Three days before they were to leave for Hong Kong—on March 31, 2006—the U.S. Embassy notified his parents that Ryan was missing. He had not been seen nor heard from for more than two weeks.

Judy and the rest of Ryan's family learned that he had entered Laos on March 6. The area, with its raw, unspoiled natural beauty and rural setting, is a magnet for backpackers and trekkers who enjoy wandering through the villages and countryside. Ryan stopped in Xieng Kok and planned to continue his journey down the Mekong River with two other travelers, but he never got the chance. He disappeared the day before they were to leave.

The last time Ryan was seen, he had left his room at the guesthouse and was said to be carrying his camera. That camera would turn up on April 7 in an area near the Mekong. Members of the Akha tribe, a group of indigenous farmers that live in the surrounding hilly areas of Burma, Laos, and China, found the camera, his key, and the shirt he had been wearing. All were clean and dry, despite heavy monsoon rains that occurred between the time Ryan disappeared and when the items were discovered. The items were located four kilometers from the village where he had stayed. The Chicovskys were able to pull the camera's memory card, which held the last photos taken of Ryan before his disappearance, including some snapped at a local marketplace. In his photos, Ryan is a gangly, smiling young man, his hair cut close to his head, with a short full beard and eyes filled with warmth, humor, and intelligence.

Judy says their family has spent many thousands searching for their child. They traveled to Laos for the first time after receiving word that Ryan was missing. At the time this book was written, his family has made twelve trips to Laos, and undoubtedly there will be more, unless Ryan is found.

Having a family member disappear in a country like Laos is not the same as someone vanishing in France or Spain. Laos is a communist country, and although all governments are mired in bureaucracy, communist regimes do things in a manner much different than the United States. Living conditions and roads in the rural areas also present challenges for Western visitors. In addition, few people in places where Ryan often traveled speak English. Judy says they have had to hire translators every step of the way.

"You have to do a lot of your own detective work," Judy says. "You're pretty much on your own."

While the American embassy staff "has been wonderful," other than our own FBI, she has not had any interaction with Interpol or other international agencies. And the embassy is limited in what it can do—the staff must abide by the laws of the country in which they are serving. However, the embassy was able to provide Judy with a list of attorneys in the area, some of whom have their own private investigators.

Judy and her family have retraced Ryan's movements many times. They hired private investigators to work the case, put up flyers, posted a reward in Laos, and maintained a strong publicity campaign. They've also made a concerted effort to keep in touch with the embassy staff, which has undergone several personnel changes since Ryan vanished.

"The file on Ryan is located in the [U.S.] embassy in Laos. New personnel are briefed when they arrive. They do try to make us comfortable, but it is a challenge to talk to new people when we have established previous relationships," she says, adding, "They always respond to me when I contact them."

Judy says she keeps close tabs on what is happening in Laos and Burma and monitors the politics in the region. She stays connected to many of the people who are searching for her son via the Internet and panics whenever she is away from her e-mail. And she reads everything she can about the locale.

Of particular help are the travelers going in and out of the area. Many who have heard Ryan's story offer to take flyers and post them in villages along the way. Judy is grateful for the kindness of these strangers.

"It's not their son," she says, explaining her gratitude. "People are good about talking to others for us."

She tries to keep her spirits up for the sake of her two other children. She says it's not easy to shrug aside the constant, nagging worry about Ryan, but she realizes she has to be there for his siblings, too. Ryan is her oldest child—he has a sister two years younger and a brother six years his junior. All have been involved in the search for Ryan; even Ryan's roommate traveled to Laos with Ryan's family in hopes of finding him.

Judy says she has one simple piece of advice for parents whose children are traveling abroad: don't let them travel alone.

"If Ryan had been with someone else, he probably would not have disappeared," she says.

She agrees that hindsight never fails. Ryan had been on his own in a foreign land and had managed quite well—in fact, he was having the time of his life. How could Judy or anyone else have stopped him from living his dream—or realized the danger that he might have faced as he traveled alone?

Judy knows the past can't be changed. All she can do now is work to find Ryan and have faith that one day she will.

"An intense belief in the strength of the human spirit sustains me; it encourages me to believe that Ryan is there somewhere and alive," Judy says.

—⚬⚬⚬—

In Mexico, police fight drug cartels and continue to investigate kidnappings like the well-publicized abduction of Felix Batista, a kidnapping expert who was plucked from the crowd as he stood outside a Saltillo, Coahuila, restaurant. Missing since December 10, 2008, there have been no demands for ransom, nor any sightings of Batista. His family has expressed fears that they will never see him again.

Four years before Batista vanished, two pretty young women—Brenda Cisneros and Yvette Martinez—slipped over the border from their Laredo, Texas, homes to attend a concert in celebration of a birthday. Afterward, they called a friend to say they were on their way home, but they never arrived nor have they been seen since. The father of one of the women found the car the pair had driven at a police impound. It had been stripped and vandalized. Police say the car was found abandoned. The two women remain missing.

In 2009, the FBI joined forces with Mexican authorities in an attempt to determine if the unidentified remains of more than one hundred corpses in that country are that of any missing American citizens. The samples will be compared with the DNA of some seventy-five Americans who vanished in Mexico over the last several years. There are about half a million Americans in Mexico at any given time, according to the U.S. Department of State. According to statistics, approximately fifteen out of every one hundred thousand are murdered. It is unknown how many Americans vanish since not all disappearances are reported.

North Americans like to travel, and many independent spirits enjoy venturing abroad alone. Often these are younger people who thrive on the exotic and who are unafraid to step into new cultures. They are the ones who avoid the guided excursions and all of the usual touristy stuff, opting for experiences that take them on paths less traveled. But those paths can be dangerous—or, at the very least, much less predictable.

Canadian Matthew Vienneau knows what sparks the curiosity and spirit of someone like Ryan Chicovsky: several years ago his like-minded, beautiful, and beloved sister, Jacqueline "Nicole" Vienneau, vanished on a solo trip through West Africa and the Middle East. Now Matt and his family are passengers on a hellish journey that consumes their lives.

With her long brown hair and slight, athletic frame, Nicole is an adventurous and experienced traveler who has never considered surrendering her independence. Instead, she has tackled her wanderlust by letting it lead her into some of the most remote places for a Western woman traveling by herself. Never, says Matt, has Nicole been afraid to go it alone.

"She is very levelheaded; she is not someone who is flighty in any way," says her brother.

Nicole was thirty-two when she disappeared on the last day of March in 2007. It was a Saturday and she was in the fifth month of a half-year trip. The day she vanished, Nicole was in Hama, Syria, two hours north of Damascus.

According to Matt, his sister was staying at the Cairo Hotel at the time of her disappearance. From what the family has managed to piece together, the last morning she was known to be at the hotel, Nicole spoke with the hotel clerk who claims she asked about the beehive houses—homes constructed from brick and shaped like beehives: their unique construction keeps the interiors cool despite searing desert heat and are an area tourist attraction. Matt also says Nicole inquired about the location of Qasr Ibn Wardan, a palace complex built in the sixth century by Byzantine Emperor Justinian, which was designed to help ward off invaders.

The Vienneau family has been unable to find anyone other than the hotel clerk who saw Nicole leave on Saturday, and there is no record of her visiting either location. There are also no indications that she planned to move on: her backpack, journals, and guidebook were found undisturbed in her room. Matt says that the night before Nicole vanished, she tried to send some e-mails, but couldn't connect to the Internet because service so far out in the desert is unreliable.

The Vienneau family has traveled to Syria to look for Nicole. Her fiancé spent weeks crossing the country, but thus far not a single lead has turned up. Her brother acknowledges there is a chance his sister was abducted into the slave trade, but he believes she would never have submitted to such a situation.

Nicole Vienneau. Courtesy of the Vienneau Family.

"She is a fighter," he says of Nicole. He doesn't want to contemplate what life is like for his sister if that is her fate, but if that's what happened, Matt and his family want to know the truth. And their present truth is that they don't have much more information on Nicole's disappearance now than they had when she first went missing. Looking for her in a country like Syria has also been a bureaucratic nightmare.

Matt Vienneau puts it this way: "If you don't know the country, you're screwed," he says. "You're not going to get any help."

He adds that being familiar with the local culture is key. "You have to understand the local rules, laws, and culture. It's very difficult."

Although Matt says the people with whom they dealt in Syria promised help, little was forthcoming. "They don't want to be confronted or made to look bad in public," he says.

Matt believes the Syrian government is not alone in its failure to act on Nicole's behalf. He also does not think the Canadian government has been very forthcoming. Matt says the experience has shattered for his family the long-held belief that government is going to help.

"The reality is, it just doesn't happen," he says.

Nicole Vienneau is not a novice traveler. She's been to more than fifty countries and seeks out unusual places on her own. She understands the safety issues confronting a woman traveling by herself, her family says, and she respects local customs and traditions. That is important in Syria, where the social expectations are different for women.

Her brother admits Nicole would have stood out in that predominantly Muslim Middle Eastern country. Unlike most Syrian women, she wore Western-style clothing. She traveled by public conveyance—buses and cabs—or she walked. She stayed in hotels that reflected the local culture and ate on the economy. Nicole is not the kind of tourist who hotfoots it to the nearest McDonald's or checks into a room at the Marriott.

Since the day Nicole was reported missing, Matt and his family have become de facto experts in keeping her case alive in the media. They blog, give interviews, and keep the drums beating loud enough to attract reporters and the occasional book author. The Vienneaus have spent a small fortune shuttling across the Atlantic Ocean, and even though their efforts thus far have been fruitless, Matt says it is not only the right way to search, but also the only way.

"You're going to have to do it yourself. If you're serious about finding the person, give up whatever you're doing with your life right then and just go wherever they went missing," he says, adding that support at home while one is searching is both irreplaceable and a must.

"But make sure you have a presence where they went missing as fast as possible, especially if it's a third-world country. They won't know what to do; they won't be investigating at the level you want. No one cares as much about it as you do," Matt says.

———— ∞ ————

The laws governing missing persons differ from country to country, as does the individual country's approach. In Japan, for instance, officials are compelled by law to spend three days searching for a missing person. Many investigations go on much longer. The Japanese, known for their intensity and single-mindedness in pursuit of their goals, do not throw in the towel until they find the person or are sure of his or her fate—as exemplified in the case of Craig Arnold.

When the award-winning American poet disappeared on the Japanese island of Kuchinoerabu-jima in late April 2009, the Japanese launched an intensive search. Investigators traced Arnold's movements along a trail up a mountain where it is conjectured that he planned to view a volcano. Despite the deployment of police, professional search teams, dogs, and a helicopter for aerial search purposes, no trace of Arnold was located. Evidence found later indicated that Arnold fell, broke his leg, then plunged from a steep cliff into an area with dense forestation. Authorities say there was no possibility Arnold could have survived the fall and, considering the remote location, recovering the body would be dangerous.

In the United States there is no official time frame required for an agency to search for a missing person. Most searches are based on the feasibility of the victim's survival, as well as the availability of resources. Some searches are brief and successful.

When forty-one-year-old Kenneth Knight of Ann Arbor, Michigan, vanished on the Appalachian Trail in 2009, searchers found him by following a brush fire he lit to attract their attention. Knight, who is legally blind, was uninjured in the brief ordeal, but not all searches end so well. When Shannon Joy Schell went missing while hiking the Tanque Verde Ridge trail in Saguaro Monument East near Tucson, Arizona, in 1994, more than 120 searchers using tracking dogs and the most sophisticated equipment of the day failed to find her, despite a prolonged search. She remains missing to this day.

In countries with fewer resources or unstable governments, the extent of an investigation or search can be disappointing. Officials at the U.S. Department of State say it's not unusual for the family of the missing person to spring for private search teams out of their own pockets. Some have even paid for police expenses. For others, like Jeff Dunsavage, who searches for his lost brother, Joe Dunsavage Sr., off the coast of the Caribbean island of Roatan, Honduras, the process has proven both frustrating and fruitless.

Thirty-seven miles long and less than five miles wide, Roatan is known for its beautiful beaches, tropical weather, and water sports. A charming place with postcard prettiness, it is populated by the Caracol, an English-speaking mix of European, African, British, and Caribbean peoples. There is also a large expatriate population in the area, as well as a constant river of tourists.

At the time he disappeared, Joe Dunsavage Sr. was neither a tourist nor a resident of Roatan. The forty-nine-year-old New Jersey resident worked as a mortgage banker, but he also had a small glass-bottom boat business on the island, so he traveled to and from the Caribbean on a frequent basis. On

Joe Dunsavage. Courtesy of the Dunsavage Family.

May 10, 2009, Joe climbed onto a catamaran to spend a couple of hours in the shallow blue-green waters close to shore. Neither he nor his boat has been seen since.

The family was told Joe had gone fishing, but Jeff says his brother did not take his fishing gear with him.

"The first couple of days we figured we'd find him—either him or his body," says brother Jeff. But as days dragged into weeks and weeks turned into months, no sign of Joe or the boat ever surfaced. What did surface, however, was a curious story: Jeff says "credible rumors" reached them that at about the same time his brother vanished an American was being treated for dehydration in La Ceiba, a port city located on the country's northern coast.

"The drift assessments have him making landfall within twenty hours," Jeff says, pointing out that landing in La Ceiba is in line with those assessments.

A drift assessment is a tool often used by search-and-rescue operations conducted in large bodies of water. It employs science to estimate where the water would carry an object such as a boat, plane, or, in the worst-case scenario, a person. Based upon those projections, Joe's family believes it possible that Joe could have been the American described in those rumors. How could Joe end up in a hospital and then vanish without a trace? The idea worries Jeff, who thinks the answer could be something better suited to a Robin Cook or

Tess Gerritsen novel: he believes his brother could have fallen into the hands of criminals who traffic in illegally harvested human organs for transplants.

"I don't like to think about it, but I can't rule it out," he admits. "With no money on him and no ransom request, what other value could he provide?"

The Dunsavage family has advocated for Joe since the moment they heard he was missing. Jeff says they encountered little assistance from the U.S. Department of State or anyone else from the U.S. government. According to him, no immediate search was launched, but after three days the Dunsavage family managed to secure a little help from the U.S. military. Search aircraft deployed from the U.S. Southern Command (SouthCom), based in Miami. The Blackhawk helicopters failed to find any sign of the missing man or his boat.

The Dunsavage family is a vocal bunch. They don't believe in treading lightly and haven't done so in this case. Jeff says they wasted no time contacting their U.S. congressional representatives and insisted someone help them find their son, brother, and father.

"After the military pulled out, the embassy told us they were mobilized and had people on the ground. We thought they were reaching out to the [very large] expat community," he says. "But there was no indication that was the case. We had to build from the ground up."

Jeff says they cast a wide net for information, contacting everyone they could think of who might shed light on Joe's fate. Along the way, he discovered his brother wasn't the only foreigner to disappear in the area.

"We had the idea that it was this charming Caribbean island. There was this impression that it was fairly safe down there. Then we found that seven [people] have gone missing [recently] and that doesn't even take into account the murders," he says.

Jeff points to mysterious vanishings in both Honduras and Costa Rica that he categorizes as "disturbing" and, he charges, not well explored by the U.S. government. Among them is the disappearance of a Chicago-based doctoral student who went missing about three months after Joe.

According to reports, on Tuesday, August 11, 2009, David Gimelfarb parked his rented car at the entrance to the Rincon de la Vieja National Park outside of Liberia, Costa Rica, then entered the rambling 34,800-acre park and vanished like a drop of water on a hot sidewalk.

"You could not just wander off that trail; in places it's so thick you would need a machete [to walk]," Jeff says. "He vanished without a trace and, like my brother, there's been no ransom [demand]. [David's] money and passport were still in the car, securely locked up."

David's parents have made several prolonged trips to Costa Rica to search for their son. Thus far, none has proven successful, although there has been at least one report of a sighting of a dirty, homeless man who bore a resemblance to David. Although that lead has not borne fruit, the Gimelfarbs have refused to abandon their search.

Another American searching for a loved one lost in a country south of our border also refuses to quit. Jeff says his friend Cindy Scheepstra, wife of missing Dutch American Ron Scheepstra, continues to search for her missing husband despite discouraging results.

Ron, forty-nine, went missing on April 11, 2009, while on a fishing trip with friends in Xcalak, Mexico. It was an area with which Ron, whose home is in Lufkin, Texas, was very familiar: a longtime sports fisherman, he had visited that wild and remote part of Mexico three times in as many years. On the day he vanished, his friends and fellow fishermen said Ron told them he was going to change locations to fish in a more remote spot in hopes of improving his luck. He has not been seen since.

Both his friends and wife believe Ron was abducted. They say they found nothing at the scene to indicate otherwise. Officials have indicated that they believe Ron may have planned his disappearance, a charge his family disputes. Cindy, his wife, is now stuck in a curious and difficult limbo: the couple was looking forward to retirement and had refinanced their home in order to put in a new swimming pool, according to Jeff Dunsavage. With Ron gone but not declared dead, she can't sell the house or do anything else with it. Jeff says Cindy works three jobs to make ends meet, while continuing to look for her missing husband.

"Cindy and her daughter flew down to Mexico and where Ron disappeared is a pretty remote area on the Yucatan. The American Embassy told them what bus to take to get there. It's a $200 bus fare and they didn't offer them any help at all. Because Ron has dual citizenship, though, the Dutch Embassy provided them with a car and driver and took them to where he went missing. When they got there, they were bullied by local authorities, locked in a room, and made to sign documents in Spanish [that they didn't understand]," Jeff says.

Jeff says Mexican officials accused Scheepstra of engineering his disappearance and Cindy of helping him. They offered no further assistance to the women.

The car Ron drove was found, but it was worthless in terms of evidence. The authorities in that area have no forensics capabilities, but also, according to Jeff, local police officers drove it around for days. If there had been any evidence to recover from the car, it would have been destroyed.

Jeff believes Americans who go missing in Mexico and Central America do not receive adequate help and support from their government. He says families must struggle with foreign legal systems, corruption, and customs they do not understand. He believes things can be better handled, and that is one of the reasons he founded the Missing Americans Project (www.missing americans.ning.com).

In the process of obtaining nonprofit status, Jeff says the Missing Americans Project will advocate for improved government response and better attention to the needs of the families of the missing. He claims current official responses are all over the map.

"They say, 'What do you want us to do?'" Jeff says. "When my brother disappeared, we had to reinvent the wheel throughout our entire experience. Every [other] family we have dealt with has come up with a similar story."

———— ⎯⎯ ————

According to its Web site, this is the U.S. Department of State's official policy on "American citizens missing abroad":

> As concerned relatives call in, consular officers use the information provided by the family or friends of a missing person to locate the individual. We check with local authorities in the foreign country to see if there is any report of a U.S. citizen hospitalized, arrested, or is otherwise unable to communicate with those looking for them. Depending on the circumstances, consular officers may personally search hotels, airports, hospitals, or even prisons.
>
> Privacy Act—The provisions of the Privacy Act are designed to protect the privacy and rights of Americans, but occasionally they complicate our efforts to assist citizens abroad. As a rule, consular officers may not reveal information regarding an individual American's location, welfare, intentions, or problems to anyone, including family members and Congressional representatives, without the expressed consent of that individual. Although sympathetic to the distress this can cause concerned families, consular officers must comply with the provisions of the Privacy Act.

Michelle Bernier-Toth, director of American Citizen Services and Crisis Management for the U.S. Department of State, admits that sometimes there is little the State Department can do in missing persons cases. But she says she understands the mixed reviews.

"A lot of it depends on host country capability. We obviously do not have . . . the resources or the capabilities or the expertise to conduct missing persons searches," says Bernier-Toth.

Bernier-Toth says the State Department receives thousands of calls every year from worried relatives who cannot find or contact family overseas. State Department consular officials do their best to locate the individual and report back to the families. Most of the reports turn out to be unfounded—a student who fails to call his mom or a case of crossed wires. The staff also takes into consideration the circumstances surrounding the individual's disappearance: is there anything that lends special urgency to the search?

"Someone who is hiking in a remote area—that is a great concern. Someone who is a tourist wandering through Prague, perhaps not as much," she explains.

Sometimes the strain of travel can bump travelers out of their comfort zones, causing them to wander off the grid. Schedules are off, tempers are strained, and important medications are neglected.

"The most common subject of our welfare and whereabouts calls are those who have mental illnesses and whose families are concerned," she says.

While some, like Jeff Dunsavage, believe the government doesn't do enough to help the families of those who turn up missing, Bernier-Toth points out that consular officials are constrained by both privacy laws and the laws of foreign countries from doing many things.

If, for instance, an individual chooses to disappear and he is located, the State Department cannot force that person to contact his family, return, or even pass pertinent information along without his permission.

"We may, at least initially, be circumspect with the information we provide back to you. If we locate your loved one . . . we will do as much as we can within the Privacy Act. We will urge them to contact the family, but sometimes they don't want to be found," she says. "That's the fine wire that we walk."

She says consular officials take a caseworker approach to their search for the missing. They use their contacts to check hotels, hospitals, morgues, tourist bureaus, and other places that might shed light on the individual's whereabouts. But, as she points out, consular officials are not law enforcement officers and have no jurisdiction or investigative powers in foreign countries.

When a member of the U.S. Armed Forces disappears in a foreign country while on official duty, that service's intelligence or criminal investigations unit will conduct a search there in conjunction with local authorities. There is no comparable organization for civilians, but sometimes the FBI becomes involved in these cases. In fact, each embassy has a legal attaché who is often also an agent for the FBI.

In the case of MaxGian Alcalde (see chapter 12), a child from Idaho who was allegedly abducted by his mother and taken to Nicaragua, both the U.S. Embassy and FBI were involved in the boy's recovery and return to his father. Other American law enforcement agencies may also assist with a missing persons investigation.

"In Latin America we have a strong narcotics program, and that's a resource where we can say, 'While you're out there talking to local authorities on the ground in various places could you put out the word?' [We] try and use it as a force multiplier," says Bernier-Toth.

Not every country wants to cooperate in a missing persons investigation. Like the victims' families, the consular staff sometimes runs into roadblocks that, depending on the sophistication of the nation and its relationship with the United States, can range from red tape to ignoring staff efforts.

"We keep pushing, we keep trying, and sometimes resources are very limited in those countries, and it's really hard," she says.

Complaints about the U.S. Department of State's response—or lack of response—to missing persons abroad often grow out of frustration with the system. Adding to that frustration is the task of dealing with foreign customs and laws. Victims' families are not coping with one bureaucracy but several. And the more rural and unsophisticated the area in which a loved one vanishes, the more devilish the investigation can become.

Nations like Laos, China, Syria, Somalia, and Indonesia can be difficult and dangerous for travelers. Increasing violence in some South and Central American counties also creates unsafe conditions for those who travel alone. But communist and emerging nations and countries with growing criminal elements aren't the only places American travelers disappear. They also vanish from the streets of sophisticated cities like Rome, London, Paris, and Madrid. In fact, one of the most famous unsolved missing persons cases in Ireland is that of American-born Annie Bridget McCarrick, a twenty-six-year-old who lived in Dublin, Ireland, and disappeared on March 26, 1993. Almost two decades and many searches later, she remains unfound.

Annie, who is from New York's Long Island, moved to the British Isles and studied to become a teacher in 1987. She came back to the United States for three years and returned to Ireland in January 1993. A police investigation revealed that on the day she disappeared, Annie took a bus to Enniskerry to visit the Wicklow Mountains. Her case remains open. Some believe her disappearance is linked to an unsolved series of homicides in the area, but nothing has been proven.

Annie's disappearance is not the only one to confound modern, municipal European police agencies. In Florence, birthplace of the Renaissance and a mecca for art students, Matthew Allen Mullaney disappeared following a night spent relaxing with friends. The Scituate, Massachusetts, native was studying art in the Italian city when he vanished after leaving a local Irish pub. Although his family has not ceased searching for Matt, who was born November 5, 1981, and went missing January 31, 2003, like Annie McCarrick, his disappearance remains an enduring mystery.

Americans are not alone in vanishing from foreign soil. It is a worldwide problem. Each year, for example, hundreds of Britons vanish while visiting other countries—in some cases, the United States.

According to the U.S. Department of State, there are no statistics that track the number of Americans who go missing in a foreign country in a given year. The British do a better job of tallying those numbers: in 2008, 481 Brits disappeared abroad, an increase from 401 the previous year and 336 in 2006. Some of the families of missing British citizens are as unhappy with their government's efforts as their American counterparts, but the family of Eddie Gibson, which has been working with both the British Foreign Office and the Suffolk Police, believes their government has done a good job.

Eddie, who hails from Hove, England, disappeared in Cambodia when he was twenty-two. His mother, Jo Clark, discovered her son was missing on November 1, 2004, when she and Eddie's father went to Heathrow Airport to meet his plane.

"I was so excited to see him," Jo remembers. After his flight landed she watched as the crowds began to exit the baggage area. As she waited for her son to appear, Jo says she began to experience a growing disquiet.

"After the last person had gone through . . . there was just emptiness. I dashed over to the Thai Airways ticket desk to ask them about Eddie. They looked at the manifest of the flight, and although Eddie's name was on it, they told me he did not check in at Bangkok Airport. My heart [sank]," Jo says.

A handsome, strapping fellow more than six feet tall with indigo blue eyes, Jo says Eddie is an affable guy who received high marks in school and was popular with the girls. "He was often in trouble but he always smiled his way out of any tricky situations," Jo says.

The family has made nine trips to Cambodia to search for Eddie. They've appeared on television and given dozens of interviews. All of that publicity has generated many tips, but thus far none of them has panned out. In addition, detectives from the Suffolk Police also traveled to Cambodia in 2006 to join forces with Thai police in their search for Eddie.

"The hardest part for me was not knowing where to start," she says. "The whole experience has just been one big nightmare."

Intelligence Officer Arianna Stucchi of the United Kingdom Missing Persons Bureau says families like Eddie Gibson's have a number of nonprofits to which they can turn when crisis strikes.

"In the U.K. there are many agencies and NGOs [nongovernmental organizations] dedicated to helping families of the missing. We have, for instance, the charity Missing Abroad (www.missingabroad.org). This is a charity that has been created from individuals that have unfortunately experienced such an ordeal [and] . . . have created this charity to support those left behind. They are especially well informed on ways of getting [the] families of [the] missing to the country [where] the individual vanished from and helping them deal with such a traumatic time." Stucchi says other charities include

Children and Families across Borders (CFAB), Missing People, Reunite, and International Commission on Missing Persons (ICMP), and all can be found on the Web.

———— ∞ ————

"Nightmare" is the most accurate term used to describe what American Amy Bradley's family and friends have been going through since the twenty-three-year-old disappeared from a family cruise.

The Bradley family was aboard the *Rhapsody of the Seas*, a Royal Caribbean Cruise Line ship out of Miami when they docked at Curacao, Netherlands Antilles, and found that Amy—a recent college graduate with a bright future—had vanished. That was March 24, 1998, and there is still no sign of the athletic, gregarious Amy. Her family says she had many plans for her future and no reason to leave. There has been some speculation that Amy could have been kidnapped and sold in the sex trade, but that allegation has never been substantiated.

While not common, cruise ship disappearances also are not all that rare. Since most of these disappearances take place in international waters or when the ships are docked in foreign ports, the victims' families must not only deal with other governments, but also with the cruise companies. These companies do not welcome the scrutiny such incidents bring to their businesses.

In 2008, sources report cruise ship operators officially documented thirty unexplained disappearances on their ships in the preceding five years. While the numbers may seem small compared to disappearances on land, for the families of these missing people, the statistics are much too high. When someone vanishes on the high sea, the obvious outcome is much too grim.

———— ∞ ————

For the families of individuals missing in foreign lands, frustration is a continent—or two—away. They must deal with multiple government agencies from various jurisdictions, most of the time at a distance. Depending on the area of the country in which the person disappeared, forensic and investigative techniques can be light-years behind the curve. And then there is the delay: often families don't even realize their loved ones are missing until days after they have vanished. That leaves them far away from the center of the investigation, playing catch-up in a game that unfolds on anything but a level playing field.

Searching in a foreign country is also expensive. Families report that, in addition to time away from work and the expense of hotels and flights, they often must retain an attorney or private investigator in the foreign country to keep the lines of communication open with the authorities.

The U.S. Department of State helps—but often finds local laws and the Privacy Act tie their hands. Some families claim they don't do enough, but officials counter that they do what they can, although admitting it's often not as much as the families would like. And what the families would like most of all is quite simple: to find their missing loved ones alive and safe, then bring them back home.

· 9 ·

A Story of Rumors, Gossip, and Innuendo:
A Family's Tragedy Feeds the Gossip Mill

Ill deeds are doubled with an evil word.—William Shakespeare

*O*n a stifling summer's day in 1990, Helen Aragona's life crashed with the savage velocity of an out-of-control airliner. There were no sirens or blinking lights, no forewarnings at all, not even a fleeting moment's intuition her universe was about to buckle and break around her.

Up until then, Helen had defined her life as ordinary, perhaps pedestrian. She cooked, cleaned house, worked, spent time with her kids and friends, and made the occasional trip back to her hometown. Helen's roots were in New York, where many of her Italian Catholic relatives still lived.

Widowed by the death of her Italian husband, Gildo, in 1984, Helen has dwelt for decades in the same unpretentious, square brick home in the quiet Bryn Marr subdivision of Jacksonville, North Carolina. Until Gildo died, he and Helen ran a tiny restaurant where New York-style pizza with basil-infused tomato sauce sold at a gratifying pace to Jacksonville's mostly marine clientele.

Jacksonville leans against not one, but three Marine Corps installations: Camp Lejeune, which bills itself as the world's largest amphibious marine base; Camp Johnson, a training facility for bright, shiny recruits fresh from boot camp; and Marine Corps Air Station New River, home base to thousands of helicopter and Osprey pilots and their support personnel.

In 1990, Helen's eldest of six children, thirty-year-old Phyllis, lived fifteen minutes from her mother on a narrow paved road in the southwest community, which skirts the nearby air station. Phyllis shared a small, wood-frame house with Scott Gasperson, her fiancé, who was a few days shy of his twenty-sixth birthday.

Physically, Scott and Phyllis embodied the Chinese concept of yin and yang: Phyllis stood under five feet; Scott, well over six. Phyllis was delicate and fair; Scott was dark and bearish, with liquid eyes and an easy, generous smile. Although different in appearance, the two had been together for several years and shared a common work ethic and unbreakable family values. They also planned to spend the rest of their lives together. Their future wedding occupied a good portion of Phyllis's spare time. She liked to leaf through bridal magazines and look at invitations in preparation for those nuptials. Phyllis had no way of knowing there would never be a wedding.

Scott and Phyllis's home sat well off Ben Williams Road, on a spacious rural lot with plenty of room for animals. Phyllis decorated the little house in the casual country style so trendy in southern homes in the mid-1980s: lots of blues and pinks, ribbons and lace, ruffles and bows. It was girly—like Phyllis.

Cats, dogs, and chickens roamed their land, and the pasture hosted Phyllis's horses. She couldn't pass up a stray. Once, after a mother hen died, Phyllis housed a batch of baby chicks in the bathroom, treating the tiny peeping birds as her own babies. Scott tolerated the menagerie well; he was a gentle soul. The couple's shared reverence for life was one of the things that brought them together. Phyllis could never love a man who wasn't kind. And Scott's kindness extended not only to the woman he loved, but also to her family.

Scott enjoyed sliding by Helen's house for a meal. Jennifer, Helen's youngest child and an almost eerie echo of her older sister, often cooked his favorites for him. As a teen, Jennifer enjoyed Scott's affectionate banter and gentle teasing. Of all the Aragona children, then-fifteen-year-old Jennifer was the sibling closest to Phyllis and Scott. In fact, Phyllis, who was twice Jennifer's age in 1990, acted as a sort of surrogate mother to the family's baby, doting on the little sister who worshipped her. Jennifer embraced her sister's boyfriend not only because he was funny and paid attention to her, but because she knew he loved Phyllis as much as she herself did.

During that time period, Helen slept over at Phyllis and Scott's little home once in a while. Her car was out of commission, so it was easier to let Scott or Phyllis drop her off and pick her up than to ride with one of her coworkers. Helen worked the graveyard shift at Charles McDaniel Nursing Home, a new complex at the time, located on the edge of town. Helen's 11:00-to-7:00 shift as a nursing assistant meant she slept during the hot, humid Carolina days, which was fine with her. She liked the night shift.

On July 11, 1990, Helen spoke with Phyllis on the phone as she always did, but decided not to stay the night with her. Instead, for no particular reason, Helen chose her own bed. It was a small, insignificant decision, but it saved her life.

At 8:50 p.m. on Wednesday, July 11——the same day Helen chose to sleep at her own home—Scott spoke with his father, Robert Gasperson, for what would be the last time. Later, Robert remembered how unremarkable the conversation was. He would muse that he would not have recalled a word of their exchange if things were different. Now, two decades later, Robert can still repeat every single syllable they exchanged. And although he had a good relationship with his son, he still agonizes over the things he wishes he'd said.

But on that July day in 1990, ten minutes after Scott and his father hung up from their phone conversation, Phyllis finished closing the business where she worked. She managed one of the seven pawnshops owned at the time by Scott's father. Scott ran Woodson Music and Pawn, also one of his father's stores. Even then, Robert was a veteran of the pawn industry, a lucrative enterprise in this military town, where young marines often hock their valuables to get them through until the next payday.

Sometime between the moment after Phyllis would have turned the key in the massive bolt that locked the heavy glass doors at the pawnshop before driving home and the seconds that held back the succeeding day, Helen tried to call Phyllis again. The phone in the small house on Ben Williams Road rang, but no one answered. With no success, Helen gave up and returned to her duties in the dim nighttime halls at the nursing home, not sensing this day marked the beginning of a change in her life as abrupt and final as a played-out game of Russian roulette.

By dawn the next morning, Thursday, July 12, it was clear the day would turn blisteringly hot. The pitiless coastal sun and shirt-drenching humidity drove local residents off the streets and back into offices, banks, or stores, where overworked air conditioners were kneecapped by the typical midsummer weather. Sitting behind the wheel of an open-window car was like piloting a coffin. Outdoor work crews labored in glistening sweat with kegs of water nearby, but most stayed off the streets and avoided the crushing heat.

On the outskirts of Jacksonville, Cyrus Brinson pulled out of his driveway onto Ben Williams Road and passed the house where Scott and Phyllis lived. In this part of the county, everyone knew everyone, as well as everyone's business, but it wasn't simple nosiness that caused people to note the comings and goings of their neighbors. Instead, in this sparsely populated area where sons built next door to their fathers and family land rarely sold to other than blood kin, there was a strong sense of obligation to each other. Brinson drove by Scott and Phyllis's home that morning and noted neither of their cars—a blue Chevy Blazer and a red Chevy Beretta—were there. The time was 5:30 a.m.

———&&&———

Paul Wiedner arrived at Woodson Music and Pawn to clean the business as he did most other mornings, but on this day no one was there to let him in. Wiedner wrote a quick note and stuck it in the metal gate that stretched across the front. After lingering a bit outside, Wiedner decided Scott was running late and left.

Meanwhile, a little red Beretta streaked down narrow, twisty, sometimes congested Rocky Run Road—away from the pawnshop. The car passed a woman named Vicky Barber, who registered the driver's recklessness as a small irritation, the kind that's common in a military community resplendent with platoons of nineteen- and twenty-year-old males.

Kimberly Paulson also observed the red Beretta as it roared past her and noted its multiple occupants. Paulson didn't see it, but after the red Beretta went by, the car veered off Rocky Run, making its way down another, more isolated, dirt road.

Paulson worked with Scott and was supposed to help him open the business that morning, but was behind schedule. When she arrived at the store, it was still locked, but the metal gate to the front door was open. Peering through the thick glass, Paulson saw a jewelry box on the floor. Concerned, she drove to the home of the store's assistant manager, Donald Whalen.

Alarmed by Paulson's story, Whalen headed for the store, and discovered it had been ransacked. The safe was open, and an inventory would reveal thousands in cash and jewelry taken from the business. The most ominous discovery, though, was not the open safe nor the items scattered about the store, but a pillowcase. The percale material was covered with bloodstains.

When members of the Onslow County Sheriff's Department arrived, they wrapped the outside of the store in crime-scene tape. After ascertaining that Phyllis also failed to show up for work, deputies issued an all points bulletin (APB) for both Scott's and Phyllis's vehicles.

Investigators didn't yet know what they had, but whatever it was, they knew it couldn't be good.

———&&&———

Deputies drove to the home Scott and Phyllis shared and found the back door ajar. Once inside, it was obvious they were encountering another crime scene. Among the evidence collected that day was a plastic wrapper discarded from a roll of duct tape and a piece of tape stuck to one of the beds.

Helen Aragona was told her daughter and Scott were missing. The bearer of the news was a deputy who watched for Helen's reaction. Fear slithered into her stomach and knotted there. She wanted to stay positive for teenaged Jennifer's sake, so Helen tamped down the panic as best she could. Her oldest daughter was missing, not dead—that's what she kept telling herself. For the moment, at least, there was hope and that had to be enough.

When questioned by deputies, Jennifer recalled that Phyllis and Scott came separately to eat lunch with her the previous day, Wednesday, July 11. In good spirits, they both spoke about the future and their upcoming wedding plans. There was no hint of anything amiss, nothing that would have indicated anything was wrong.

At 3:00 p.m. on Thursday, July 12, after Helen and Jennifer were interviewed, Phyllis's Blazer was found abandoned behind the Econo Lodge, a hotel a couple of miles away from the pawnshop. Helen performed mental surgery, trying to suture this development into a positive outcome, but she couldn't quite do it. Nausea swept in and threatened to overwhelm her. She wanted to stay strong for Phyllis, but all she could think about was that her child—her baby, her firstborn—was missing, and each new development was taking her closer and closer to a dark place where she did not want to go.

Where was Phyllis? Where was Scott? And what in the name of God was going on?

———— ✖ ————

Whenever the telephone in the Aragona house rang, Jennifer pounced on it. Like all teens who came of age before cell phones evolved into common currency, Jennifer's life was predicated on the sound of the household phone. When Phyllis disappeared, Helen started to guard it. If and when Phyllis called, she wanted to be the one to answer. She also didn't want Jennifer to take a call if the news was bad.

Helen daydreamed that she would pick up the receiver and Phyllis would be on the other end, alive and healthy and with a good explanation for whatever happened in that store. She was afraid to leave the house because she didn't want to miss that call. Until Helen could speak to Phyllis, her life was as off balance as a car with two wheels speeding along a mountain road.

Helen's mind kept circling the investigators' implications. She worried about where the evidence might lead them, and worse—where it might take Phyllis. She believed that if she thought the worst, it might come true.

Helen knew it was irrational to believe dark thoughts could inspire a similar outcome, but she couldn't help herself. In the back of her mind, the niggling idea that her missing daughter could be dead sat like a cancerous tumor, draining her reserves. If she allowed herself to confront the idea that

Phyllis was gone forever, then it was like giving up on her. Still, the mother in her couldn't help but acknowledge how afraid Phyllis must be. She prayed Phyllis and Scott were still together. He would comfort her. He would stand by her. He would protect her.

In those first few desperate hours after the news of Phyllis's disappearance broke, there was nothing Helen could do but wait and pray. If the phone rang, it was most often a detective calling to check a detail or ask another question. Some of what law enforcement officials wanted to know drove Helen crazy. She didn't understand why they asked these things about Phyllis, her relationship with Scott, her bills, her habits. Helen answered them as best she could, reasoning the deputies were, after all, on her side, and they shared the common goal of wanting to find Phyllis alive and well and as fast as possible. They had not said so, but she knew time worked against them. The longer it took to find Phyllis and Scott, the worse their chances of being whole and unhurt.

As Helen prayed someone would find her missing child, what deputies discovered, instead, was Scott. And the news sent Helen into a downward spiral unlike anything she had ever experienced.

Sergeant David West of the Onslow County Sheriff's Department was one of the dozens of law enforcement officers fanned out in the county searching for the couple that Thursday in July. The investigation into Scott and Phyllis's disappearance was hours old and already the day had grown long and intense. West, like the rest of the officers in his department, scoured parking lots, streets, and wooded areas for signs of the missing couple's vehicles.

Old leaves crackled under West's shoes as he made his way through the woods. Tree branches and bushes snatched at West's light, mud-brown uniform, now wet with perspiration. Mosquitoes buzzed, delighted at the intrusion. West swatted them away as he pushed farther into the musty-smelling underbrush. Off the road, he could hear the sounds of cars approaching and passing the spot where he'd parked his patrol car on the road's shoulder.

It was a little before 6:00 p.m. as West crept through the wood. There were still a good two or more hours of sunlight left before the shadows would lengthen, and he wanted to finish searching that particular area before moving on to the next spot. There was a lot of land to cover before night fell, and the department was stretched thin.

The deputy was more than two hundred feet into the forest when he spied a jolt of red visible through the trees. As he moved closer, West found a small clearing. In the center of that clearing stood Scott's candy-apple red Beretta. And on the ground between the car's open door and the vehicle itself, curled up as if sleeping in a bed of leaves, was Scott, his head wrapped in a makeshift hood. He had been shot once at point-blank range on the left side of his head. Later, investigators would determine his hair contained traces of duct tape adhesive.

In addition to their grief and horror, Helen and her family were panicked at the news of Scott's murder. They knew his killing meant Phyllis's chances of being found alive had ebbed away.

As each day passed and the investigation into the robbery of Woodson Music and Pawn and the kidnapping and murder of Scott Gasperson progressed, Helen also began to sense a shift in the way the community regarded her and her family. Although her lifelong friends and those who knew Phyllis well continued to stand by and comfort her, terrible rumors began to creep into the subtext of the Aragonas' lives. Phyllis, people whispered, had been in on the robbery and helped kill Scott. Even now, these voices said, she was on the run.

"My friends would call me up to say teachers had told the class my sister did it," Jennifer says. Helen received telephone calls that were even nastier than Jennifer's.

"I'd get calls at work, a voice saying, 'Help me, Mom, help me,'" Helen says.

Jennifer was also on the receiving end of cruel, personal intrusions. "People would call and tell me that I was a tramp," she says. For a fifteen-year-old girl mourning her big sister, the telephone calls were both crushing and astonishing. She didn't understand how a world that was orderly and normal could turn sour and unsure so fast.

Speculation about the circumstances of Phyllis's disappearance continued to spawn gossip and rumor: Phyllis was after Scott's money. He had a big life insurance policy and she was the beneficiary. She was on the run, hiding out, pretending to be a victim, but she'd come back soon to claim the cash.

The officers investigating the case also conjectured on the petite redhead's possible involvement. The discovery of Scott's body with no sign of Phyllis placed everyone close to the missing woman, including Helen and Jennifer, under suspicion.

Onslow Sheriff's Deputy Mack Whitney, now retired, has decades of experience as a cop. In addition to his law enforcement duties, Whitney serves as an ordained minister, a combination some might find odd, but not uncommon in southern law enforcement. Whitney's mellow personality and soft, persuasive voice make him easy to talk to, even when the subject is murder.

Five days after Scott and Phyllis were discovered missing, Tuesday, July 17, a man named Miguel Angel Guzman contacted Whitney. Guzman told the officer that about three months before Scott and Phyllis disappeared, he was approached by two acquaintances, a Cuban refugee named Gary Fernandez and his son, Orlando. Gary and Orlando asked Guzman to participate in a robbery. Their target: Woodson Music and Pawn. Guzman declined. He also failed to mention it to anyone.

Guzman said Gary and Orlando Fernandez once again contacted him on July 1, still talking about the pawnshop robbery. After Woodson's was robbed, on Thursday, July 12 and again on July 13, they told Guzman in two separate conversations they were going away.

Based on Guzman's information, deputies searched a storage unit and mobile home rented by the fugitives. By then, they'd left Onslow County far behind. Gary Fernandez, his girlfriend, Maria Monserrate, and Gary's son, Orlando Fernandez, were in Miami.

The way most successful detectives investigate any case is a bit counterintuitive: they do not try to unearth enough evidence to prove someone is guilty of a crime but instead attempt to exculpate each suspect. When they cannot build a case for innocence, they usually have their answer.

Phyllis's disappearance left them with a hurdle that would prove difficult to overcome. Since they had no inkling of her whereabouts, investigators treated her not as a victim, but as a party to the crime. Helen later said she knew they were doing their jobs, but it was still painful.

Why wasn't Phyllis cleared once deputies knew about Gary Fernandez? Because until she was found and an arrest made, everyone associated with the case remained a suspect, even Phyllis.

When a loved one vanishes, even if the evidence points to a dark ending, it's often difficult for the family to accept what may seem inevitable to others. The Aragonas continued to hold onto their faith that Phyllis would be returned to them alive and whole, even when most expected the worst. Mothers often find hope in the bleakest of scenarios. Helen Aragona was no exception.

As the search for Phyllis continued, investigators tracked Gary Fernandez and his accomplices. With Phyllis still missing weeks after the robbery, Helen traveled to New York to visit one of her other daughters. Detectives followed her on the premise she could be meeting Phyllis. Helen feels conflicted at the premise she might have been in league with her daughter or that Phyllis was suspected of involvement in Scott's slaying.

But Helen and Phyllis were not alone in the spotlight. Detectives couldn't rule out anyone who might benefit from Scott's death, even his father, Robert.

"They thought Robert might have killed Scott for the money," Helen says, her voice derisive at the implication this father would sacrifice his child for cash. Although their relationship was strained at first because Phyllis remained missing after Scott's body was found, Robert Gasperson has become a good friend over the years.

As long as Phyllis remained missing, her absence became almost like a living thing—the elephant in Helen Aragona's life. Though she arose each day with the hope that Phyllis would be found, even she admitted as the days passed, it seemed less and less likely. But never once did she buy into the theory Phyllis was involved in the robbery or Scott's murder.

"She loved him. She loved him more than anything," Helen says. "She would never, ever do anything to hurt that man. He was the center of her world."

Meanwhile, Helen continued to endure rude comments and finger-pointing. People yelled at her on the street from passing cars. She hated going out. The abuse also affected Jennifer.

A counselor at Jennifer's school called the stricken student into her office and advised her to "get over it." An honors student, Jennifer's grades slipped, and she grew morose. She could think of nothing but her sister. Soon things grew so nasty that Helen sent Jennifer to Texas to live with another sibling. There, the fragile teen was spared the cruelty and idle speculation of classmates and strangers, but her life would remain altered and broken beyond repair. To this day, she still weeps for Phyllis and Scott, and her trust in others has all but evaporated.

"I don't feel safe anymore," Jennifer says, trembling.

Months passed and the investigation continued. The Aragonas observed their first Thanksgiving without Phyllis. The Christmas holidays ahead promised little peace. The struggle to return to business as usual and put their lives back together remained difficult. Without knowing where Phyllis was and what happened to her, they felt as though they lived in some sort of hellish alternate universe.

Winter stripped the trees of their leaves and turned the grass brown and lifeless. Helen Aragona went through the minutiae of living, but there was no longer any joy in her life. Still, she was convinced, as she had been since the beginning, that her daughter was innocent of the things people said about her. The ugly speculation and scrutiny continued to wound, but she tried not to think about it and focused instead on the continued search for Phyllis.

By this time, the agencies involved in the case, including the FBI, read like a book of acronyms. Authorities were now convinced Gary and Orlando Fernandez and Maria Monserrate killed Scott Gasperson and robbed the pawnshop. They tracked the threesome from Miami to the Dominican Republic, where they had traveled by boat.

A couple of weeks before Christmas, they had them: Gary, his son, and Maria, the girlfriend. Arrested in the Dominican Republic, the three were brought back to stand trial for Scott's murder. Phyllis was still missing.

The story behind the crime was so bizarre and so heinous that the case would be reenacted on John Walsh's television program, *America's Most Wanted*. When Gary, Maria, and Orlando were apprehended in the Dominican Republic, one law enforcement agency involved contacted the television program to announce the arrests, even though Helen Aragona had not yet been notified. Helen found out when the news media called for comment.

Helen's quest to clear her daughter's name would continue until April 1991, as the sun warmed the cold hard earth.

On Sunday, April 7, almost nine months from the day that Phyllis Aragona was abducted, her skeletal remains were discovered in a wooded area in nearby Pender County. Like Scott, Phyllis had been shot once in the head. Over time, her bones were scattered, and authorities were forced to use dental records to identify her. Bits of hair and duct tape also were found at the scene.

The news brought mixed emotions to the Aragonas. When she heard, Helen experienced intense pain, but also a grim sort of relief—not because Phyllis was dead, but because Helen could stop hoping.

"That year in limbo, that was the worst time of all," Helen says.

Now her phone could ring unanswered and Helen could do something no mother ever wants to do: lay her child to rest.

It took almost three years to find all the people responsible for the deaths of Phyllis and Scott and bring them back to Onslow County to stand trial for the murders. Helen went head-to-head with the investigators during the entire process. She demanded to know their progress, to stay in the loop.

In addition to the Fernandezes and Maria Monserrate, Eli Ocasio, Maria's teenaged son, also was charged with murder. After a long, intense search that saw the case stretching into the spring of 1993, authorities located and arrested Eli in New York City.

After the trials, after the sentencing, after the young lovers' names were chiseled on their headstones, the full story emerged about how Scott and Phyllis were kidnapped to facilitate the pawnshop robbery. And Gary, who master-minded the crime, turned out to be more than a Cuban refugee; he was also a government informant enrolled in the federal witness protection program.

During the trials, testimony revealed the crime was one of swiftness, brutality, and an underworld far removed from the lives of ordinary, decent people like Scott and Phyllis. Gary was involved in drug dealing and theft, and his past had caught up to him. He needed money fast. Gary cased Woodson Music and Pawn and made plans to take the couple hostage, then force them to open the safe so it could be looted.

Scott and Phyllis were captured at their home and then held at the trailer. Two of their abductors left the trailer early on the morning of July 12 and drove to the pawnshop Scott managed. After opening the door and going in-side, they departed and waited to see if their actions would trip a silent alarm and trigger a police response. No alarm sounded; no officer came by.

They drove back to the trailer and retrieved Scott. They brought Scott to the pawnshop in his own car—the car witnesses would pass as it sped toward Smith Road, where Scott's execution-style murder took place. Maria also drove back to the pawnshop, but in Phyllis's Blazer. Phyllis was held in Maria's mobile home, where she was beaten and raped.

At one point during their capture, Scott broke free and tried to run but was chased down and forced back inside the residence. The morning of the robbery—July 12—was the last time Scott and Phyllis saw one another.

A few hours after murdering Scott, the killers took a terrified Phyllis and drove her to a location even more remote than the one where they left Scott. As they walked her deep into the woods, she clung with fraying hope to her captors' promise that they would leave her there so she could be res-cued. She knew that they took Scott away but not that he was murdered. That hope died with Phyllis when she was shot in the back of the head and abandoned to the elements. The bullet, from a .380 caliber handgun, exited near her eye.

Gary was the first one tried and convicted of robbing, kidnapping, and murdering Scott Gasperson and Phyllis Aragona. Arthur Bollinger, an inmate imprisoned with Gary Fernandez, testified at Gary's trial that Gary told him he shot and killed Phyllis, and his son, Orlando, killed Scott. Gary also admitted to Bollinger that he beat and raped Phyllis.

The jury convicted Gary but hung during the sentencing phase, which meant he did not receive the death penalty. Instead, Gary Fernandez was given a mandatory life sentence for each of the first-degree murder convictions, plus 130 consecutive years for the other charges.

The four defendants are each serving life sentences. It is doubtful any of them will ever be paroled.

TODAY

In the corner of one room of Helen Aragona's pastel-hued home sits a huge blue stuffed rabbit. It is the size of Helen's four-year-old granddaughter. The rabbit has seen better days. Its stuffing is lumpy, its fur bedraggled and the ears look as if they've been used to drag the bunny around.

Helen's kitchen, all sky blue and white, has a little country feel to it. It's a look that went out of fashion more than a decade ago, but Helen doesn't care. Most of what hangs on the walls of her antiseptically clean home has been taken from the little house on Ben Williams Road that Phyllis shared with Scott.

Jennifer, grown and married now with children of her own, resembles her oldest sister so much that Helen's voice breaks when she remarks on their similarity. Both mother and daughter remember with absolute clarity the moment they heard about Scott's death. His killing disassembled what remained of their faith that Phyllis would come back home to them alive.

Helen fiddles with some papers on the table while, from the corner of her eye, she watches her young granddaughter play. In the playroom stands a giant wooden horse Scott had made for Phyllis.

All these years have passed, and Helen finds herself in disbelief at the things people still say to her about Phyllis and the Aragona family's loss.

"People would say to me, 'Well, she was thirty years old,' and 'You have other children,' as if that means I shouldn't mind losing my daughter," Helen says. "I have never gotten over it, and I never will."

Helen's home is full of Phyllis's things, but visitors would not get the impression that she has built a shrine to Phyllis.

"I have her shoes," Helen says in a soft voice. She strokes Jennifer's hand as her youngest daughter sits white-knuckled at the table.

"I still run into people to this day who ask about the case and want all of the juicy details," Jennifer says, disbelieving. "I don't always want to relive that."

Helen's windows are open, and the smell of cut grass wafts in from the yard. She is drinking water, and ice tinkles in the glass as her granddaughter babbles to her toys in the other room.

Phyllis, Helen says, wanted to be a veterinarian. It seemed like a natural extension of her affinity for animals. But Phyllis forgot all about veterinarian school when she met Scott. "He was all she wanted," Helen says.

Her family says Phyllis was so short she had to sit on something to drive. But in direct opposition to her feminine personality, Phyllis preferred muscle cars, like Ford Mustangs.

She listened to Neil Diamond and Barbra Streisand and Bon Jovi. Always cheerful, she was feisty, hardworking, and the kind of kid who makes a mom proud. After all this time, Helen still can't believe she lost this happy-go-lucky child to the random greed and cruelty of someone like Gary Fernandez and his co-conspirators.

"See these letters? They've [the killers] written me," Helen says, holding the papers in her hand. She shakes her head at the ordinariness of Phyllis and Scott's killers. "I've met Gary and Maria and Orlando, and I did not see the evil in them."

They have asked for her forgiveness, but it's a request Helen will never grant.

"I don't understand why they killed them," she says. "And I will never understand it, never in a million years."

She finds the community's response to her daughter's initial disappearance just as perplexing. After all, those driving the rumor mill were friends, neighbors, and classmates. Of all people, Helen says, they should have shot down the whispers and kept the good Aragona name out of the muck. They should have acted as her defender. Instead, many seemed not only willing, but eager to dirty her name.

"It was like losing my child all over again. First to the people who killed her and then to the people who decided it was their business to crucify her," Helen says.

· *10* ·

Foul Play Suspected:
What Happens When All Hope Is Gone

Fear is a journey, a terrible journey, but sorrow is at least an arriving.—Alan Paton, *Cry the Beloved Country*

$\mathscr{K}$eith Call, a handsome twenty-year-old from a tight-knit family, stopped by his brother's place on April 9, 1988, to borrow a shirt for his first date with a classmate. It was the last time his brother or anyone from his family would see him alive.

Later that night, Keith and his friend and fellow student, Cassandra Hailey, eighteen, a vivacious young woman with a crown of curly dark hair and sparkling eyes, would vanish like an unfinished thought, leaving not a single clue as to their whereabouts.

The two disappeared along Colonial Parkway in Virginia, where Keith was driving his red 1982 Toyota Celica. They had planned to take in a movie; they ended the evening with a spur-of-the-moment appearance at a local party.

The parkway itself is not a sinister place. In truth, it is a beautiful, scenic route for travelers, with twenty-three miles of roads connecting the historic Virginia cities of Jamestown, Williamsburg, and Yorktown. The drive is filled with trees, colorful bushes, and flowers, as well as wildlife. With abundant waterways along the route, ducks and geese crisscross the skies; raccoons, opossum, and deer fill the wooded areas. A drive along the parkway would have taken Keith and Cassandra past many secluded spots prized by lovers as quiet places to park.

But no one knows whether the couple chose to park and talk that night or if someone else forced their car to stop on the parkway. In either case, Keith and Cassandra never made it home. Instead, they vanished sometime in the early hours of April 10, leaving behind the little Toyota with most of their belongings in it, under circumstances that compel investigators to theorize they were the latest victims of what has been dubbed the Colonial Parkway Killer—or killers, since aspects of the crimes indicate the presence of more than one perpetrator.

The case of the Colonial Parkway Killings began on October 12, 1986, with the discovery of the bodies of Cathleen Thomas, a titian-haired Naval Academy graduate who worked in nearby Norfolk, and twenty-one-year-old Rebecca Ann Dowski, believed to be Thomas's lover. The two women were found strangled, their throats cut, in Cathleen's car, which was parked on an overlook. The killer had tried without success to torch the vehicle, and there were signs the victims fought for their lives.

As investigators continued to search for Thomas and Dowski's killer, a second set of bodies was discovered. A little more than eleven months after the first killings, twenty-year-old David Lee Knobling and his fourteen-year-old companion, Robin Edwards, were found shot to death and dumped at a game refuge, three days after Knobling's truck had been found abandoned on the parkway.

It was a little more than six months after the discovery of Knobling and Edwards in 1988 that Keith Call, of Gloucester, and Cassandra Hailey, a York County resident, disappeared. Multiple searches conducted over the years have failed to turn up indications of the couple's whereabouts. But their disappearance did not signify an end to the string of violence and mystery in the vicinity of the Colonial Parkway: on September 5, 1989, twenty-one-year-old Daniel Lauer and his brother's eighteen-year-old girlfriend, Annamaria Phelps, were found dead and decomposed after they disappeared from a rest stop along Route 64, near the parkway.

Six families lost children and siblings, but they could lay their loved ones to rest. They say that it is small comfort, but it's something. However, for the Call and Hailey families, there have been no funerals, no grave markers, and no chance to bring their children home. And, as terrible as it is to have proof of loss, the limbo of not knowing a family member's whereabouts can be worse in a way. Keith's sister, Joyce Call-Canada, says that their parents both died without ever knowing what happened to their bright, popular, attractive son. Their loss haunted the Call family, leaving a hole in their lives that could never be filled.

"It was devastating. Agony. I had to watch my parents [go] to pieces. It was very hard. We never found any bodies, and [after] many, many years . . . we still are searching," Joyce says.

Letting go of the hope that a loved one is still alive is one of the hardest steps for the family of a missing person to take. Joyce says her own family didn't want to give up on Keith. "For the first few years we had the hope that someone had them, and that was very hard, too," she says.

"Keith was very good-hearted, easy-going, loved his family. He had just started college for computer science, worked part-time at a boatyard, and commuted to nearby Christopher Newport College," says Joyce. Keith and Cassandra were both freshmen at the college, just starting to move into adulthood and find out what they wanted to do with their lives. Joyce says Keith had broken up with his steady girlfriend and asked Cassandra out. The two were on their first date and following the movie had stopped by a small cookout at an apartment complex.

Despite many searches in and around the area near where the two students disappeared, no trace of either has ever been found or at least acknowledged by law enforcement. Authorities located most of their clothes and belongings in Keith's abandoned car, along with evidence that makes some believe that the person or persons who abducted the students might have pretended to be law enforcement officers or were indeed connected to some type of police agency. Similar evidence was reportedly found in at least one of the other cases.

The six murders and the abductions of Keith and Cassandra grew cold. Although the victims' families have stayed active in urging officials to continue to investigate the murders and disappearances, other cases have pressed to the front of the line. While all of the victims' families want justice for their children, Joyce says their continuing pain comes from not having brought her brother home again. While finding Keith's remains won't end their tragedy, it would allow the Calls the opportunity to refocus their anger and energy.

"We've never even had the experience to have closure. What do I want? I would like some accountability," Joyce says.

She and the families of the other victims saw their cases make headlines again when some of the original crime scene photographs surfaced and were made public—very public. In addition to being handed around to strangers not connected with the investigation, they were leaked to the media. The families were outraged. An internal investigation conducted by the FBI found the crime scene photographer, who had since retired from the federal agency and died, had retained copies of the photos. Although the victims' families were furious at their release, something positive did come out of this act: the incident brought fresh attention to the case. Joyce and other family members hope that the renewed interest will help solve the cases, as well as bring them the news they have anticipated for more than two decades: the whereabouts of the bodies of Keith and Cassandra.

"It's difficult," Joyce says. "We went for many, many years without any response. Now I'm glad new agents have taken it over and they have been more receptive."

Still, even with new investigators on the case, information sifts through official channels at a slow pace. The Calls, like the other families, are often told they can't climb into the loop. "We want to know what happened to him and I don't understand; it's not like it's a fresh case. We get very frustrated that they cannot give us more information," Joyce says.

Some have theorized that the Colonial Parkway murderer, or murderers, have died, relocated, or were incarcerated, bringing the local killing spree to an end. Whatever happened to those responsible for so much heartache, the Call family has come to terms with the knowledge Keith will never walk back into their lives again. Unlike cases where a disappearance could have a happy ending, the evidence suggests that will not be the result with Keith and Cassandra. And after more than twenty years, the Calls wish for something they have long been denied: the chance to bury their loved one.

The name Jodi Huisentruit may ring a bell for many, even if most can't quite place the name or face. Back when she disappeared on June 27, 1995, the attractive blond television personality was all over the news—and not just in the local Mason City, Iowa, market where she worked.

Jodi, an angelic-looking twenty-seven-year-old Minnesota native, anchored the morning news for KIMT-TV when she went missing. The morning Jodi disappeared, she had overslept and was running late to work. Official accounts say Jodi went to work around 3:00 a.m., but that day she was awakened by her producer at a quarter to four in the morning. From the evidence found at the scene, it appeared that Jodi grabbed her things and was trying to open the door of her car, a red Mazda Miata, in the parking lot of her apartment complex when she was attacked. Investigating officers found a bent car key in the door of the vehicle and blood at the scene. Personal articles—a pair of red shoes, a hair dryer, her purse, and other items—were found scattered, as if dropped during a struggle. A palm print, which remains unidentified, was also located during the initial investigation.

Police canvassed the area and found someone who reported hearing screams around 4:30 a.m. but did not contact police. A man told investigators he had seen a light-colored van in the area at the time, but thus far the van has failed to materialize.

According to reporter Josh Benson and death investigator Gary Peterson, two veteran investigative reporters who maintain a Web site dedicated to Jodi (www.findjodi.com) and have kept pressure on officials to solve the case, hundreds have been interviewed in connection with the missing anchorwoman. Dozens of searches have taken place, but unless investigators are playing their hands close to their chests, little information of value has resulted.

The courts declared Jodi Huisentruit dead in 2001. The declaration follows what most believe: that she was abducted and killed. Who did it and where they left Jodi's body is a mystery that Benson and Peterson, as well as Jodi's family and friends, want to see resolved.

The fate of the independent and high-profile young career woman remains the Mason City area's most puzzling case.

———∞∞∞———

Sometimes when an individual goes missing, it is apparent that foul play is involved, as in the cases of Keith Call, Cassandra Hailey, and Jodi Huisentruit. Law enforcement classifies those cases as "missing, endangered." The press sums it up with "foul play is suspected." But despite the impression offered by the occasional sensationalized case in the media, the vast majority of disappearances are not sinister: kids become lost; people grow unhappy and walk away from their lives; the mentally disabled quit taking their medications or do not receive adequate treatment and join the throngs who live on this nation's streets; and some fall prey to accidents.

In 2009, 719,558 persons were reported as missing to the National Crime Information Center (NCIC). Of those, 22,993 children younger than the age of twenty-one were classified as "endangered," while 59,571 adults received the same classification. Another 10,055 persons younger than twenty-one were recorded as "involuntary." Of those twenty-one and older, 10,136 also received an "involuntary" classification.

"Endangered," for purposes of the NCIC report, is defined as a person who is missing under the types of circumstances that would indicate that he or she might be in physical danger. The NCIC definition for "involuntary" is that the person appears missing under circumstances that indicate the disappearance may not have been voluntary, as in a parental abduction, although these types of abductions can also be classified as "endangered."

Another 41,272 persons received an NCIC classification of "other," which means that the known circumstances do not meet the criteria for "endangered" or "involuntary" but there is reason to be concerned about that person's safety. The "other" statistics for 2009 break down as follows: 9,496 younger than age twenty-one, with the remainder of 31,776 being twenty-one and older.

It is worth noting that the majority of these cases are cleared, most with positive results: often, the person is found, alive and well, and the case is closed. However, because NCIC has no category for cases opened and closed in the same reporting period, it is impossible to say how many of 2009's cases originated and closed in that year. Many cases from previous years are often included in the "closed" statistics. So, hypothetically, the case of a seventeen-year-old whose 2005 disappearance is classified as "endangered" but is found and whose case cleared in 2009 would play out like this: her disappearance would appear in the 2005 statistics and her recovery in the 2009 numbers. Because there is this overlap in national statistics, under the current system, it is impossible to tell what percentage of cases that originate in a given year are cleared. However, local agencies may keep running accounts of clearances and may be able to better correlate the years of origination and clearance.

Also worth noting is that some missing persons cases are never recorded. Either the person disappears and no one knows or cares enough to report him or her missing or officials decline to report the individual missing. Official numbers reflect the cases that are reported—not the true numbers of missing in this country. Outpost for Hope founder Libba Phillips calls these missing persons the "missing missing" and estimates their numbers in excess of a million people—maybe even twice that. She believes the overwhelming majority who fit into this category would also by official definition be considered "endangered." No one will ever know how many are deceased and never found or are recovered and kept in a morgue or buried in an unmarked grave.

Since the airwaves and newspapers often carry headline-grabbing stories about missing persons, it's easy to come away with the misconception that police are quick to label a disappearance "suspicious." This is not true. Police are taught to deal in concrete evidence and leads, not supposition. Even when evidence tends to support a darker reason for a victim's vanishing, law enforcement leans toward conservative conclusions—at least for the record. They do not like to speculate aloud because it can hurt the families of the missing, and very often those speculations impede the investigation. But a cautious approach can also have a negative effect on a missing persons case because it can hold back the initiation of the investigatory process. Time is a precious commodity in these kinds of investigations. When too much time elapses before a probe gets rolling, evidence—and even the opportunity to find the missing person—can be lost forever. Preventing this lag was the guiding principle behind the enactment of Suzanne's Law.

Suzanne's Law amended section 3701(a) of the Crime Control Act of 1990. It requires originating law enforcement agencies to enter into NCIC anyone who goes missing between the ages of eighteen and twenty-one. A law requiring the entry of children up to age eighteen already existed (the National Child Search Assistance Act of 1990).

The law was named after Suzanne Lyall, a nineteen-year-old student enrolled at the State University of New York at Albany, who disappeared in 1998. When Suzanne, who was last spotted taking a bus following her shift at a local mall, disappeared, police reportedly waited almost two full days before they launched an investigation. The petite student has not been seen since, despite her parents' continuing and unwavering advocacy for their daughter and, indeed, for the rights of all missing persons. Passage of the law named after their daughter is hoped to speed investigatory efforts into the disappearance of college-age students.

Teenagers in general are often lumped into the runaway, or "throwaway" (also called "thrownaway"), category even when little evidence exists to support the child leaving of his or her own free will. A throwaway is a child who is not wanted by the family or guardians and is forced or encouraged to leave the home.

In decades past, most law enforcement agencies considered a missing teen, without any evidence to the contrary, to be a runaway. Many times this turned out to be true, but not always, as the Clark County (Washington) Sheriff's Department discovered in 1971 when a high school student named Jamie Rochelle Grissim vanished.

<hr />

There is no doubt that something terrible started in the Vancouver, Washington, area in the winter of 1971. Vancouver's Decembers are so cold they drive all but the heartiest indoors. Even inside, the damp chill has a way of penetrating all attempts to ward it off. But for sisters Jamie and Starr Grissim, the frozen December weather was a small thing: the two young teens were thrilled to be in a warm and loving household. It had not always been that way. The girls had lived in at least fifteen foster homes by the end of 1971 and were used to being moved around. This time, fate had been kind to them: their foster mom, an elderly woman named Grace Stilts, treated them as if they were her own. They felt loved and were happy in her home.

Starr and Jamie came from a large family of ten, but Starr—whose last name is now Lara—says there were many problems in her family situation. "There were very different age groups, and some of us had different fathers," Starr says. "My mother lost her previous children [to child welfare officials] and then had us four, and we were taken away, too."

Two younger siblings were adopted, but Starr and Jamie found themselves consigned to foster homes until their mother's parental rights were terminated when they were grade-schoolers. By then, Starr says, they were too old for most adoptive parents. They spent the next few years shuttling from one foster home to the next. "Some of them were so temporary, I can't even remember them," Starr admits.

But of all of their foster moms, Grace was their favorite. Although much older than the rest and in ill health, she wanted the girls to feel as though her home was also theirs, and she went out of her way to try to make them happy. She succeeded.

At that time, Jamie attended Fort Vancouver High School. She was sixteen years old, outgoing, and personable. Jamie didn't hesitate to try new

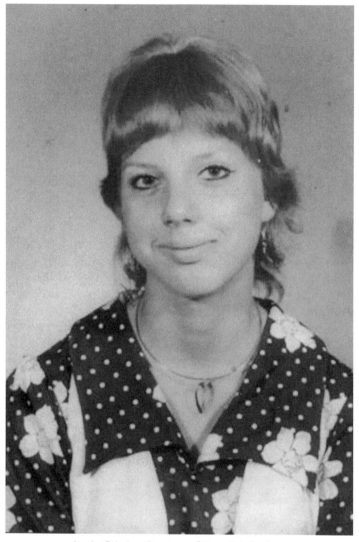

Jamie Grissim. Courtesy of Starr Grissim Lara.

things, like horseback riding. She also had an artistic streak as wide as her frequent smile and loved both drawing and writing poetry. In fact, she had already decided on an art career and had landed a small scholarship as a result of her artwork.

Her good heart brought her many friends, but she also drew animals to her with her abundant empathy. From horses to dogs to the chickens on the farm where they once lived, Jamie loved them all, and they also took to her. Starr remembers the roosters following Jamie around like a band of paparazzi. Still, no one inspired Jamie's loyalty and love more than her own little sister. Starr says they made a pact to always stick together and defend one another, no matter what.

"We had an agreement we wouldn't be separated, even if it meant one of us might [have to pass up being] adopted," Starr says.

When it came to adoption, Jamie knew the kind of person with whom she didn't want to live. The girls were once placed with wealthy potential adoptive parents, but when Jamie saw their prospective father beating one of the horses, "she said, 'We're out of here,'" Starr relates. Jamie didn't care about the money. She said she didn't want to live in a place where they would do that to a horse.

Jamie had a boyfriend, but he had already graduated from high school and was serving in the navy on the other side of the continent. Smart and capable of excellent schoolwork even with her sometimes volatile and always changing home situation, Jamie was on track to graduate a year early and excited about her prospects of studying graphic design in college.

In every way, Jamie Grissim learned to make the most of what life dealt her. Despite early years that would have broken the spirits of most kids and a proliferation of foster situations—some good, some bad—Jamie knew one constant: her close bond with Starr wouldn't change, no matter what happened. Despite the passage of decades, that bond remains even though Starr has not seen her sister since that cold, damp December in late 1971.

"It was a Tuesday and I was sitting at our kitchen table, and Jamie had to wait for the bus," remembers Starr. Her sister had gone to the school bus stop outside their door but was soon driven back inside by the chilly weather. Jamie checked in on their foster mom, who suffered from heart problems, then spoke to her sister before returning to the bus stop, reminding Starr to tell Grace, their foster mother, that she would walk home from school because she had a couple of classes that day. Jamie said she would return home around 1:30 p.m. Starr, who was in junior high school at the time, wasn't released until two hours later.

When Starr returned from school, she noted Jamie had not yet returned home, which she thought odd because her sister had been very specific that she would be out of school early that day. Hour after hour passed, but still no Jamie. As darkness fell, Starr says she knew something was very wrong. At last, Grace called the police to report her dependable, good-natured foster daughter missing.

"She didn't come home that night. The next day I went to school and it was snowing, and I kept calling home and calling all of her friends," says Starr.

The girls' caseworker, Jeannine Gillas, from child protective services, knew Jamie didn't vanish on her own, even if police did not. Starr says law enforcement dismissed her disappearance because she was a teenage foster kid. They thought she had run away, but the caseworker pressed them to take a report. They filed a missing persons report after thirty days—on January 7, 1972.

"Our caseworker was furious. She went to the school and questioned people and looked for her, but she never did find Jamie," says Starr, today a resident of Hillsboro, Oregon.

Five months later, in May 1972, Jamie's purse and identification, along with some of her other belongings, were discovered "up in the hills," in a wooded area northwest of Vancouver, according to Starr. It was a desolate area, far from their home, a place where Jamie would never have ventured by herself. But there was even worse news for Jamie's family: authorities had found the bodies of other missing teenage girls. In fact, two of those bodies would be discovered within one hundred yards of Jamie's belongings.

As the investigation into Jamie's disappearance continued over the years, the authorities asked Starr repeatedly for Jamie's dental records. Each request cut her to the heart. "Haven't you kept them?" she would inquire each time, adding, "I've given them many times, and none of the girls turned out to be her."

The truth of it is that authorities lost some of the evidence in Jamie's case. Her pocketbook vanished from police custody. Her savings account, containing $80 was confiscated by the state. "That was a lot of money back then," Starr notes. The state refunded the money to Starr in 2009 after a medical examiner issued a death certificate for Jamie.

Starr says there is an enormous difference between the way the Clark County Sheriff's Department handled Jamie's case in the beginning and the manner in which modern investigators are approaching it.

"At the time, it was harder to convince anyone that a foster kid wasn't just a runaway. Not everyone took it as seriously as my caseworker did. People heard about her and just assumed she had done something wrong in order to be a foster child. At the time they just didn't take [a teen's disappearance] seriously," she says.

Although they may be working harder to find Jamie now, one thing remains clear: teens who disappear are still considered runaways unless there is a clear indication of foul play. "The sheriff's department tells me they classify kids by age. If they are twelve and under, they are 'missing children' and above that they call them 'runaways.' That's how they classify it to this day," says Starr. "That's insane."

A park employee who was a popular graduate of Jamie's high school was arrested in connection with the murder of one of the six young girls whose bodies were found in the area, as well as an attack on one victim who survived. At least one of those bodies has never been identified; the others who died were local teenagers, all of whom reportedly had been hitchhiking. Jamie was not known to hitchhike, but Starr believes that since the suspect was a well-known, high-profile student at Jamie's high school who graduated five years earlier, she may have felt comfortable accepting a ride with him. He also lived ten blocks away from Grace and the girls, so they were used to seeing him around the neighborhood. Jamie's body, despite many searches over the years, has never been found.

The suspect received a life sentence for attempted murder following his trial in 1978. He will be eligible for release in 2014. He has never been charged with nor officially connected to Jamie Grissim's disappearance, nor with the murders of the other five women.

"My number-one thing is I'm hoping to keep this guy in jail," Starr says. "I am hoping that someday I will find her—that someday he has a change of heart when he figures he's not getting out."

In the meantime, Starr plans to attend the man's parole hearings. "It's like a form of continuing abuse," Starr says of the parole attempts. "But my sister would have done this for me, and I just can't let her be forgotten. I just can't."

Starr, like so many relatives of missing persons, needs to be able to grieve for her sister. But she faces a delicate and often incompatible balance between hope and reality: hope that her suspicions and the evidence are wrong and Jamie is still alive somewhere; reality in the form of the evidence in the case that has prompted even law enforcement to say Jamie is no longer alive.

Part of Starr's healing process includes something she both longs for and dreads: finding her sister's remains. Without a body to bring Jamie's case to a hard and inarguable conclusion, there is always the wisp of a chance that everyone has gotten it wrong and Jamie is alive after all, that despite the odds, the evidence, and plain old-fashioned common sense, Jamie really did run away or survive an abduction. It has happened before—for proof, look at Jaycee Dugard.

Jaycee, who lived in South Lake Tahoe, California, was kidnapped in 1991 at the age of eleven, after being dragged into a car while walking to the bus stop. In 2009, Jaycee, who was twenty-nine at the time, was discovered living with a man identified as Phillip Garrido and his wife, Nancy, near Antioch, California, outside of San Francisco. Held captive with two children she bore after her abduction, Jaycee and her children lived in a shed and some tents behind the Garrido home.

Unlike most stranger abduction cases, positive proof that Jaycee had met with foul play was established early in the case. Her stepfather watched from a distance as a car drove up and Jaycee was pulled into it against her will. He gave chase but was unable to catch the vehicle. In the majority of similar cases, the victim is murdered within hours of abduction.

Added to the grave circumstances of Jaycee's disappearance was the length of time she remained missing, despite hundreds of hours of searches and investigation into the case. Widespread publicity also did not help to find Jaycee, and no one could fault her family for believing her dead and moving on with their lives.

But even when the facts are as grim as they were in Jaycee's case or in the matter of Jamie Grissim or Keith Call of Virginia, there is always that tiny bit of hope nourished by the family that they, too, will one day experience a miracle.

And, the families say, if they are not going to get their miracle, if their loved one is gone, then they want proof. They want to provide a proper burial or cremate their loved ones' remains. Without this important step in the grieving process, it is difficult to advance from an emotional standpoint, even if they have already done so on an intellectual basis.

Ann Leach, director of Life Preservers, a global grief support community, says not knowing what happened to a loved one is the toughest part.

"You always wonder, 'Could I have done more?' It's part of the natural process of grieving," she says.

For the families of the missing, all of the second-guessing makes for vicious self-punishment, but Leach says it is normal to heap on the self-blame. Added to the worry and uncertainty of a missing loved one, the emotional baggage can be almost too much to bear, and that multiplies when the missing person is a child.

———— ∞ ————

Since July 2006, the mother of an Austin, Texas, teen has targeted highways and hotels, parks and alleys, city streets, and the middle of nowhere looking for her daughter. But no matter how many times or how many places Elizabeth Harris searches in her quest to find her missing daughter, Roxanne Paltauf, none of it has helped ease her heart.

Roxanne vanished on the night of July 7, 2006. Elizabeth says the striking eighteen-year-old was last seen leaving the Budget Inn in the vicinity of Interstate 35 near Austin. Wearing flip-flops, shorts, and a pink tank top, Roxy, as friends called her, stands five feet, four inches tall and weighs about 115 pounds. She has long, light brown hair and luminous green eyes, which are accentuated by a feminine, heart-shaped face and generous, pouty lips.

Elizabeth says that from what she knows, Roxanne and her longtime boyfriend had apparently engaged in an argument earlier that day. Her daughter is reported to have stormed out of the motel, carrying nothing more than the clothes she was wearing and some identification. Roxanne has not been seen since, despite multiple media campaigns, a billboard in her hometown, and her family's efforts to keep Roxanne's case on the front burner.

"We celebrated her twenty-second birthday on January 3, [2010]," Elizabeth says. "Her family gathered to sing . . . happy birthday to her, and we hung balloons and a banner along with her missing flyers. It was bittersweet."

Roxanne is the eldest of five children, and Elizabeth says the younger kids have trouble putting her disappearance into context, but they lean on one another. "We are a strong family and support each other through the ups and downs of this journey that we are going through," she says.

Elizabeth works hard to keep her daughter's name and face in the news. She gives interviews, tacks up posters, and talks about Roxanne whenever the opportunity presents itself. Sometimes the despair overpowers her attempts to keep her hopes up: after the passage of several years, it has become more and more difficult to stay optimistic that Roxanne will be found alive. Elizabeth wants to find her, no matter what her fate. Until she does, she will never stop looking and never find the peace she needs. It is like falling down a rabbit hole. Elizabeth sums it up: "It's a strange trip to be on."

———⊗⊗⊗———

It *is* a strange trip, and a lonely one, too. And no one knows it better than other families who have walked the same twisted path. Lisa Ann Murray is another traveler on that long, terrible, infinite highway. Lisa last saw her younger sister, Lynn, on December 4, 1985, and she has never stopped searching for her.

Jeffery Lynn Smith, who goes by Lynn, was born on October 12, 1969, to Clarice Minner Hay, who was was working as a babysitter and housekeeper for Virginia Clinton Dwire, former President Bill Clinton's mother. Lynn was named for Virginia's third husband, Jeff Dwire.

Lisa says her younger sister by three and a half years led a quiet, unremarkable life and dreamed of becoming a gymnast until she ended up in a volatile relationship. Then the petite sixteen-year-old disappeared. Lynn says her sister, who was dressed in a brown jacket and pink pants, was last seen walking with a boy she knew.

"There were all kinds of rumors—that she was a runaway, that she was staying with one of her girlfriends, all those kinds of things," Lisa says. "None of those rumors ever panned out and we often felt as if we were on a wild goose chase."

Lisa returned home from college and joined the family's search for the missing teenager. After no success, her mother notified the police that Lynn could not be found. She was listed as a runaway—a classification that persisted

Jeffrey Lynn Smith. Courtesy of Lisa Ann Murray.

for weeks. A ring Lynn received as a gift for her fifteenth birthday turned up at a local pawnshop. Police confiscated it, but after that, official interest in the case seemed to dwindle.

"The police [at that time] just let it go, and that, basically, was that. [After that] it was just us looking for her," Lisa says.

Lynn's disappearance forever changed her family's dynamics. Her mother slipped in and out of depression—a depression that continues until this day, according to Lisa. And although they held out hope that Lynn would return alive and unharmed during the first year after she vanished, Lisa says she now believes her sister was murdered—and she has a suspect in mind, but police have yet to make any arrests.

"Unless we find her body, it's going to be pretty difficult to prove, though," Lisa admits.

Lisa hasn't quit looking for Lynn, even though more than two decades have passed since she last saw her younger sister. Although she now lives and works in Pennsylvania, Lisa continues to act as her sister's advocate in every way: she has talked to her sister's friends and neighbors—anyone she can find who might shed light on what happened to the shy, quiet girl with the large, luminous eyes and high cheekbones. Lisa has done her best to get her sister's case out to the press. She created a YouTube video about Lynn, made posters, and prevailed upon the National Center for Missing and Exploited Children to create an age progression on Lynn to show what she would look like at the age of thirty-eight.

Lisa also has found a new ally in her search for a conclusive answer to the question of what happened to her baby sister: a police detective now assigned to the case who has shown an interest in this coldest of cold cases.

"She has been wonderful," Lisa says, remarking on the contrast between current attitudes and those of investigators when Lynn first disappeared. She is somewhat bitter that authorities dismissed her sister as a runaway.

"I think it was racially motivated," Lisa says of the police department's lack of interest in the case when it first hit the blotter. Lisa also believes the media is less inclined to publicize crimes when minorities are the victims.

"Look at the media. It's all about what appeals to the majority. You don't see many minority kids profiled anywhere, especially ones that are missing. In fact, in all honesty, you don't see much about the missing at all," she says.

Lisa wants nothing more than to bring her sister back—alive or not. "I want to see my sister in a final resting place . . . in peace next to our sister who is buried in Topeka, Kansas. I want some closure, but I also want justice for my sister and our family," says Lisa.

And although it has been more than twenty-five years since she saw Lynn, she won't stop trying until she finds her.

Reza Jou tries to apply logic to his own daughter's disappearance and to what the man who claims to be the last to have seen her alive says happened to her, but Reza fails each time. There is no logic to what transpired when the intelligent, vivacious Donna Jou vanished, and his sense of loss is palpable, as well as heartbreaking.

Donna Jou. Courtesy of Reza Jou.

Reza, the system integration manager for the International Space Station, finds himself almost unable to speak his daughter's name without tearing up. Only nineteen when she disappeared, Donna is an all-around good girl who never gave her close-knit family a minute of worry.

A brilliant, straight-A student with an almost perfect SAT score, Donna hoped to attend Johns Hopkins University or Harvard Medical School in her quest to become a neurosurgeon. She was in the process of obtaining her undergraduate pre-med degree from San Diego State University—a feat she planned to accomplish in three years.

Donna is well known for her kindness and generosity, which are at a level quite unusual for one so young. She volunteered with battered women's shelters and at a hospital laboratory. She tutored math students at her high school. She played basketball, worked hard at her studies, and told her father she was studying medicine so she could be his physician when he grew old.

Donna seems to have no enemies. Born as the youngest in a family where academic achievement is high, Donna set lofty goals for herself and always met them. She is not one to brag or nurture conceit—she is modest, good-natured, and devoted to her family. Donna has always been the kind of daughter to make a parent proud.

Reza says he fell in love with his baby girl the first moment he laid eyes on her. She did not cry like other newborns, he says, his voice stumbling over the memory. Instead, she opened her big bright eyes and looked at her father for the first time as if she were sizing him up. Over the years, their bond would grow unbreakable. She would never disappoint him nor bring him pain. And she possesses an unusual amount of common sense for one so young.

On June 23, 2007, Donna vanished, splintering the happiness Reza and Nili Jou had always known and shared with their three children. The Jou family's lives imploded into a blur of worry, pain, and sorrow.

Reza says their nightmare began when Donna advertised her tutoring services on Craigslist, a free online classified advertising Web site. She was trying to earn a little extra money and was very advanced at math. Her father says he warned his youngest daughter to be careful in her dealings with strangers and to never go to their homes. He says she assured him she would remain cautious, but Reza was still uneasy.

Donna, like many teens, was naive, according to Reza. No matter how much her parents cautioned her, she believed she could take care of herself. Never having faced true evil, she didn't understand it and never imagined she would ever cross paths with someone capable of hurting her. Reza says she was wrong.

Although her father asked her not to advertise as a math tutor on Craigslist, Donna met thirty-seven-year-old John Steven Burgess, who also went by the alias Sinjin Stevens, when he answered her ad on the online site. After exchanging e-mails, the pair arranged to meet for a tutoring session. On the night Donna disappeared, she left on a motorcycle with a man police believe to be Burgess.

The following night, on June 24, Donna's mother received a text message sent from her daughter's cell phone that said her cell phone battery was dying and that she was in San Diego and would be home soon. The Jou family lives in Los Angeles.

On June 25, two days after they last saw her, Donna failed to show up for work or attend classes. Her parents went into panic mode. They felt certain Donna would not vanish on purpose.

They started calling everyone they knew, as well as everyone Donna knew or had ever mentioned, looking for clues to her whereabouts. Police told the Jous that since their daughter was over eighteen, she could go wherever she wanted without notifying them. They intimated Donna had left on her own, not because someone forced her.

"I told them that was impossible. We are very close. She wouldn't do anything like that," Reza says.

Leads poured in, says Reza. They piled up, one on top of the other, a mountain of information. The family passed them along to authorities. "I forwarded [the leads] and trusted them to follow them up. Later on I found most of them were not pursued," he says.

Police developed Burgess as a suspect, naming him a person of interest in connection with Donna's disappearance. Burgess reacted by packing up and vanishing. On July 9, a search warrant was executed on the suspect's house. His roommate was also questioned. A little over two weeks later, Burgess was picked up in Florida on drug charges and extradited to California, where he was allowed to post bond.

In the meantime, the Jou family hired a search-and-rescue team to conduct a search for their daughter. They found nothing. Reza and Nili hired well-known California attorney Gloria Allred to represent them in their quest to find out the truth about their daughter.

Burgess, who is a convicted sex offender, was once again arrested in the state of Florida. This time he was charged with a multitude of offenses, including theft. Again he was brought back to Los Angeles where he was sentenced to prison for three years in connection with another California case. Meanwhile, a large search-and-rescue effort throughout the Santa Monica Mountains was conducted. No clue as to Donna Jou's whereabouts was found.

While the Jou family continued seeking their daughter, Burgess was released from prison on March 14, 2009. The state then ordered him arrested in connection with Donna's disappearance, and he was charged three days later.

On May 6, he pleaded guilty to a felony count of involuntary manslaughter and misdemeanor concealment of an accidental death. He was sentenced to five years in prison followed by three years of probation for his role in Donna's death. The Jou family was told he could be released as early as 2011—serving about two years.

Burgess told investigators that he and Donna were partying the night of her death and that she wanted drugs. He says she used a mixture of heroin and cocaine and he left her sitting there, on a drug high, while he went to bed. When he awakened the next morning, he said, he found the bright, young college student dead in a chair in his living room. He says he panicked because he was on probation for performing a lewd act on a child, so he placed Donna's body in a bag. Burgess told investigators he put the bag with her body into the bed of his truck and drove to the waterfront. Then he moved Donna's remains to a boat, took her to an area in the vicinity of Cabrillo Bay and Wilmington Marina, and dumped her in the water. A police spokesman later told the press that others at Burgess's house during the party corroborated both Donna's presence at the party and her drug use. The Jous believe the people at that party covered for Burgess.

Reza has hired a private company to search the waters for his daughter's body because he does not believe the story Burgess told police. For one thing, he says, his daughter has no history of drug use. He does not believe she would ever have taken drugs—especially a mixture of such strong and potentially lethal narcotics. Donna was a pre-med student. She understood the effects of drugs like heroin and cocaine. Why, Reza asks, would an ambitious, intelligent, otherwise levelheaded individual like Donna allow herself to be drugged with a highly addictive substance like heroin? Other parts of Burgess's story don't add up for the Jous, either.

"He said he put her in a bag and put her in the bed of his truck, and the truck was there parked on the side of a narrow street in his overcrowded neighborhood from the early morning hours of Sunday until Monday evening, in June, all night long, and nobody could smell anything or see anything in the bed of that truck? And he drove through the narrow streets to San Pedro and lowered her into a boat and dropped her into the water near a lighthouse and no one saw anything. It's so crowded [in those areas] it's impossible for somebody to do those things and nobody sees anything," Reza says.

Reza believes Burgess fabricated the story in order to hide what really happened to his daughter. But whether Burgess is telling the truth or lying in order to draw the least possible sentence, as the Jou family suspects, there is one thing that can help Reza Jou come to terms with what has torn his life to pieces: finding his daughter's remains—if she is dead.

Without a body, there is always reason to hope, no matter how strong the evidence to the contrary. That is one reason Reza persists at the task of searching for Donna.

"[Police] told me many times their job is not to look for Donna; their job is to put Burgess behind bars. They are not looking for my child," says Reza.

Reza says the experience changed his life in ways he cannot articulate. "Sometimes I have difficulty recognizing myself. The pain is unbelievable: her image is always in front of my face," he says.

"She had such a promising future and now this person gets two years' prison time [the amount of time Burgess most likely will have served by the time he is released] and he gets the chance to do it one more time to other families," says Reza.

He will not rest until he finds Donna or her body. "I'm not alive anymore. It's the new me, not the same person I used to be. Now I live only to be a champion for Donna," Reza says.

Deborah Bowen, coauthor with Susan Strickler of *A Good Friend for Bad Times: Helping Others through Grief*, says for many it is impossible to move on without recovered remains, even when there is no doubt the loved one is gone. "It's an individual thing, but for some people [a body] is really important for them to let go," says Bowen.

Those with a missing loved one say there is no such thing as closure, but crippling grief inhibits the ability to live one's life. Siblings of lost children often see dramatic shifts in family dynamics, particularly when a case is unresolved. Although not the hoped-for ending, in worst-case scenarios finding the loved one's remains can allow the grief process to run its natural course.

Bowen says different people need different things to get through the "not knowing." Some find solace in religion. "All the world's religions believe in life after death and the spirit lives on: it's a good thing to focus on that point," she says.

"Grief can keep you from moving on," Bowen says. Even if solace is found through religion or other pursuits, Bowen recommends counseling. She says, "It doesn't mean you are going to quit grieving." But it may help kick-start the healing process.

Melanie Brady Drury of Cincinnati, Ohio, and her sister Michele Walker of Gallatin, Tennessee, each devote part of their day to searching for their sister, Melisa Brady Sloan. Melisa, a petite blond with brown eyes and a warm, generous smile, had moved with her husband, John, from Kentucky to Orlando,

Melisa Brady Sloan. Courtesy of Merle B. Brady.

Florida, where she found employment as a nurse. But on May 1, 1994, the twenty-three-year-old vanished.

Police went to the home she shared with her husband at the request of her worried family and found Melisa's car there, along with her pet cat. Her husband told the officers that Melisa left him for another man. Melanie says Melisa's credit cards and Social Security number have not been used since she disappeared. Official records confirm the marriage was troubled—police responded to calls at their home at least twice in the months preceding Melisa's disappearance.

John divorced Melisa eight months after she vanished. Melanie says he has remarried and lives on the other side of the country. Orlando detectives reviewed Melisa's case again in 2007, obtaining DNA samples from the Brady family for future use. Melisa is listed as "missing endangered."

"Not knowing where Melisa is probably is the most frustrating [thing] of all," Melanie says.

Melisa's family struggles to keep her name in front of the public. They don't want their bubbly sister with the outgoing personality and a knack for music forgotten. And the Bradys understand all too well how important it is to keep a case alive: their father, Francis "Frank" Brady, was kidnapped and murdered in October 1991. His killers were apprehended following a broadcast of *America's Most Wanted*.

"The thing about having two tragedies happen to your family is that you never, ever seem to feel like you come up for air. It's never over. It never leaves you. It's always there," says Melanie. "We just want to bring Melisa home and place her beside my father."

On the other side of the country, in Niagara Falls, New York, Sharon DeLuke understands Reza Jou's emotions. She has walked in his shoes, and it was a painful journey.

On Thanksgiving Day in 1990, Sharon's seventeen-year-old son, Ron, laid his glasses on a table in the home he shared with his family and left to go to a friend's house. His family would never see him alive again.

A happy-go-lucky young man with brown hair and a stocky build, Ron loved racquetball, the family dog, and riding the four-wheeler he bought with money he earned from his paper route. He was a good student and one of Sharon's five children. A senior in high school, he hoped to become a math teacher. Ron's future was brimming with possibilities, and he couldn't wait to move to the next phase: college.

But that's one place he would never go. Ron DeLuke vanished as he traveled the short distance between his house and that of his friend.

When they discovered him missing, his family mounted a search. The local media printed photos of Ron, and television stations ran stories on his disappearance. He was entered into the police database as a runaway—something standard to police departments when the missing individual is a teenager. But his mother and family knew that Ron DeLuke never ran away. He was too well adjusted and happy to abandon his life and dreams.

The family did everything they could think of to find Ron and bring him back home. There were helicopter and ground searches in and around the Niagara Gorge, which lies blocks from the DeLuke residence. Nothing was found. Sharon even consulted psychics who claimed to have information on Ron, but she came away disappointed and despairing. "We turned over every stone looking for him," she says.

Meanwhile, everyday life became a nightmare. "It was tough to get up and go to work; in fact, it was hard to go anywhere. All I kept thinking of was that I had to find him, that someone was holding him hostage, someone beat him up—you can't control what you are thinking," she says.

Sharon never gave up hope that her son was alive, yet she understood implicitly that the longer he was missing, the worse the possible outcome. That outcome crystallized on Easter Sunday in 1993, about two and a half years after Ron vanished. Sharon, who works in a hospital lab, says a nurse told her that a body had been found in Niagara Gorge, which is part of the state park system. Goose bumps rose on Sharon's arms. She knew without being told that the discovery was connected to Ron's disappearance.

She spoke to the doctor in charge of the hospital's forensics unit, and he confirmed that he believed the body to be Ron's. Sharon, her police officer nephew, and her former husband (Ron's father) went to identify the clothes and personal items found on the remains, which some kids playing in the gorge had stumbled across on the night before Easter.

"They had his clothes lying on the floor and his wallet," she said.

Examination of the skeletonized remains proved the victim was indeed Ron DeLuke. Because so much time had passed, the medical examiner could find little in the way of how he might have died. All Sharon knows is that his clavicle was broken.

Does she suspect foul play? She has her opinion about what happened to Ron but realizes that chances are she will never know the truth. Ron never made it to his friend's house the night he disappeared, and he didn't like the gorge, says Sharon. She finds it hard to believe he would go anywhere near it, especially by himself, in the dark.

"When you have a missing child, you don't know if he's hungry or hurt or if he has a warm bed," she says. But until his body was found, she never gave up on him nor did she believe he could be dead.

"At least God gave him back to me and I was able to give him a decent burial. That was the most important thing, to give him a proper burial," she says.

Sharon says she knows that her son is at peace now. During his funeral she looked up at the window in the church and saw a column of sparkling dust in the air against the backdrop of stained glass. She believes it was "angel dust."

"I saw his spirit leave and go to heaven, and that's when I got my peace. I knew he would be all right and God would take care of him," Sharon said, her voice breaking as she recalls that long-ago moment.

"It's very important to be able to bury your child. Some people never have that," she says.

• 11 •

The Searchers: The National Center for Missing and Exploited Children, Project Jason, Search and Rescue, Private Eyes, and Others

> You will never close the hole in my heart.—Clark County, Nevada, Coroner P. Michael Murphy quoting the family of a missing person.

*T*he last time Kelly Jolkowski saw her son, Jason, he was in the process of leaving his childhood behind. At nineteen, Jason wanted to be a radio sportscaster. A sweet boy who had never been in trouble, he was earning money to return to college in the fall by working at a local restaurant. He lived with his mom, dad, and younger brother, Michael, in Omaha, Nebraska.

Kelly says Jason suffered from some minor learning and speech issues, but he'd tried hard to overcome them. While a student at the local community college, Jason had discovered a gift for working as a disc jockey at the school's student-staffed radio station. Combined with his almost encyclopedic knowledge of sports trivia, Jason believed he'd found his calling.

The Nebraska youth didn't drink or smoke. His idea of a great time was to play video games with his brother. Michael, who is seven years younger than Jason, worshipped his older sibling. The two were as close and inseparable as fingers on the same hand.

On June 13, 2001, after Kelly and her husband, Jim, left for their respective jobs, Jason received a call from his place of employment asking him to come in early. Jason told his boss his car was in the shop and he didn't have a ride. His boss said he would send another employee to pick him up.

Jason directed the coworker to the high school where he graduated, which was about seven or eight blocks away. He said he would meet her there because she wasn't sure where his house was. But first, before he left, he had a chore to do.

Jason Jolkowski. Courtesy of Kelly Jolkowski.

It was Jason's job to put the trash cans away after the sanitation trucks came and went. At about 10:00 that morning, Michael glanced out the window and saw Jason, dressed in his work clothes, rolling the trash cans to their usual place. Michael had no idea his brother would soon vanish into that hot summer morning.

The first inkling Kelly had that something was wrong came when Jim called her at work sometime in the afternoon asking if she'd had a call from Jason. "And I am thinking, 'Why would I?' I had no idea this stuff had transpired," she says.

After her husband explained Jason had not shown up for work, Kelly says she grew concerned. "That was not like him. Jason would not promise to do something and then not do it."

They called his cell phone and he didn't answer. They drove the route Jason would have walked and found empty sidewalks.

"I had a dark, horrible feeling in the pit of my stomach," Kelly says.

Believing they had to wait twenty-four hours to file a missing persons report, Jim and Kelly spent a sleepless night searching for their son, then called the police the next morning.

"The police officer who took the report said, 'Oh, he's probably just spending the night at a friend's house and will be back any minute,'" Kelly says. At the time she felt the remark trivialized what the family was going through but now says, "I understand he was trying to be comforting." Ten days later detectives came out and interviewed the family.

When Jason still didn't come home and no trace of him was found, extended family members traveled to the Jolkowski's Omaha home and helped distribute flyers. In the meantime, Kelly and her phone were inseparable. She was afraid Jason would call and she wouldn't be there to answer it. For the first six months after he went missing, she even carried it into the bathroom when she showered.

Her days blurred. "I became an emotional zombie," she says.

Even worse, she didn't know where to turn for help. Other than dealing with the police, there was no real guidance, nothing to help her figure out where to go, what to do, how to search for Jason.

"There were never any leads, never any clues. It was an absolute zero," she says. Police interviewed friends and coworkers and turned up nothing. No witnesses, no possibilities.

The family called in the media. Stories ran in newspapers and on television, but no solid leads developed. It was as if Jason had dropped off the map. Kelly couldn't stand to talk about it—she asked that coworkers not discuss the case with her until she was ready. They complied. But her desire to not talk about it with the people in her life didn't undercut her obsession with finding Jason.

Kelly found accounts on the Internet of other missing persons and was determined, "That would never be us. We wouldn't be like those families. I told myself that one day he would be home," she says.

In educating herself about missing persons, Kelly found little in the way of organized help for families but knew the Internet could be a good resource. She built a site for Jason and once again attracted widespread media attention. Others with similar situations also contacted her. Kelly—working on a budget—began looking for ways to publicize their disappearances without breaking the bank: Project Jason was born.

A nonprofit that offers assistance, advice, and a place for the families of missing persons to communicate with others who are going through the same heartbreak, www.projectjason.org is often one of the first places families turn to for help.

Over the years, Kelly has initiated programs like the 18 Wheel Angels, in which long-haul truck drivers distribute posters of the missing as they travel. Other Project Jason programs developed by Kelly include

- Awareness Angels Network, a source where the public may access and disseminate printed posters for the missing;
- Come Home, in which posters of the missing are distributed in homeless shelters around the country;
- Faces of the Missing, profiles and images of the missing are posted on projectjason.org for public viewing and to help get the word out; and
- an annual retreat to teach families of missing persons coping strategies.

Kelly and Project Jason also work with law enforcement and other agencies to ensure that appropriate training is available. She doesn't limit her reach to helping police—she also has worked on legislation in a number of states to make individuals who have disappeared a police priority.

Kelly cautions those with missing friends or relatives to check out an organization before engaging with it. Although there are hundreds that claim to be able to help, some are run by individuals with questionable motives and even more questionable skills and advice. Families of missing adults can check the organization's resource page for trained and ethical nonprofits.

When dealing with missing children, she recommends checking to see if the organization or nonprofit belongs to the Association of Missing and Exploited Children's Organizations (AMECO) at www.amecoinc.org. AMECO has stringent membership qualifications. Project Jason is a member.

Dynamic and untiring, Kelly has turned her tragedy into a source of strength for thousands. Stephanie Cook is one of the many who have turned to Kelly and Project Jason for guidance.

"The most helpful thing for me was Project Jason. Kelly Jolkowski helped me get in touch with the missing persons clearinghouse in my area to submit DNA. Kelly also had an age progression done on my mom of what she may look like now," says Stephanie.

Stephanie's mother, Bobbi Ann Campbell, disappeared in late December 1994. The twenty-four-year-old blond had gone to pick up her paycheck and stop at the grocery store, leaving behind her five-year-old. The petite young woman has not been seen since, but her car was found not too long after her disappearance, abandoned near the Jordan River in Salt Lake City, Utah.

Stephanie has not stopped looking for her mom, whom she says once worked at a zoo and loved animals. She remembers camping and fishing together and reminds the public that a missing person leaves behind heartache and uncertainty. "All missing adults have a family and friends. People love them," she says.

In June 2010, Stephanie channeled her grief and longing for her mother into a memorial service to commemorate Bobbi Ann's life. But she still hasn't given up on finding her.

"The hope gets harder every year that passes," Stephanie says.

Kathy Wormington understands Stephanie's reference to time all too well: more than three decades have passed since Kathy saw her father, Frederick Leach. Like Stephanie, Kathy also turned to Project Jason when she saw no progress in her dad's case.

Frederick vanished under suspicious circumstances on March 17, 1976, from Laytonville, California, where he lived and worked as a mechanic. Kathy says the facts surrounding her father's disappearance have led her family to believe he was murdered, although no body has surfaced. After years of dealing with law enforcement agencies and searching on their own, the family asked Kelly Jolkowski for help.

"We realize it's been a long time," Kathy says. But she, like many others, has learned to put her faith in grassroots efforts like Project Jason, Outpost for Hope, and the Doe Network.

The Doe Network (its full name is the Doe Network: International Center for Unidentified & Missing Persons) is operated by a volunteer administrative team and concentrates on missing persons and unidentified recovered remains in North America, Europe, and Australia.

The organization's Web site, www.doenetwork.org, posts cases online and gives amateur sleuths a platform from which to do some of the difficult searches and comparisons that law enforcement often has neither the time nor the manpower to accomplish.

Todd Matthews, who is also with NamUs, the National Missing and Unidentified Persons System, has a long affiliation with the Doe Network. He says the Doe Network was founded because "until NamUs came along, there really was nothing out there. The Doe Network was born of a need." The volunteers are still vital, he says. "The existence and progress of Doe Network proved it is possible to harness the power of the people."

Doe Network volunteers work from their homes. They are store associates, cooks, homemakers, teachers, mechanics, nurses, lawyers, and college students all united by one goal: they want to help people find their loved ones.

"Families are sometimes under the impression they can make the report [that someone is missing] and sit back and do nothing," Matthews says. He urges them to avoid adopting the "wait-and-see approach." Instead, he pushes people to become proactive in the search and to demand accountability from law enforcement.

The Doe Network has about five hundred volunteers, according to Matthews. He admits that they get their share of people who don't understand the organization's goals.

"'I've seen every episode of CSI. I want to match up photographs.' We get a lot of that," he says.

---❦---

Brian Sullivan's family says they will find him no matter how long it takes. Brian vanished on July 8, 2007, from Rochester, New York. A community college student, he was in the process of deciding whether to continue school or to move and go to work. Brian's mom, Barbara Sullivan, says his red 1995 Pontiac Sunfire was found on a dead-end street, his wallet and bank cards on the seat. Brian's cell phone, iPod, and car keys were not found. Nothing in the nineteen-year-old student's apartment was disturbed, and some expensive mail order purchases he had made were delivered soon after his disappearance.

Barbara stresses that Brian was neither unhappy nor depressed in the days prior to his disappearance. Like many young people, he was exploring his options and hoped either to go into some aspect of the music business or to become a social worker.

Brian is a gentle soul, according to his family. He cooks perfect fried chicken, has a broad interest in music that ranges from hip hop to jazz, and loved his late cat—Congo—who used to sleep with him. Brian, who is remembered as a sensitive, considerate kind of guy, also has a goofy sense of humor.

"He has a way of making you laugh when you [are] mad as heck at him," says his mom.

Barbara and the rest of Brian's family have searched nonstop for him without success. She says they are pleased with the way local law enforcement has handled his case. The police stay in constant touch with the Sullivan family, and a poster seeking information on his whereabouts was even put up in the jail, in hopes that someone might recognize him and come forward.

Barbara claims that of all the individuals who go missing, adult males get the least amount of media attention. She's right. Children, young women—and in particular, pretty, young, white women—and celebrities monopolize the news. Those whose loved ones fall into different demographics must work hard to keep them in the public eye. Barbara urges them to never give up.

"We have relied on many outside agencies: NCMEC, Project Jason, Center for Hope," she says. The family also has created a MySpace page for Brian and he is featured in the New York deck of missing persons playing cards distributed to prisoners. (Created by the parents of missing college student Suzanne Lyall, the playing cards feature photos of missing persons and are given to jails for the inmates to use.)

"We are devastated," says Barbara with a simplicity that underscores how terrible these situations are for families. "As with many that go missing, the answers are a long time coming."

For Susan Burg, the passage of time has left her standing in the same spot for more than eight years. That is when the search for her daughter, Sabrina Kahler, began. Sabrina disappeared from Erie, Pennsylvania, under suspicious circumstances after swimming at a local pool. Although she had just celebrated her twentieth birthday, Sabrina was little more than a child—she still had braces on her teeth and was mentally challenged. Her mother misses her sweet girl and never stops pushing for answers to her disappearance.

Neither do Joy Little or Janey Caravallo, who seek missing siblings on opposite sides of the country. Joy's sister, Linda Lois Little, vanished from Daytona Beach, Florida, in 1991 and hasn't been seen since. Linda disappeared while biking home from her job in the early morning hours. A tall woman with long, wavy brown hair, Linda's family says she would never leave on her own. They've hung posters, distributed flyers, and taken advantage of every opportunity to bring her story to the media. Still, Linda Little's case remains unresolved.

Janey also uses print media to search for her brother, Gilbert Caravallo, who disappeared from the home he shared with their mother in Pearl City, Hawaii. The thirty-five-year-old Gilbert vanished in 2004 while hanging out with some friends. He has not been seen since despite the efforts of his family to find him. Janey says losing a child this way has been tough on their mother. In addition to getting the word out on the Internet, dealing with the press, and putting up posters, Janey also wrote and published an account of her brother's disappearance. She hopes the book she wrote will focus media attention on Gilbert, but thus far no sign of the missing man has surfaced, and the Caravallo family keeps looking.

―――∞∞∞―――

When children disappear, they fall under the auspices of the National Child Search Assistance Act, which was passed in 1990. It prohibits law enforcement agencies from requiring a waiting period before taking a missing persons report and provides that certain information be entered into the national database known as the National Crime Information Center (NCIC). It also directs that this information be made available to the various state clearinghouses, which are designed to follow up on missing persons. A list of state clearinghouses can be found on the Klaas Foundation's Web site at www .klaaskids.org/pg-mc-stmisschildclearing.htm. The foundation was founded in memory of Polly Klaas, who was abducted from the bedroom of her home by a stranger and then murdered. The KlaasKids Foundation, which is a member of AMECO, works to further the cause of child safety and offers aid and support to parents of missing children.

In addition to federal law, each state may have its own set of laws on missing children. In Massachusetts, for example, police agencies are required by statute to enter the child without delay into state and federal databases, even if the report is incomplete.

———— ✺ ————

"The only thing that gets to me is the body of a three-, four-year-old wearing Winnie the Pooh pajamas. I have flashbacks to my granddaughter," says Jerry Nance.

Nance is sitting at his desk in the crowded office space he shares with other case managers at the National Center for Missing and Exploited Children (NCMEC). Long legs stretched in front of him, Nance's hangdog expression makes him appear sad. In view of the things he has seen during his four decades as a criminal investigator, Nance is entitled to a touch of gloominess. But he's a gentle soul, an introspective man who believes in what he is doing and never stops hoping for those random miracles like the recovery of Jaycee Dugard, found alive eighteen years after she was abducted by a stranger.

Nance is a realist, though. He understands that cases like Jaycee's are rare. But like the rest of the crew at NCMEC, he is dedicated to fighting that uphill battle. He and his coworkers are often a missing child's best hope of being found.

Nance worked as a certified death investigator with the Naval Criminal Investigative Service and established their cold case program. He retired on a Thursday in 1998 and began work at NCMEC's Arlington, Virginia, office on the following Monday.

Back in 1998 when Nance first arrived, NCMEC had about 175 employees and volunteers. That number has shot up to 500, with about 300 in the Alexandria, Virginia, area. The rest are in Florida, Texas, and New York.

NCMEC (referred to as "Nick-Mick" by cops) was founded at the urging of individuals like Reve and John Walsh, host of *America's Most Wanted*, both tireless advocates for missing children. The Walshes' activism grew out of the tragic 1981 kidnapping and slaying of their son, Adam.

The Virginia-based organization offers a wide range of assistance to law enforcement and the families of the missing, from counseling to following complicated leads. Nance's job is to work with law enforcement. He handles the kinds of things that would guarantee most individuals years of nightmares.

Earlier, he received a call from a police department that had hosted a motorcycle rally. "It was a pretty calm event, and on Sunday [the participants] all started taking off. On the way out of town, one of them passed a vet's office. On Monday morning, the assistant goes to open up the door and finds a Walmart bag on the doorknob. Inside she finds a human skull of a child about four to six years of age. It's too young to tell if it's a boy or a girl. The mandible [jawbone] was separated from the rest of the skull and some of the teeth were glued in. Makes me think it was some kind of trophy," he says.

It was a horrific find, Nance agrees, but not the cut-and-dried criminal case it seems at first blush. He points out that there are professional skeletons—the kind used in medical schools—out there, too.

"Our job will be to tie all of the information together. We'll search through the databases and give the police suggestions," he says. Facial reconstruction is another method by which NCMEC might try to identify the child.

What happened to bring this nameless youngster to such a disturbing denouement? Nance's job is to help authorities working the case to maximize the reach of their investigation. Since he stays on top of cutting-edge forensic techniques and has access to multiple databases, he can connect the dots that others can't.

But when it comes to missing children or unidentified recovered remains, Nance finds it hard to take satisfaction in resolving his cases. "You can have DNA, do skull reconstruction, help make a case, but at the end of the day, there is a dead child out there," says Nance.

He empathizes with those parents who are resigned to a bad outcome. "One mother said it drives her crazy to think of her daughter out in the cold. She wants to put a blanket on her," Nance says.

Although police now have better and more sophisticated tools with which to work, the tide of missing children continues, fueled by the Internet. Nance and other law enforcement officers share a growing concern about the sheer number of victims that can be reached over the information superhighway.

The case manager says he once attended a conference where an FBI cybercrimes expert gave a talk about chat rooms. He went online in front of the conference attendees, entered a chat room, and typed in, "Hi, my name is Heather and I like puppies."

"There were eighty replies within one minute. This is 10:00 in the morning. It shook me," Nance admits.

Although nonfamily abductions are the least common reason behind a child's disappearance, it's still too much of a factor for Nance. "Most abductions lead to death—what happens, happens fast," he says.

Nance says his wife has learned not to ask about his day and he has learned not to share it. It's how he keeps his head on straight, how he sleeps at night. But he's proud of what NCMEC and his forensics unit accomplish.

"We're the only unit in the U.S. who does what we are doing. Sometimes we're their only chance. And even though we look for the dead, we put most of our resources into the living," he says.

Adult males. As Barbara Sullivan says, their disappearances draw the least amount of press attention. Sometimes their families feel like they are the only ones looking for them, the only ones who give a damn.

Trevor Morse. Anthony Holland. Justin Burkhart. Three adult men, missing from three different states, all leaving behind three desperate, devastated families.

Trevor's father, Rick Morse, says that his son disappeared from Las Vegas, where he lived and worked as an electrician, on May 6, 2007. Trevor is a transplant from El Paso, Texas. Rick says police in Las Vegas have tried to convince the family that Trevor committed suicide, but he denies his son was suicidal and says there was every indication that things were going well for Trevor. In fact, says Rick, Trevor was planning on moving back home to El Paso to be closer to his family.

"Dealing with the [Las Vegas Police] was a nightmare. They showed very little understanding . . . and absolutely no compassion," says Rick. "On the other hand, [the] El Paso Police, though they had no responsibility in the case, were compassionate."

A handsome young man with defined cheekbones beneath cornflower blue eyes, Trevor was twenty-six when he vanished. Rick says he spends part

Trevor Morse, left, with his mother, Linda, and brother Dan. Courtesy of Rick and Linda Morse.

of every day looking for his son—he searches the Internet and tries to keep press interest from flagging.

"We do not have the financial resources to post billboards and rewards," says Rick.

On June 21, 2009, Anthony Holland walked out of the door of his Cordell, Oklahoma, home to run a business errand. He never returned. His family, including his cousin, Teresa Goughan, continues to look for him, but all of their efforts have thus far turned up little to indicate what happened to the successful businessman.

Anthony was fifty-one when he disappeared. With his white hair and charming smile, he resembles a favorite college professor. Teresa says Anthony is bighearted and generous. He comes from a large, close-knit family.

"We all have faith that we will find Anthony one day and this faith keeps us going," says Teresa.

Searchers found Anthony's abandoned truck, but no sign of Anthony, nor any indication of his whereabouts. His personal effects—wallet, checkbook, cash, and identification—remained undisturbed in his home.

Teresa says the family is pleased for the most part with the way local authorities have handled the search for her cousin. They've called in air and ground searchers and worked with cadaver dogs on the assumption that Anthony has fallen victim to an accident and perished. She says the Washita County Sheriff's Office stays in touch with them, and "appear[s] to be actively working the case. They have not ruled it as foul play, but I don't think they have ruled that out, either," she says.

Teresa says she isn't certain the officers conducting the investigation are trained for the task, and when family members ask questions, they are stonewalled. "In general, we are typically told that our questions cannot be answered as it is part of the investigation," she says.

"Each day that goes by is another day without Anthony. We hope and pray that he is safe," she says.

When the searches lead to nothing and leads dwindle, all that is left for some families is hope and prayer. Eloisa Chavez finds herself praying a lot these days. Most of those prayers are for her missing son, Justin Drew Burkhart.

Justin, a young Hispanic man who had been working hard to leave his troubled youth behind, left his Bend, Oregon, apartment in the early morning hours of August 1, 2009, to pick up something to eat and never came back. His mom says there was no reason for Justin to vanish on purpose, and when he left, it was obvious he intended to return: the lights were on in his apartment and music was playing.

Justin had a promising social life. Engaged and planning to move to Alaska to follow his fiancée, he had overcome drug addiction, although his family says he still drank—sometimes to excess.

They continue to search for him and celebrate his life, but investigators have little to go on in this case. There are no clues, no smoking gun, nothing that gives any indication of where Justin could have landed when he left his place. Did he have an accident? Was he kidnapped or injured and left somewhere to die? Those are questions they are beginning to believe they will never answer.

When answers are few and the trail grows cold, some resort to private investigators like Harold Copus to keep the search going when things look their dimmest.

Reflecting on his long career in private investigation, Copus estimates his success rate in finding missing persons is about 90 percent, which is a pretty good clearance rate. He's proud of those numbers, but it's the 10 percent he doesn't find that haunts him.

Middle-aged, with glasses perched on his nose, Copus speaks of those cases in vowels that wind as long and endless as a country dirt road. A product of Alabama, he resides in Athens, Georgia, a college town not far from Atlanta. After his own graduation from college, Copus made his way to the FBI, where he worked as a special agent for almost a decade, leaving, he says, when the constant transfers proved too hard on his home life. He settled into a job directing private investigations for a large law firm, but after a decade of telling other people what to do, he decided to parlay his experience into a private investigations agency of his own.

Over the years, Copus worked his share of the private eye's steady diet: divorces, employee thefts, evidence gathering for criminal defense attorneys; however, the missing persons cases he signed on for were the vehicles for both his greatest accomplishments and most devastating failures.

Parental abduction cases and runaways are typical of the missing persons cases that cross a private investigator's desk. Copus will say without hesitation that not all private investigators are equal, not all are qualified to work these cases, and it helps to know the difference between a good private eye and one who is in it for the quick bucks.

Nationwide, it's impossible to say how many missing persons cases are brought to the private sector, since no one even knows how many private investigators there are. Some states, including Mississippi and Colorado, lack licensing requirements. But the majority of states do regulate private investigators, if only to make them buy a license and submit to a criminal background check.

Private investigators' associations abound, and like state standards, association standards differ. Some seem to exist to sell gear and training to their members; others set high standards and expect their members to adhere to them. With plenty of muscle in place to enforce their rules, they also interact with state licensing agencies.

Training and education also vary. Some private investigators come to the profession as did Copus: via the military or prior law enforcement. Others decide to become a private investigator, then buy a newspaper advertisement or invest in a Web site. Like people who call themselves "actors" after having headshots taken, it's not technically a lie but also not the absolute truth. Many times, amateurs dabbling in the business do the most harm.

Private investigators like Copus work a steady diet of runaway cases. They understand police will take those cases just so far; once it is clear a child has taken off on his or her own and is of a certain age, official enthusiasm levels off. It's not because police are not interested in getting the child back to his or her parents—that's in everyone's best interest. A kid who returns home is less likely to be holed up somewhere with a boyfriend, turning tricks on the street, stealing, doing drugs, living homeless, or cluttering up a police blotter.

Most departments don't have the budgets or manpower to pursue a runaway past the state line. For the most part, they are entered into the system and local police are told to be on the lookout for them. If kids are older than sixteen, police can't even make them go back home if they find them. All they can do is notify the parents that they are alive. A private investigator, however, does not have all those official roadblocks.

Hired help can cross any jurisdictional boundary their client can afford, and they can pass the results of their investigations back to the client. Hiring a private investigator can be a real win-win for the clients if everything works out. But it can also lead to questions of cost and competency.

Some private investigators are upfront about how much they charge. One who claims to specialize in missing persons advertises $850 a day for his services, more when he's out of town on a case. Any additional expenses, including plane fare, meals, and hotel rooms, are on top of his regular fees and must be prepaid, which is not untypical.

Copus recalls a case where the mother of a runaway paid a private investigator between $8,000 and $10,000 to find her daughter. When he took over the case, he visited the private investigator that had been hired to see what the initial investigation turned up. The private investigator had found nothing at all. In fact, she seemed to be successful only in billing her client.

When a parent is faced with the trauma of a missing child, and the police can't or won't help, money becomes a small consideration next to finding that child. Driven by emotion and the need to know that they are doing something, many parents open the phone book or use the Internet to pick a private investigator. Few check on the private investigator beyond finding out whether the firm handles missing persons cases, and the parents often end up hiring individuals who lack even the basic skills to conduct a thorough search. The unvarnished truth about the private investigation business is that they are not all created equal. Those investigators that lack a great deal of prior legal experience must rely on their relationships with law enforcement.

And unless investigators have a good working relationship with the police, it is doubtful they are going to get any information from them. They can tap a phone, but it's illegal, and so are most of the methods used by the private detectives in the movies: using electronic devices to tail cars, going through mailboxes without permission, hacking into databases. What is illegal for most civilians is also illegal for private investigators.

But it's important to know what good private detectives know, and that is that they can also do things police cannot or will not do: They can cross jurisdictions. They don't have to worry about evidence and courts and probable cause. They can avoid problems that occur when working with other agencies. And they don't have to deal with the media or public opinion.

For many, hiring a private investigator is the measure of last resort: leads have run cold, the police aren't responsive, and the family is desperate to find their missing loved one. There is nothing wrong with bringing in outside help. A private hire can tip the balance in favor of the victim. But hooking up with someone who knows what he or she is doing is paramount to a successful conclusion.

Those considering hiring a private eye should ask to talk to other clients, check the investigator's record on missing persons cases, and know what is expected in return for the fee. Hiring those who don't know what they are doing won't make it better. It will only waste time.

Melanie Methany has been through a few rough patches in her short twenty-one years. Struggling to make ends meet, she has three young children by two different men and is no longer with either man. She enrolled in college-prep classes in hopes of going back to school to become a nurse and making enough money to pull her kids out of poverty. But the Belle, West Virginia, woman would never make it to those classes. Instead, she would disappear on July 19, 2006, leaving behind little but rumors and sorrow.

Deborah Daniel, Melanie's mother, says that after her daughter vanished, "psychics came out of the woodwork wanting to help." One met the family at Melanie's apartment and gave them a "reading." Another Florida psychic sent Deborah and her family maps to track Melanie's movements. Exhausted and out of options, they took a chance and followed those maps into the nearby mountains, finding nothing. In the meantime, the rumor mills worked overtime to provide fresh new torture for Melanie's family.

"I [sank] into a deep depression and fell into denial," says Deborah, who also says the self-proclaimed psychics didn't help her daughter's case. "This all ended up being a fabrication of someone's imagination," she says.

Police caution families of the missing to beware of scammers and people who claim to have a psychic knowledge of the loved one's fate. They often pretend to have information to sell to the family—a ploy very common in international disappearances. Families, desperate to grab any straw, often fork over the money without realizing until it's too late that they've been had. Police say trained investigators should handle leads.

People who claim to have a psychic connection to the missing person are very often individuals who want to be involved in the case. Like rock star groupies, they are drawn to high-profile cases. Again, families are wise to hand over these individuals and their information to the authorities. They bring additional pain to people who can least afford it.

"I have often referred to our ordeal as a never-healing wound that only scabs over. In my daughter's case, our scab is constantly picked off with each new horrific rumor, leaving a deeper wound each time," says Deborah.

———

When search-and-rescue personnel looked for Randy Spring, he was a twenty-eight-year-old hiker, out to enjoy a few days in the San Jacinto Mountains near Whitewater, California. Randy disappeared after his mother, Arlene, dropped him off with a backpack for a few days of hiking on October 10, 1988. The former army sergeant is well versed in outdoor survival skills and enjoys spending time in the wilderness. But this hiking trip was different—when Randy failed to contact his family after ten days in the woods, his mother called the police. They found nothing.

If he is alive now, Randy is middle-aged. Arlene, now in her eighties, still mourns the son who left that October day and is afraid that she will never see him again. She has never stopped looking for her child.

Bethanie Dougherty's father, Terry Curtis, watched official search teams laced with volunteers comb the area around his daughter's home in the days following his grown child's disappearance. Bethanie has been missing from her home in rural Broome County, New York, since April 2, 2008.

A striking redhead with long tresses and big, round eyes, Bethanie was forty when last seen. She lived with her eighteen-year-old son in a home in the hamlet of Killawog. On the night before she disappeared, Bethanie put on her pajamas and said goodnight to her son. He awoke the next morning to find her car in the driveway and her personal effects still in the house. When he returned

Bethanie Dougherty. Courtesy of Terry M. Curtis.

home from school, nothing had changed. Investigators later said area residents reported hearing some screams outside at around 3:00 in the morning. State troopers called to the scene had investigated and found nothing suspicious.

Search teams formed across the area. The initial search covered about two hundred acres and lasted several days. Authorities used both air and land teams, as well as trained search dogs, but no sign of Bethanie has ever been found.

"The sheriffs have told us some, but very little, about Bethanie's disappearance. They say it is because they know very little. They have found no trace of her and no physical evidence of any kind," says Terry.

Benjamin Roseland disappeared from the middle of a bustling city like an icicle melting from an overhang. He stepped from a friend's house onto the frozen streets of Clinton, Iowa, on February 9, 2008, on his way to a nearby store and vanished. His family spread out across the town and searched for Ben but found nothing. They say they are somewhat bitter that search teams were not called in to look for him right away.

Benjamin Roseland. Courtesy of Julie Connell.

Nineteen when he vanished, Ben has blue eyes and a mischievous smile. His face bears the scars of a car accident. His mother, Theresa, says Ben liked his job, saved his money, and has a "big personality."

She isn't satisfied with the way local law enforcement has searched for her son. Instead, she says, the family relies on friends to help them look for him.

"Thousands of flyers have been distributed throughout the neighboring communities. Local trains, barges, and city bus lines have all carried Ben's poster in the hope that someone will give us answers. The Cue Center for Missing Persons [www.ncmissingpersons.org, a nonprofit with a good reputation for helping families search for their missing loved ones] and a local advertising agency worked together to make two billboards of Ben for our community," says Theresa.

Three missing persons, three very different types of searches: Randy Spring disappeared in a vast wilderness; Bethanie Dougherty in a rural community; Ben Roseland in a city. But even though the approach, equipment, and personnel may vary depending on the terrain and circumstances of the disappearance, there are two things that remain the same when it comes to physical searches of an area: in order to minimize mistakes and maximize the potential for recovering evidence, searches should be controlled by professional search-and-rescue personnel, and timing is critical. Waiting too long to search—a frequent complaint fielded in reference to law enforcement—can result in the destruction of evidence.

Search and rescue is a skill and not everyone can do it. In Randy Spring's case, it would have been important to use professional searchers familiar with the territory to avoid the possible tragedy of losing a volunteer to an accident. In Bethanie's case, local volunteers had the right sort of equipment to navigate the back roads and hills—four-wheel drive vehicles and trucks. In a city-based search, the physical features surrounding the search area might necessitate the use of special skills and equipment. And in all types of search and rescue, using the right type of K-9 team can make the difference between finding a trail and missing one.

----✆----

On the day after Christmas 2008, Liz Lingenfelter's forty-nine-year-old daughter, Beverly Meadows, walked out or was taken from the Marshall, Texas, nursing home in which she lived. She never returned.

Liz says her family tried to keep Beverly at home, but she suffered from severe medical problems they could not handle. They placed her in the home because they believed it was safe for her.

Since Beverly disappeared, Liz and her family have become search experts. They made and distributed posters, drew maps of the area, and looked

Beverly Meadows. Courtesy of Liz Lingenfelter.

for her using the routes she would have traveled. They also posted a reward for information about her case.

They searched the nearby motels, checked churches, abandoned houses, hospitals, jails, and morgues. They kept in touch with law enforcement. They worked with groups like the Cue Center and Project Jason. Today, they try to keep the case before the media. And they are hopeful Beverly remains alive.

"It is extremely hard to get news out there about my daughter. For some reason most of the news reporters don't think it's important enough to keep reporting," says Liz.

For Liz, like many with loved ones or friends who are missing, keeping the buzz going and her daughter's name and face in front of the media is both difficult and maddening. One Miami woman understands Liz's feelings better than most.

Frustrated with the lack of interest in the disappearance of her friend Lily Aramburo, Miami resident Janet Forte decided to take matters into her own hands and work the Internet on Lily's behalf. Although the missing young mother still has not been found, it's not for lack of trying on Janet's part.

Lily, a tiny, delicate Hispanic woman with luminous eyes, was last seen on June 2, 2007, leaving her boyfriend's Miami condo at around 2:00 in the morning. The devoted mother of a small son, she is smart, energetic, loyal, and much tougher than her small (four foot, eleven inch, one hundred pound) frame would suggest, say her friends. Janet, who maintains a blog dedicated to the search for her friend, says Lily's case has attracted a disappointing amount of media attention.

But like the friend she seeks, Janet is strong and determined. She is also very, very good at finding her way around the Internet social networking maze.

"I started with Craigslist, locally," Janet says. She says she progressed from there to Facebook, Twitter, and YouTube. Janet points out that even if an individual doesn't have a lot of fancy technical knowledge or equipment, "You can do YouTube videos with a cell phone. An emotional plea can work wonders, even if it's just ten seconds."

Janet's determination has paid off. She has attracted the national media to her friend Lily's story. But the real payoff, finding Lily, has yet to happen.

"It's a daily struggle and a painful one," she admits.

Find her comprehensive blog post on how to work the social media in missing persons cases here: http://subliminalpixels.com/non-profit/50-free-online-resources-for-finding-a-missing-persons-using-social-media/.

———⟨∞⟩———

Melissa Cabana doesn't know what to think. Years after Melissa's father, Ronald, vanished (on June 9, 2002), there has been not a single sighting of him. Like most families of the missing, she hopes for the best and is prepared for the worst.

Melissa is the first to admit her father had problems: when he went missing, he had just been released from the hospital where he'd been confined for depression. Later police found broken glass with traces of blood in the bathroom of his small Alford, Florida, home, as well as medications for the treatment of bipolar disorder and schizophrenia. Melissa says her father's reading glasses were still there, and his clothes were laid out as if he planned a trip.

She says her dad had filed a bogus insurance claim and was wanted for insurance fraud, but the family has no idea whether Ronald Cabana took a powder to escape the consequences of his actions, suffered a psychiatric incident that led him to homelessness and life on the streets, or something more sinister.

All Melissa knows for sure is that her father is missing and she misses him.

Melissa's story is far from unusual. Although the number of missing persons reports that are filed has dropped in recent years, the National Crime Information Center held 93,192 active missing persons records in 2009. Of those, more than half are for adults, ages eighteen or older.

Several hundred people shift in their seats as the annual National Conference for Responding to Missing & Unidentified Persons kicks off in Appleton, Wisconsin (www.fvtc.edu). Sponsored and administered by Fox Valley Technical College, the conference brings together an eclectic mix of criminal justice professionals, agency heads, victim advocates, and families of the missing. They are all there for one reason: to improve the way missing persons cases are handled in the United States.

Ed Smart, father of Elizabeth Smart, who was abducted as a child from the bedroom of her Utah home while she slept, is the keynote speaker. He leads the crowd through a step-by-step description of his family's experiences during the harrowing minutes, days, and months that transpired between his daughter's abduction and her miraculous recovery. The main conference room is cavernous and a bit noisy when the heating unit kicks in, but the crowd sits transfixed as this father talks with raw emotion and honesty about his child and her ordeal.

In the audience are a number of families who understand better than anyone how hard it is to not know where a loved one may be. They are the families whose children or parents or siblings are missing. They are the real reason for this annual conference, which looks for ways to bring the disparate segments of this community together for a common goal.

And there is a common goal: they all want to bring home the missing. But investigating a missing persons case isn't like investigating any other case. Barbara Nelson, the conference coordinator, says, "Although adults have the right to disappear without notifying anyone, the substantial issues surrounding adult disappearances are often sensitive and recovery resources are limited. In order to make a determination that an individual is 'at risk,' law enforcement agencies must focus on a number of serious social issues that contribute to disappearances, like domestic violence, Alzheimer's disease, substance abuse, prostitution, human trafficking, mental illness, suspicious circumstances, and foul play."

Nelson says the three-day conference, which is held each February, helps provide leadership in changing attitudes, policies, and practices. And most important, it opens a platform for those who search for the missing to talk to others who are doing the same thing, often in a different way or from a different perspective.

In the end, it is this exchange of ideas that helps police understand the human equation involved in these cases, and that is the most important lesson they can learn.

<hr/>

On June 8, 2010, one day after the arrest in Peru of a man believed to be involved in the disappearance of her daughter, Beth Holloway presided at the opening of a new resource center for the families of missing persons.

The Natalee Holloway Resource Center at Washington, D.C.'s National Museum of Crime and Punishment will offer better access to materials and the press for families of missing persons. Natalee disappeared while on a group high school graduation trip to Aruba in 2005.

Beth told reporters at the opening that she hoped the center would "act as a point of light for the missing."

• *12* •

Happy Endings:
These Loved Ones Came Home

> We hope that our story focuses attention on all of the children
> still missing and on their need to be found. We must keep look-
> ing for them. As Jaycee shows, miracles can happen.—Terry
> Probyn, mother of Jaycee Dugard

$\mathcal{J}$aycee Lee Dugard was eleven years old when she was abducted from the
street near her family's home in South Tahoe, California. Her stepfather,
Carl Probyn, saw a gray sedan occupied by two people pull up to Jaycee,
open the car door, and yank her into the vehicle before speeding away. He
chased the car on his bicycle but was unable to keep up, and the car, with
Jaycee inside, vanished. The date was June 10, 1991, and the little girl was
in fifth grade.

Police and other law enforcement organizations were brought into the
case. Days became months; months turned into years. The National Center
for Missing and Exploited Children continued to update Jaycee's photograph,
progressively aging her image to enhance her chances of being found. But
privately, given the time and circumstances, many believed that Jaycee was
already beyond help.

Terry Probyn, Jaycee's mother, put her time to good use. Like many
of the families of the missing, she advocated not only for Jaycee, but also for
other missing children.

Then in August 2009, police investigated a report that a convicted sex offender named Phillip Garrido—on parole and forbidden to have contact with
children—had two little girls and their young mother living with him and his
wife, Nancy. They found Jaycee Dugard and her two young daughters in the
backyard of the Garridos' Antioch, California, home. Jaycee told detectives
that Garrido fathered both of her children.

195

Jaycee reunited with her family and became reacquainted with her younger sister, who was a baby at the time of Jaycee's abduction. The police, who had received multiple tips concerning the odd living arrangements at the Garridos' home and had done little about them, came under severe criticism. They apologized to the Dugard family at a press conference, and the California state legislature voted to award Jaycee $20 million in victim's compensation funds.

As of this writing, the Garridos await trial in connection with Jaycee's abduction and captivity. She and her daughters are reported to be adjusting well to their new lives.

Stories with endings like Jaycee Dugard's are rare, but they do happen. In 2007, police found Shawn Hornbeck alive. The eleven-year-old victim of stranger abduction had been missing since October 6, 2002. The break that led the police to Shawn came while they were investigating the disappearance of another Missouri youth, Ben Ownby. Authorities followed a tip from an observant teenager and discovered a man named Michael Devlin was holding both boys captive. Tried and convicted of kidnapping and imprisonment in addition to other charges, Devlin was sentenced to life in prison.

Spending four years, or in the case of Jaycee Dugard, eighteen years, in captivity makes it hard to qualify a case as a "happy ending." Jayee's family lost almost two decades with their child and the circumstances in which she lived were both abnormal and difficult. But for a parent whose child has been abducted by a stranger, finding the child alive and well is an amazing outcome.

The good news about stranger or nonfamily abductions is that despite what news accounts lead us to believe, they are not that common. According to Stacy Daniels and M. A. Brennan (Department of Family, Youth and Community Science, Florida Cooperative Extension Service, Institute of Food and Agricultural Sciences, University of Florida, Gainesville), who conducted a study of missing children:

> Nonfamily abductions are rare. The U.S. Department of Justice estimates that in 1999, 33,000 children (a rate of .47 per 1,000) were victims of nonfamily abduction. The perpetrator is often a stranger, is more likely to be male, and more often victimizes females. Teenagers are at higher risk for this form of abduction, mostly because these attacks take place when the child is alone and in some type of public area. Most victims of nonfamily abductions are between the ages of fifteen and seventeen, but twelve- to fourteen-year-olds are more likely to be victims of stereo-typical kidnappings. Sometimes the perpetrator, or perpetrators, asks for a ransom, but more often the motive in these attacks is sexual. Just less than half of all victims of nonfamily abduction are sexually assaulted. In a very few cases the victims die. A 1997 study by the State of Washington's Office of the Attorney General calls the murder of an abducted child "a rare event." They concluded that about 100 such incidents occur each

year in America. This is less than one-half of one percent of the total number of murders committed each year. However, they warn that 74% of abducted children who are murdered are dead within three hours of the abduction.

—⊶∞⊷—

In 2002, two teenage girls made conscious decisions not to join that .5 percent of murdered children. They fought back when abducted by a stranger who took them from a lover's lane area. After tying up the girls' boyfriends, thirty-seven-year-old Ron Ratliff, a two-time loser and rape suspect already on the run from authorities, forced the girls into his car. Seventeen-year-old Jacqueline Marris and sixteen-year-old Tamara Brooks, of Lancaster, California, would emerge as the test case for the state's new Amber Alert system, which both worked and failed simultaneously.

Named for nine-year-old Amber Hagerman, an Arlington, Texas, girl who in 1996 was abducted and slain, the Amber Alert (which sometimes goes by a different name, depending on the state) is an electronic system used to notify the media and public when a child has been abducted.

The Amber Alert itself grew out of a model program conceived by Bruce Seybert, a volunteer who had joined the tragic search for Amber, and Marc Klaas, father of Polly Klaas and the force behind the Klaas Foundation, which promotes child safety. Seybert mentioned their concept in an address during a media symposium. When word of Klaas and Seybert's idea filtered to the Dallas police chief, the Amber Alert system, which initially used local radio stations to impart crucial information, was created. Soon, other states followed Texas's lead and implemented their own systems.

In 2002, five-year-old Stanton, California, resident Samantha Runnion was snatched from her own front yard. Samantha had been playing outside when a man named Alejandro Avila approached and told her he was looking for his lost dog. Her body was later found in the mountainous areas near Riverside, California. She had been raped and strangled. Avila went to trial and in 2005 received the death penalty. On July 24, 2002, California reacted to the senseless abduction and slaying of the curly-haired little girl by instituting the statewide Amber Alert system.

In October of that same year, a federal effort was launched to encourage states to adopt the Amber Alert system. Included in the legislation was a national alert coordinator, as well as funding for the effort. But California's system was only a few days old and the national system nonexistent when Jacqueline and Tamara, the two California teens, were kidnapped by Ron Ratliff.

The girls later told police that they waited for a vulnerable moment, then fought back against their attacker, cutting him with a knife and hitting him in the face with a whiskey bottle. Communicating with one another by holding hands and tracing words in one another's palms, the girls were prepared to go down fighting. They almost did: only when Ratliff, their captor, confronted them with a gun, did they give up their effort to escape.

In the meantime, as Ratliff drove the young women in his Ford Bronco about one hundred miles north to Kern County, an Amber Alert went out across the state. After freeing themselves, the boys had called authorities and provided a thorough description of both Ratliff and his vehicle.

That first California Amber Alert almost didn't work: there were expensive delays getting the information out to the media. But in the end, when seconds were precious currency, that alert helped save the girls' lives. A Kern County animal control officer who heard it and paid attention spotted the Bronco and reported it. When deputies responded to the call, they found Ratliff aiming a gun at them. They shot and killed him. Jacqueline and Tamara, who had been forced to crouch down on the floorboards of the Bronco by Ratliff in order to avoid detection, suffered minor injuries in the incident. Both girls have been candid about the fact that Ratliff raped them. Their unique courage has been credited not only with dispelling much of the stigma associated with rape, but also with encouraging other victims to fight back and speak up.

Rescue for Jacqueline and Tamara came not a moment too soon. Deputies say they believe Ratliff planned to kill them within the next few minutes.

———⊶⊷———

Not every person who goes missing and is found alive and well is recovered as a result of random good luck. Some are located because the person searching for them is determined not to fail. Oklahoma resident Cathy Wilson is one of those seekers who wouldn't give up.

When Cathy's son, Matthew, disappeared on December 17, 2007, she knew from the beginning that something was wrong. Matthew was on a full scholarship to Rice University in Texas. When Cathy tried to contact Matthew prior to his holiday visit, she instead reached his roommate, who told her that her son had disappeared. Although at first she believed something had happened to Matthew, a closer look convinced her he had walked away.

Matthew is a good kid—smart, hardworking, and close to his family. His father died when Matthew was two, but he is close to his mom and three sisters. Cathy knew he was under self-induced pressure at college and refused to entertain the possibility she might not see her son again. Instead of waiting and hoping the police would locate him, the preschool teacher dedicated herself to finding Matthew.

Although Cathy wasn't well versed in the ways of the media, over the next few months she would make herself an expert, both at tracking her son and at attracting media coverage. She worked with university police at Rice and the police agencies she encountered in her search for Matthew. She also hired two private investigators during her crusade.

"I could never give up; I took time off from my job and lived my life searching for Matthew," Cathy says.

Six months after Matthew disappeared, his car was found on a street in Berkeley, California, prompting Cathy to fly there. She had already crossed the country in her search, raised a reward, put up thousands of posters, given dozens of interviews, and kept Matthew's name in front of the public. She would not rest until she found her son—and find him she would—eight months to the day he first went missing.

Matthew was in Berkeley. Under enormous pressure at school, tired, and feeling alone in the world, he fled and made his way to the University of California's Berkeley campus, where his mother discovered him. Cathy, who is working on a book about her efforts to find Matthew, says he came back to Oklahoma, where he continues to put his life back together with the support of his family.

"It was hard. I remember being jealous when friends would say their kids were home from college and I would think, 'I don't know where mine is,'" Cathy says about the time Matthew was missing. "But if I had [the search] to do all over again, I would."

―≈≈≈―

In October 2008, two Goldsboro, North Carolina, men traveled across the country to renew a relationship with someone they had neither seen nor heard from in thirty-eight years—their father. The reunion was made possible by persistence and smart sleuthing.

William Schafer met his wife and the future mother of the two men in Long Beach, California. The former sailor and his new spouse relocated to Durham, North Carolina, but when their sons, John and Robert, were ages three and eighteen months, the couple separated. Custody went to their father, but John told a newspaper reporter that, unknown to their father, their mother took them from a day care center one day and moved with them to Lillington, North Carolina, where her family lived.

She changed the boys' last name to that of her first husband, with whom she had other children. The two Schafer boys spent a decade believing they were Hewitts by birth.

John said he learned about his real father from his mother's former boyfriend. Although he continued to ask his mother about his birth father, she refused to discuss him. Later, he would learn his father had never stopped searching for his boys, even hiring a private investigator to look for them.

John's wife, Kerri, knew that her husband had many unanswered questions that could only be resolved by finding his father. William Schafer had been forty-two when John was born. Kerri knew there was a chance he might not be alive. Still, she persisted in her efforts to locate him, using her instincts and amateur sleuthing skills. Kerri's efforts produced a lead.

Their dad was eighty-three years old when John and Robert saw him for the first time since their abduction. Almost four decades had passed since their mom had taken them from the day care center. William Schafer had neither remarried nor had any other children. The family reunited in Long Beach, California, and spent many hours discussing the intervening years. They vowed to make the most of each moment they still have together.

⸎

The National Center for Missing and Exploited Children's age-progression technology has resulted in more than one child being reunited with his or her family. Thanks to a dedicated investigator and the NCMEC's finesse for nailing age progressions, another long-overdue reunion took place in 2003.

Special Agent Colleen Maher of the U.S. Department of Education was investigating a possible fraud case involving student loans. A man later identified as Brent Austin took out thousands in federally financed student loans using the Social Security number assigned to his son, Michael David Johnson Jr. Austin, who was going by the name of Michael David Johnson Sr., admitted to the fraud, and Maher discovered an age-progressed photograph that looked a lot like his son.

The boy, Michael David Johnson Jr., turned out to be Aric Austin, who was abducted from his mother's care during an ugly custody dispute in 1981, when the child was six weeks old. Although infants are difficult to age progress, the NCMEC staff did such an expert job of it that Maher had no trouble recognizing Aric, who was at last reunited with his mother, Pennygale Gusman.

In Florida, an eleven-year-old girl with Asperger syndrome disappeared in a swamp infested with alligators near her Winter Springs home. Searchers blanketed the area, but after four days even the most optimistic among them discounted the chances of finding Nadia Bloom alive and unharmed.

Sometimes things do go right: a volunteer who attends church with the Bloom family spotted the little girl on a dry patch of land in the swamp. Nadia was dehydrated and covered in bug bites but otherwise fine. It was the happy ending for which her family had prayed.

Three years earlier the prayers of another family were answered when rescuers discovered a starving and fragile Ora Doris Anderson just days shy of the memorial service scheduled on behalf of the missing seventy-six-year-old woman. Ora vanished in the wilderness of the Wallowa Mountains in Oregon in what rescuers described as "extremely rough terrain." She had spent thirteen days without food or water in thick brush. Although she sustained a hip injury, medical authorities said Ora was in good shape for someone who had spent the better part of two weeks unable to move.

Ora and her husband, Harold, were on an elk-hunting trip when their truck became stuck in the mud. The couple started to walk for help, but Ora became fatigued and turned back to wait in the truck. She lost her way and ended up stranded, spending evenings in temperatures that plunged into the thirties.

Harold later told the press that he would never hunt elk again.

Some reunions between searchers and the lost are bittersweet. Parents can't help but mourn the time that was stolen from them along with their children. But getting their loved ones back alive trumps everything else. For others, finding a missing family member, even though the outcome is not good can be a relief. It lets the family complete the circle, no matter how sorrowful the journey.

Although it may seem counterintuitive to include the recovery of the body of a missing person in a chapter about happy endings, for families who already are aware that the outcome will not be good, finding their loved ones' remains can help them move on with their lives. As Sharon DeLuke, whose ordeal in losing her son Ron was described in chapter 10, puts it, "Knowing was terrible, but not knowing was worse."

To the families of lost loved ones whose bodies were never recovered in times of war, the simple act of bringing them home for proper burial is monumental. The case of Michael Blassie illustrates how science is helping to bring our boys home, where they belong.

Blassie was a first lieutenant in the U.S. Air Force when he was shot down in 1972 while on a mission over South Vietnam. The twenty-four-year-old was an Air Force Academy graduate from St. Louis, Missouri, who came from a close-knit family of five children.

Although attempts were made to find Blassie after the crash of his A-37B Dragonfly, they were unsuccessful. Later, South Vietnamese army troops discovered human remains and artifacts that, because of their location, could have belonged to the missing pilot. But tests were inconclusive and rather than rule the remains as Blassie's without sufficient scientific proof, they were placed in the Tomb of the Unknown at Arlington National Cemetery in 1984.

As time and scientific know-how progressed and the use of DNA to identify human remains became more refined and standardized, Blassie's family asked that the remains in the Tomb of the Unknown be tested. The results were a positive match against family DNA. In 1998, more than a quarter of a century after his death, Michael Blassie was buried in Jefferson National Cemetery, a stone's throw from where this true American hero spent his childhood.

Michael Blassie is not the only American service member to be identified and returned to his family through the application of DNA testing. Stories of remains found in Vietnam and Laos that are matched with identities surface all the time. The U.S. Armed Forces make identifying their lost service members a priority. They now have a method to ensure that those killed in the service of their country are identified.

Since 1992, the U.S. Armed Forces Institute of Pathology has built and maintained a DNA registry that holds DNA samples of all personnel serving on active duty. The registry, established due to problems that arose from matching human remains during the Gulf War, will prevent situations like the one faced by the Blassie family from recurring.

The DNA is maintained in a huge warehouse located in Rockville, Maryland. Stored as tiny blood samples, they are kept in vacuum-sealed envelopes and frozen to ensure their integrity.

Officials say the samples will be used only for identification purposes, but they are sometimes asked to compare DNA for missing service members whose disappearances are not connected to a military action. The DNA is not released, however, and the comparisons are done on-site. DNA samples are maintained for at least fifty years and are not released to law enforcement, except by court order.

Although he was not a member of the U.S. Armed Forces, DNA helped another family put to rest a loved one who had been missing for six decades. Joseph Van Zandt, a merchant marine who died in a plane crash in Alaska on March 12, 1948, was identified through his mother's familial DNA.

Van Zandt was one of twenty-four merchant marines who were passengers on a flight from China to New York City when the DC-4 they were in crashed into the side of Mount Sanford. The plane, its passengers, and six crew members vanished on a nearby glacier.

Fifty-one years later, two pilots—Marc Millican and Kevin McGregor—would discover mummified remains. The remains—a mummified arm and hand—were turned over to Alaskan authorities. Although attempts were made to identify them, they proved unsuccessful. But in 2006, through new techniques, usable mitochondrial DNA was obtained.

Because thirty individuals perished on that flight fifty-eight years ago, finding relatives with whom to compare the DNA was a formidable task. Forensic genealogists working on the case tracked down family members connected to sixteen of the victims but there were no matches. In the meantime, scientists worked to rehydrate the fingers in order to secure a fingerprint match—the merchant marines' fingerprints were still on file at Arlington's National Marine Center. After all those years, they were able to identify the remains as belonging to Van Zandt. A DNA comparison to a relative they located made the ID complete, and the remains could be brought home to rest.

—————

Every case in which a missing person is found has an angel of some sort. In some it's an observant witness, in others a dedicated investigator. Many times it's a family member who refuses to give up—like Heather Miller.

Heather's cousin "Mike" grew up on the West coast, while she calls Pennsylvania home. Heather says she always knew Mike suffered from mental illness and the two weren't close growing up, but he's family, and when his life turned upside down, she made it her business to find him and assume the role of his advocate. A social worker by profession, Heather understands the system better than most.

Mike's current problems began after his mother passed away and his father became very ill. Unable to cope, he vanished. When she couldn't locate Mike, Heather filed a police report with authorities in the town where he lived.

"We were lucky they found him," Heather says of his disappearance, but her relief would not last long. Unstable and incapable of making good decisions, Mike then bounced from one apartment to another. Then he made the decision to leave home and travel to Pennsylvania to see Heather.

Once again Mike disappeared from the radar for several months, resurfacing in a state where he had no real ties. Heather tracked Mike there and tried to stay abreast of his situation, which changed almost daily and included incarceration. Her biggest fear was that he would disappear again.

"Most of his arrests stemmed from trespassing. He has an inability to get food and shelter. He didn't understand when he was doing the wrong thing," Heather says.

She says some of the police both she and Mike dealt with were great—and others not so much. "Many don't really understand how to deal with people with paranoid schizophrenia," Heather says.

"Back then, everyone told me I should not get involved with this: he has a brother; he has a sister. Everyone said it was going to be a nightmare. The homeless advocacy people told me, 'Do you know what it is like, keeping an eye out for him, but probably not being able to do anything?'" she says.

Heather secured a good lawyer through the local bar association and she was able to gain emergency conservatorship of Mike. By becoming his guardian, she also waded into more red tape than she ever imagined.

"I understand why family members back off from this. It took about a year [to obtain permanent guardianship]. I got emergency guardianship three times before I obtained it permanently. He had to be served the petition in person, and we only knew where he was for sure when he was in jail. As it turned out, he was kind of grateful someone was willing to be involved," Heather says.

Despite the bureaucratic issues that accrue with her guardianship of Mike and the struggle to keep him from vanishing again, Heather persists. Heather has flexed her social worker's muscles to help her cousin: she managed to get records of his visits to emergency rooms, shelters, and hospitals. Most followed a pattern of him asking for help and getting something short of what he needed: a bus pass, a cursory examination, a bed for the night—a short-term patch job instead of a real, long-term fix.

Heather knows that Mike will vanish forever or die on the streets without substantial intervention. People who are homeless and have no one to advocate for them often don't stand a chance, and that is even truer in places where the winters are long and harsh and the facilities for the homeless in short supply.

"They take most people into the shelter there on cold nights. However, if you're asked to leave, then you can't go back for four months. So I asked, 'Where do people go?' The response I got was, 'I don't know,'" says Heather.

Mike is different from some of the homeless and mentally ill, though. His family has managed to keep up with him and remains his advocate. Although Heather says that while sorting out all of the bureaucratic red tape associated with her cousin's problems is like handling flypaper, she persists, and because of that persistence, she also makes progress.

Throughout her efforts to help Mike lead a safe, productive life, Heather has run into government roadblocks, particularly where privacy issues are concerned. Heather went to deal with the issue on Mike's home turf. She received help from Libba Phillips's organization, Outpost for Hope (www.outpostforhope.org). Outpost for Hope works with families of missing persons who fall into several categories neglected by traditional agencies, including the homeless, mentally ill, and substance abusers. Now Heather has reason to believe that she will one day settle Mike in a safe and loving environment where he can live out his life without fear.

"I'm not a hero, just a cousin doing the right thing. If I don't do it, who will?" Heather asks.

Although he is a work in progress, Mike is a success story because, as a result of Heather's devotion to his cause, he went from missing to found. And Heather has no plans to give up on Mike, even though many tell her she is "crazy for doing this."

"It's the right thing to do," she says.

For Marco Alcalde, the right thing to do was to never stop searching for his missing son. And on Tuesday, March 30, 2010, Marco boarded a flight to Managua, Nicaragua, as part of the last leg of a sixteen-month journey to find and bring the boy, MaxGian (pronounced Max-Jon), back home to Boise, Idaho. Father and son were reunited in that Central American country after federal agents, following a lead, found the child there with his noncustodial mother.

MaxGian is an adorable little boy with bright blue eyes, brown hair, a shy smile, and an affinity for baseball. After an acrimonious divorce, a judge awarded Marco and his ex-wife joint custody of their only child. On November 26, 2008, Marco dropped his son at school, where later in the day his mother, Margaret Sanchez Meija Dunbar Alcalde, picked him up for a twelve-day visit. It was right before Thanksgiving and MaxGian told Marco that his mother, who goes by the nickname of Maika, was taking him to visit family friends in Nevada. They never made it.

Marco believed that Maika, fluent in Spanish and well traveled, had left the country. After filing a missing persons report, Marco concentrated his search south of the U.S. border.

"My ex-wife speaks five languages. She has traveled all over the world. She has money, intelligence, and the skills to survive," Marco says. He knew finding Maika and MaxGian would be daunting. It was.

Marco retained an attorney. He pushed authorities to look for MaxGian. And he set up a Web site that displayed the child's photograph and also tracked the ISP addresses of those who frequented the site.

"We were sure [Maika] was hitting the Web site and tracking what was going on, but she was using technology that hid where she was," he says.

Marco says he knew Maika would watch what he was doing from a distance. "It is human nature to look over your shoulder," he says. He hoped she would slip up and make a mistake.

A mechanical engineer by profession, Marco approached his son's abduction and recovery with the analytical skills and precision he uses to earn his living. Marco says he survived with support from his friends and neighbors and he held regular brainstorming sessions with them.

"That was very helpful. It was a very emotional time and I was looking for action. I wanted activity; I wanted motion," he says.

False leads and dead ends piled up, especially in the first year. "It was very draining. I cried every day," Marco says. "You have to let the emotions out. If you don't, if you pretend [it doesn't bother you], then it will destroy you."

During the lengthy investigation, Marco traveled to both Costa Rica and Panama in search of MaxGian. He also hired private investigators, talked to hundreds of people, and continued his Internet campaign. Then someone came forward with information on MaxGian's whereabouts.

"They let the cat out of the bag," Marco says.

He says the FBI became involved in the case right from the beginning, working alongside the Boise Police. Using information provided by a third party, they located Maika in Nicaragua and took custody of MaxGian. Although Marco knew they were working a hot lead, he didn't realize how soon the case would turn in his favor. When he received the phone call that authorities had his son, Marco was ready to pick him up at a moment's notice.

MaxGian was seven when his mother left with him, around eight and a half when he was found. In addition to being standoffish when his father arrived to pick him up, there was also a language barrier that had not existed before.

"He wouldn't look at me. And he spoke only Spanish—no English," Marco says.

"I had just traveled twelve hours by plane and had no sleep, so I was a little off myself. I just leaned over and said, 'I don't know what you've been told or what you think, but I love you very much and have never stopped loving you,'" he says.

Marco believed it important that MaxGian know his mother was well and he made sure of that. When they returned to Boise, the child reestablished his relationship with the best friend he left behind and settled back into school. Life returned to as close to normal as it could be with such a big chunk of time carved out of their lives. Marco says MaxGian's time on the run affected him.

"We have seen solid progress, yet it will still require time and parenting consistency to work through it," says Marco.

It was difficult to rebound from the experience, but Marco is thrilled to have regained his child. "I'm elated to have him back, just elated," he says.

It is important to remember that for every Marco Alcalde there is also a Stephen Watkins—a person searching for a beloved child or sibling or parent who has disappeared. But the odds are getting better for people like Stephen. As technology shrinks the world, hiding in it—or concealing someone else—becomes ever more difficult.

Families of the missing are no longer sitting back and waiting for someone to do something. These families are strong and realize they draw their strength from standing together. Individuals like Kelly Jolkowski of Project Jason and Libba Phillips of Outpost for Hope advocate for the rights of the missing. They rally families to find their voices, flex their muscles, and keep their cases alive.

Their tragedies do not define these families: they fuel them. They turn into lions, demanding better from their police and federal authorities and urging the passage of new laws that give their missing loved ones and the missing of the future a better shot at happy endings.

Sympathetic legislators who push for the truth and sponsor bills that make a difference; police haunted by the faces of the missing who continue their investigations off the clock; private investigators who donate their services for free to those whose wallets are empty—these are the dramatis personae of happy endings.

And more happy endings are possible. As Jaycee Dugard, Shawn Hornbeck, and Ben Ownby prove, they are out there waiting to be found. If only people didn't mind their own businesses but acted upon their suspicions; if only police had the resources to follow up on all leads instead of having to choose the most viable; if only the ball got rolling sooner instead of later—who knows how many opportunities for happy endings are out there, waiting to be discovered?

And if we start paying attention, if we demand better training for our police, better laws, better resources, better efforts, and we all get involved, who knows how many of our missing can be brought home?

It is time to find out.

Resource Guide

$\mathscr{T}$he best resources now can be found online. In fact, the Internet has revolutionized the way missing persons cases and the matching of unidentified remains are investigated. Most publications devoted to missing persons are also on the Internet or can be downloaded. Here is a list of good resources for those starting this terrible journey, as well as for anyone interested in helping others confronting the loss of a loved one. But, as always, the very first resource should be your local, state, and, if applicable, federal law enforcement agencies.

These sites are listed in no particular order. Also, please be careful when navigating these legitimate organizations so that you do not accidentally end up on a site capitalizing on the name of the person you are attempting to find. Some fraudulent sites attempt to exploit missing persons for profit and scam unsuspecting visitors.

VOLUNTEER ORGANIZATIONS AND WEB SITES

Project Jason (projectjason.org)

Offering advice, support, and publicity and named for Jason Jolkowski, Project Jason is a comprehensive starting point for the public and for families of the missing. The organization hosts an annual coping skills retreat, the only one of its kind.

The Charley Project (charleyproject.org)

A comprehensive and well-maintained database, the Charley Project is the archived home for more than 8,500 cold cases and more than 500 missing persons cases, which can be searched in many different ways. It is not an assistance organization.

Cue Center for Missing Persons (ncmissingpersons.org)

A site devoted to working for the recovery of missing persons, the Cue Center for Missing Persons hosts a respected yearly conference.

Outpost for Hope (outpostforhope.org)

Libba Phillips's site shines a light on those most often neglected by investigators, including foster kids and the homeless.

Shawn Hornbeck Foundation (alostchild.com)

Founded by a recovered abducted child, this foundation seeks to help the families of the missing with their publicity efforts.

AMECO (amecoinc.org)

This association of nonprofits specializes in missing children. Many of their member organizations also serve missing adults. AMECO is a good place to research other organizations. If they belong to AMECO, they're valid.

The Center for Hope (hope4themissing.org)

The Center for Hope was created by missing college student Suzanne Lyall's parents, also the originators of the state playing card program, which prints playing cards with photos and identifying information about missing persons. They are distributed to prisons and jails for the use of inmates in hopes someone might recognize the victim or know something about the case. The Center for Hope offers a number of resources for families of the missing.

Jacob Wetterling Resource Center (jwrc.org)

Named after an eleven-year-old boy who was abducted while with a group of children, this organization offers, among many things, advice and safety information for at-risk children.

Laura Recovery Center (lrcf.org)

Established to honor Laura Smither, a Texas child who was abducted and later found murdered, this organization works with law enforcement and communities to reinforce the safety of children.

Morgan Nick Foundation (morgannick.com)

Set up to honor an abducted six-year-old who has never been found, this foundation assists parents and others facing similar circumstances.

The Polly Klaas Foundation (pollyklaas.org)

With the aim of fostering child safety, this foundation promotes awareness and helps keep missing kids in the news.

radKIDS (radkids.org)

An effort sponsored by the family of abduction victim Elizabeth Smart, this organization teaches kids how to defend themselves from abduction attempts or attacks.

Child Quest International (childquest.org)

This nonprofit works to prevent and recover abducted or missing children worldwide.

International Cruise Victims (internationalcruisevictims.org)

Families and victims of crimes and disappearances aboard cruise ships can find individuals with similar experiences here.

Bring Sean Home (bringseanhome.org)

The Web site built around the parental abduction of the now recovered and returned Sean Goldman advocates for laws making it harder to conceal a child stolen from a custodial American parent.

GOVERNMENT AND OTHER RESOURCES

America's Most Wanted (amw.com)

John Walsh, who lost his son Adam to abduction, has proven to be a true friend to both victimized families and law enforcement with this television show and Web site devoted to balancing the scales of justice.

National Coalition for the Homeless (nationalhomeless.org)

This large group advocates for the rights, safety, and dignity of the homeless.

National Runaway Switchboard (nrscrisisline.org)

This group sponsors efforts to get runaways off the street and, if possible, back home. Crisis line is 1-800-RUNAWAY.

The Hague Convention (hcch.net)

This international treaty governs adoption and custody issues spanning the globe.

Children's Rights Council (crcjapan.com)

This coalition of parents is involved in custody issues with Japanese citizens.

National Alliance on Mental Health (nami.org)

This organization works with families and individuals who are dealing with mental illness.

National Institute of Mental Health (himh.nih.gov)

This government agency works toward solutions for persons suffering mental disorders.

National Center for Victims of Crime (ncvc.org)

This coalition dedicates itself to victims' rights.

Federal Bureau of Investigation (FBI.gov)

Site includes a list of current missing and kidnap victims, both children and adults.

National Center for Missing and Exploited Children (missingkids.com)

Home base for this organization founded by the Walshes, this organization offers its services to law enforcement agencies without charge.

Fox Valley Technical College (fvtc.edu/public).

This Appleton, Wisconsin, college has led the way in bringing families and investigators together in the field of missing persons and recovered unidentified human remains. Their annual conference is excellent.

National Missing and Unidentified Persons System (namus.gov)

A clearinghouse for missing persons and unidentified human remains, NamUs brings together the public, law enforcement, and medical examiners in a unique project that has already resolved several disappearances.

Center for Human Identification (unthumanid.org)

The University of Texas's ongoing forensic and human identity project, the Center for Human Identification is considered the premiere program of its kind in the country.

Most states have free searchable sexual predator databases. They can be found by searching by state name.

Many states also have missing persons clearinghouses, which can also be found using your search engine.

Bibliography

Alfano, Sean. "'Runaway Bride' Sues Ex for $500,000." CBS News, October 10, 2006. http://cbsnews.com/stories/2006/10/10/national/main2076613.shtml.

The Ambrose Bierce Project. http://ambrosebierce.org.

America's Most Wanted. "American Women Go Missing across the Border." http://amw.com/missing_persons/case.cfm?id=30673.

Andrews, Suzanna. "The Runaway CFO." *Portfolio*, February 11, 2009. http://portfolio.com/executives/features/2009/02/11/Arkansas-Executive-Goes-Missing.

Armed Forces Institute of Pathology. "Armed Forces DNA Identification Laboratory (AFDIL)." http://afip.org/consultation/AFMES/AFDIL/index.html.

Associated Press. "Natalee Holloway's Mom Opens Center for Missing Persons." PetoskeyNews.com, June 8, 2010. http://petoskeynews.com/national_news/article_e2d755e2-7336-11df-a037-001cc4c002e0.html.

———. "Rescuers Find Blind Hiker Who Vanished from Appalachian Train in Good Condition." Fox News, May 3, 2009. http://fox.com/story/0,2933,518705,00.html.

Association of Missing and Exploited Children's Organizations. http://amecoinc.org.

Barrett, David. "Youth Who Had DNA Wiped from Database Is Back on List for Drug Crime." *Telegraph*, August 1, 2009. http://telegraph.co.uk/newstopics/lawandorder/595...who-had-dna-wiped-from-list-is-back-on-list-for-drug-crime.html.

Battacharya, Sharon. "Killer Convicted Thanks to Relative's DNA." *New Scientist*, April 2004. http://newscientist.com.article/dn4908-killer-convicted-thanks-to-relatives-dna.html.

Bennett, Mike. "Missing Man Found Alive after 15 Years." *Palladium-Item*, March 18, 2009. http://pal-item.com/article/2009...WSO/9031800304.

Bensman, Todd. "FBI Will Join Search for Missing in Mexico." Chronicle News Service, February 5, 2009. http://chron.com/disp/story.mpl/hotstories/6249267.html.

Benson, Josh. "The Case." October 22, 2009. http://findjodi.com.

The Biography Channel. "Richard John Bingham." http://biography.com.

Birkbeck, Matt. *A Beautiful Child.* New York: Berkley, 2005.

Bradley, Iva, and Ron Bradley. "Missing: Amy Lynn Bradley." http://amybradley.net.

215

Bresnahan, Angela Isidro, and Andrew Downie. "Saving Faces." *People Magazine*, November 25, 2002. http://people.com.people.archive/article/0,,20138568,00.html.

Brewer, Howard. "Jaycee Dugard's Mom: 'Miracles Can Happen.'" *People Magazine*, September 23, 2009. http://people.com/people/article/0,,20307746,00.html.

Brummitand, Paula C., and Paul G. Stimson. *Forensic Dentistry*. 2nd ed. Boca Raton, FL: CRC Press, 2010. http://crcnetbase.com.

Bujold, Lois McMaster. The Quotations Page. http://quotationspage.com/quote/25893.html.

Carpenter, Mackenzie, and Allen Detrich. "Children of the Underground." Dart Center for Journalism and Trauma. http://dartcenter.org.

The Charley Project. "Annie Bridget McCarrick." http://charleyproject.org/cases/m/mccarrick_annie.html.

Children's Rights Council of Japan. http://crcjapan.com/.

Clark County Coroner's Office. http://accessclarkcounty.com/depts/coroner.

CNN.com. "Rescuers Find Woman, 76, Given Up for Dead." CNN.com, September 7, 2007. http://cnn.com/2007/US/09/07/oregon.rescue/index.html.

Conrad, Chris. "Still Missing 10 Years Later, Questions Linger about Boy." *Mail Tribune*, December 5, 2008. http://mailtribune.com/apps/pbcs.dll/article?AID_120081205/812050327.

Crichton, Michael. *Jurassic Park*. New York: Ballantine Books, 1991.

CrimeTime.com. "State by State Private Investigator/Detective Licensing." http://crimetime.com/licensing.htm.

Crussell, Bud. "Two Years after Disappearance a Little Girl's Fate Unknown." *Ocala Star-Banner*, July 23, 1978. http://news.google.com/newspapers?id=SP4xAAAAIBAJ&sjid=0wUEAAAAIBAJ&pg=2002,7206625&dq=dorothy+scofield+missing&hl=en.

Dale, W. Mark, Owen Greenspan, and Donald Orokos. *DNA Forensics: Expanding Uses and Information Sharing*. Sacramento, CA: SEARCH, The National Consortium for Justice, 2006.

Daniels, Stacy, and Mark A. Brennan. "Missing Children: Incidences and Characteristics of Runaway Children and Resources Available to Them." University of Florida IFAS Extension. http://edis.ifas.ufl.edu/fy855.

Davis, Kristin. "A Cold Case Heats Up: The Colonial Parkway Murders." *The Virginian-Pilot*, April 18, 2010. http://hamptonroads.com/2010/04/cold-case-80s-heats-up-colonial-parkway-murders.

Dedel, Kelly. "The Problem of Juvenile Runaways." *Juvenile Runaways*, Guide 37 (2006). http://popcenter.org/problems/runaways/.

The Doe Network. "International Center for Unidentified & Missing Persons." http://doenetwork.org.

Downes, Lawrence. "In Mexico, on the Law with Ken Kesey." *New York Times*, March 23, 2008. http://travel.nytimes.com/2008/03/23/travel/23Kesey.html.

Earley, Pete. *Crazy: A Father's Search through America's Mental Health Madness*. New York: Penguin, 2007.

Eberhart, Dave. "Months Later, Kidnap Expert Remains Missing in Mexico." Newsmax.com, April 13, 2009. http://newsmax.com/Newsfront/basista-kidnapping-mexico/2009/04/13/id/329443.

Evident. "The Identification of Francis Joseph van Zandt." http://evidentcrimescene .com/consulting/mm/mm.html.

Felknor, Bruce. "Tragic Voyage of the SS Sunset Crew." http://usmm.org/felknoralaska .html.

Forsythe, Frederick. *The Day of the Jackal*. New York: Bantam, 1982.

Forte, Janet. "Free Online Resources for Finding Missing Persons Using Social Media." Subliminal Pixels. http://subliminalpixel.com/non-profit/50-free-online -resources-for-finding-a-missing-person-using-social-media.

Fox Valley Technical College. "Responding to Missing and Unidentified Persons." http://fvtc.edu/public/content.aspx?ID=1238&PID=3.

Gadsden Times. "Few Clues Found to Missing Girls." February 10, 1978. http://news .google.com/newspapers?id=YQEkAAAAIBAJ&sjid=RNYEAAAAIBAJ&pg=276 8,1343789&dq=dorothy+scofield+missing&hl=en.

Garrett, Ronnie. "DNA Saves." *Law Enforcement Technology*, February 2009.

Georgia Bureau of Investigation. "Mattie's Call." http://amber.gbi.georgia.gov/00/ channel_modifieddate/0,2096,67865199_74426401,00.html.

Gladwell, Malcolm. "Million Dollar Murray." *New Yorker*, February 13, 2006.

Glod, Maria. "Authorities Reexamine 'Colonial Parkway' Killings in Virginia." *Washington Post*, April 2, 2010. http://washingtonpost.com/wp-dyn/content/ article/2010/03/30/AR2010033001590.html.

Goldman, David. Bring Sean Home Foundation. http://bringseanhome.org/wordpress/.

Grudgings, Stuart. "Brazilian Court Rules Boy Should Return to U.S." Reuters, December 16, 2009. http://news.yahoo.com/s/nm/20091216/us_nm/us/brazil _usaboy/pr...r0F;ylu+X3oDMTBvajZzaTFyBHBvcwMxNQRzZWMDdG9wB HNsawNwcmludA--.

Hague Convention on Private International Law. http://hcch.net.

Hall, Charles F. "International Child Abductions: The Challenges Facing America." bePress Legal Series, 2004. http://law.bepress.com/expresso/eps/240.

Hammer, Heather, David Finkelhor, and Andrea Sedlak. "NISMART, National Inci- dence Studies of Missing, Abducted, Runaway, and Thrownaway Children." Office of Juvenile Justice and Delinquency Prevention, Office of Justice Programs, U.S. Department of Justice. October 2002. http://missingkids.com/en_US/documents/ nismart2_runaway.pdf.

Harrington, Maureen. "Braver Than They Knew." *People Magazine*, August 19, 2002.

Hartocollis, Anemona. "A Mother Relives Her Anguish; A Subway Killer Is Sen- tenced." *New York Times*, November 3, 2006. http://nytimes.com/2006/11/03/ myregion/03kendra.html.

Hewitt, Bill. "Daddy's Girls." *People Magazine*, May 11, 1998. http://people.com/ people/archive/article/0,,20125199,00.html.

HungZai.com. "Mysterious Disappearances on Cruise Ships." Cruise Ship Law Blog, Lipcon, Marguilies, Alsina & Winkleman, P.A., October 6, 2008. http://blog.lipcon .com/2008/10/mysterious_disappearances_on_c.html.

International Cruise Victims. http://www.internationalcruisevictims.org.

Jackson, Marie, and Druti Shah. "Missing . . . From Afar." *BBC News Magazine*, May 12, 2009. http://news.bbc.co.uk/2/hi/uk_news/magazine/8012485.stm?ad=1.

Jacksonville Police Department. "General Procedure 8: Missing Persons." *Standard Operating Procedures Manual.* City of Jacksonville, November 22, 2004.

Jacob, Nicole. "Recalling Girls' Brush with Death." *Antelope Valley Press*, August 1, 2003. http://www.freerepublic.com/focus/f-news/956799/posts.

Jolkowski, Kelly. "Project Jason." http://projectjason.org.

The Joyful Child Foundation. "In Memory of Samantha Runnion." http://thejoyful child.org.

Kanable, Rebecca. "Reducing the DNA Backlog." *Law Enforcement Technology*, August 2008.

Kansas City News. "Porter Pleads Guilty in Deaths of Children." *Kansas City News,* January 3, 2008. http://kmbc.com/news/14963276/detail.html?treets=kc1&tid=26 55853705813&tml=kc1_4pm&tmi=kc1_4pm_1_04000301022008&ts=H.

Karnowski, Steve. "Database Can Crack Missing Person Cases—If Used." *The Daily Caller*, March 7, 2010. http://dailycaller.com/2010/03/07/database-can-crack -missing-person-cases-_-if-used/.

Keiser-Neilsen, S., and F. Strom. "The Odontological Identification of Eva Braun Hitler." *Forensic Science International*, no. 1 (January/February 1983): 59–64. http:// ncbi.nim.nih.gov/pubmed/6337935.

Kelly, George, George Knowles, Joe McGillen, and Tom Augustine. "America's Unknown Child." http://americasunknownchild.net.

Kennedy, Helen, and Corky Siemaszko. "Christian Karl Gerhartsreiter, a.k.a. Clark Rockefeller, Found Guilty of Kidnapping." *New York Daily News*, June 12, 2009. http:// nydailynews.com/news/2009/06/12/2009-06-12_christian_karl_gerhartsreiter_ aka_clark_rockeffer_found_guilty_of_kidnapping.html.

KlaasKids Foundation. "Missing Child Statistics." http://klaaskids.org/pg-mc -mcstatistics.htm.

Kobely, Jason. "Kidnap Victim Jaycee Dugard Located after 18 Years." News10. http://new10.net/news/local/story.aspx?storyid=65885.

Kurth, Peter. "In the Name of the Sister (Seven Days, June 1999)." PeterKurth.com. http://peterkurth.com/IN%20THE%20NAME%20OF%20THE%20SISTER.htm.

L.A. Chamber of Commerce. "History of Skid Row." http://lachamber.com/client uploads/LUCH_committee/102208_History_of_Skid_Row.pdf.

La Ganga, Maria L., and Shane Goldmacher. "Jaycee Lee Dugard's Family Will Receive $20 Million from California." *Los Angeles Times*, July 2, 2010. http://articles .latimes.com/2010/jul/02/local/la-me-0702-dugard-settlement-20100702.

Lanning, Kenneth V. *Child Molesters: A Behavioral Analysis.* National Center for Missing and Exploited Children. Washington, DC: GPO, 2001.

Lenahan, Jessica Gonzales. "Jessica Gonzales' Statement before the IACHR." http:// acl.org//human-rights-womens-rights-/jessica-gonzales-statement-iachr.

Lewis, Jesse. "Dorothy's Trail Ends in Missing Persons' File." *Ocala Star-Banner*, December 1, 1976. http://news.google.com/newspapers?id=c8swAAAAIBAJ&sjid=n QUEAAAAIBAJ&pg=1727,85362&dq=dorothy+scofield+missing&hl=en.

———. "Missing Child Mystery for Year." *Ocala Star-Banner*, July 22, 1977. http:// news.google.com/newspapers?id=V9ATAAAAIBAJ&sjid=6QUEAAAAIBAJ&pg =5085,4530078&dq=dorothy+scofield+missing&hl=en.

Library of Congress. Crime Control Act of 1990. http://thomas.loc.gov/cgi-bin/ bdquery/z?d101:SN03266:%7CTOM:/bss/d101query.html%7C.

The Literature Network. "Agatha Christie." http://online-literature.com/agatha_ christie/.

Lopez, Steve. "End of an 18-Year Illusion." *Time Magazine*, May 4, 1998. http://time .com/time/magazine/article/0,9171,988299,00.html.

Lost Children's Network. http://lostchildren.org.

Lost: The Eddie Gibson Story. Documentary. Produced, directed, and written by Philip Bloom. UK. 2005. http://philipbloom.net/films/other-hd/lost-the-eddie-gibson -story/.

Lovece, Frank. "Behind the Scenes of Lost and Found by Frank Lovece." http:// takegreatpictures.com/default.aspx?path=Articles.Details&params=oject/10435/ -design.

Lyall, Doug, and Mary Lyall. Hope 4 the Missing. http://hope4themissing.org.

Manamy, John. "'Forced' Meds Treatment—The Real Issue." http://mcmcanweb .com/foced_meds.html.

Matas, Kimberly. "Recreational Hiker, 34, Vanished in Manning Camp Quest in 1994." *Arizona Daily Star*, March 17, 2010. http://azstarnet.com/news/local .article_3d59d168-41ad-58bf-aedc-ab17dc2b09b3.html?print=1.

McMahon, Barbara. "Lord Lucan Found? Well, Perhaps Not." *Guardian*, August 10, 2007. http://guardian.co.uk/world/2007/aug/10/uk.mainsection/.

McShane, Larry. "Etan Patz's Dad Wants to Keep Perv He Says Killed So-Ho 6-Year-Old in Jail." *New York Daily News*, May 3, 2009. http://nydailynews.com/ news/ny_crime/2009/05/03/2009-05-03_etan_patzs_dad_wants_to_keep_perv_ he_says_killed_soho_6yrold_in_jail_new_hope_30.html.

Meikle, James. "MI5 Suspects: John Stonehouse, Bernard Floud and Will Owen." *Guardian*, October 5, 2009. http://guardian.co.uk/2009/oct/05/three-labur-mps -history-mi5

Moore, Phyllis. "Father, Sons, Reunited after 38 Years." *Goldsboro News-Argus*, December 28, 2008.

MSNBC. "Wilbanks: 'I Was Running Away from Myself.'" MSNBC.com, May 6, 2005. http://msnbc.cmsn.com/id/7692019.

Mullaney, Terri. "Have You Seen Matt Mullaney?" http://matthewmullaney.com.

Nakashima, Ellen. "From DNA of Family, a Tool to Make Arrests." *Washington Post*, April 21, 2008. http://washingtonpost.com/wp-dyn-content/article/2008/04/20/ AR2008042002388_pf.html.

Nash, Jay. *Among the Missing.* New York: Simon and Schuster, 1978.

National Alliance on Mental Illness. "Persons with Mental Illness Who Are Homeless or Missing: A Guide for Families." http://nami.org.

National Coalition for the Homeless. "Mental Illness and Homelessness." July 2009. http://nationalhomeless.org/factsheets/Mental_Illness.html.

National Institute of Mental Health. "The Numbers Count: Mental Disorders in America." NIMH, 2008. http://nimh.nih.gov/health/publications/the-numbers -count-mental-disorders-in-america/index.shtml.

National Runaway Switchboard. 1800runaway.org.

National Silver Alert Program. http://nationalsilveralter.org.

Netter, Sarah. "Man Turns Up Alive and Well Nearly 20 Years after Fake Drowning." ABC News, January 29, 2009. http://abcnews.go.com/6761530.

New York Daily News. "Nadia Bloom, 11-year-old Girl with Asperger Syndrome, Found Alive after Five Days in Florida Swamp." *New York Daily News,* April 13, 2010. http://nydailynews.com/news/national/2010/04/13/2010-04-13_nadia_bloom_11yearold_girl_with_asperger_syndrome_found_alive_after_five_days_in.html.

O'Connor, Thomas. *Forensic Odontology.* http://aspu-edu/occonort/3210/3210lect02c.htm.

The Official Website of the Executive Office of Public Safety and Security (EOPSS). "Laws Governing the Reporting of Missing Children." http://mass.gov/?pageID=eopsterminal&L=5&L0=Home&L1=Law+Enforcement+%26+Criminal+Justice&L2=Law+Enforcement&L3=Missing+%26+Wanted&L4=Massachusetts+Missing+Children+Clearinghouse&sid=Eeops&b=terminalcontent&f=msp_missing_missing_children_msp_missing_children_laws&csid=Eeops.

Oliu, Brian. "Poet Craig Arnold Missing in Japan." April 29, 2009. http://htmlgiant.com/author/news/poet-craig-arbold-missing-in-japan/.

Oregon State Police Missing Children Clearinghouse. http://oregon.gov/OSP/MCC.

Outpost for Hope. http://outpostforhope.org.

Paton, Alan. The Quotations Page, no. 31438. http://quotationspage.com/quote/31438.html.

Pauling, Linus. "No More War!" The Quotations Page, no. 5174. http://www.quotationspage.com/quote/5174.html.

Pavese, Cesare. *Goodreads.com.* http://goodreads.com/author/quotes/76241.Cesare_Pavese.

Pawlik-Klenlen, Laurie. "Mental Health and Psychology Quotations." Suite101.com. http://psychology.suite101.com/article.cfm/psychology_quotes.

Poets & Writers. "Searchers Say Craig Arnold, Missing since April, Has Died." May 11, 2009. http://pw.org/content/searchers_say_craig_arnold_missing_since_april_has_died.

Ratliff, Evan. "Gone: How to Disappear without a Trace." *Wired,* September 2009. www.wired.com/images/press/prf/WIRED_1709_Vanish.pdf.

———. "Vanish." *Wired,* December 2009. http://wired.com/vanish/11/ff_vanish2/.

Rice, Stephanie. "Father Accused of Taking Son in '81." *The Lookout Magazine,* December 29, 2004. http://operationlookout.org/Lookout_Magazine/2004/12/father-accused-of-taking-son-in-81/.

Rossiter, Leonard. Reggie Online. http://leonardrossiter.com/reginaldperrin/Real.html.

Sam and Lindsey Porter.Org. http://samandlindsey.org.

Segal, Kim. "Traffic Stop Leads to Man Believed Dead since '89." CNN, January 29, 2009. http://cnn.com/2009/CRIME/01/29/faked.death.arrest.

Semple, Kirk. "Runaway Spent 11 Days in the Subway." *New York Times,* November 24, 2009.

Seybert, Bruce. "Amber Alert." http://amberalertcreator.org.

Shakespeare, William. "The Comedy of Errors." *The Riverside Shakespeare.* Boston: Houghton Mifflin Company, 1972.

Smothers, Jim. "Man Arrested for Murder in 17-Year-Old Case." *The Daily Home*, May 6, 2010. http://dailyhome.com/view/full_story/7343202/article-Man -arrested-for-murder-in-17-year-old-case?instance=home_right_bot.

Stevenson, Mark. "Mexico's Drug War Takes Growing Toll on Americans." Associated Press, March 10, 2010. http://news.yahoo.com/s/ap/it_drug-war_mexico/.

Telegraph. "John Stonehouse Shed His Guilt by Adopting New Identity." December 29, 2005. http://telegraph.co.uk/news/uknews/1506526/John-Stonehouse-shed -his-guilt-by-adopting-new-identity.html.

Treatment Advocacy Center. "Remembering Kendra Webdale, Her Family and So Many Others." http://psychlaws.blogspot.com/2007/01/remembering-kendra -webdale-her-family.html.

Tuscaloosa News. "Another Girl Missing in Florida." February 10, 1978. http://news .google.com/newspapers?id=li4dAAAAIBAJ&sjid=950EAAAAIBAJ&pg=6172,19 02485&dq=dorothy+scofield+missing&hl=en.

United Way of Connecticut. "Child Abduction Prevention." http://211ct.org/ InformationLibrary/Documents/Child%20Abduction%20Prevention%20fj.asp.

U.S. Department of Justice. *National Institute of Justice 2004 Annual Report*. Washington, DC: GPO, 2004.

———. Office of Juvenile Justice and Delinquency Prevention. *A Family Resource Guide on International Parental Kidnapping*. Washington, DC: GPO, January 2007.

———. Office of Juvenile Justice and Delinquency Prevention. Federal Task Force for Missing and Exploited Children. *Federal Resources on Missing and Exploited Children*. 5th ed. Washington, DC: GPO, 2007.

U.S. Department of State. "7 FAM 150, MISSING PERSONS." *U.S. Department of State Foreign Affairs Manual*. Vol. 7, Consular Affairs. http://state.gov/documents/ organization/86569.pdf.

———. Bureau of Consular Affairs. *International Parental Abduction Philippines*. http:// travel.state.gov/abduction/country/country_514html.

U.S. Federal Bureau of Investigation. "James J. Bulger." *FBI Ten Most Wanted Fugitive List*, December 22, 2009. http://fbi.gov/wanted/topten/fugitives/bulger.htm.

———. *NCIC Missing Person and Unidentified Person Statistics for 2008*. http://fbi.gov/ hq/cjisd/missingpersons2008.htm.

———. *NCIC Missing Person and Unidentified Person Statistics for 2009*. http://fbi.gov/ hq/cjisd/missingpersons2009.htm.

U.S. National Library of Medicine. National Institute of Health. "Michael Blassie Unknown No More." http://nlm.nih.gov/visibleproofs/galleries.cases/blassie.html.

Walker, Simon. "The Secrets of Stonehouse." *Daily Echo*, October 11, 2009. http:// dailyecho.co.uk/news/4675564.

Walsh, John. BrainyQuote.com. Xplore, 2010. http://brainyquote.com/quotes/ quotes/j/johnwalsh187485.html.

Index

About the Author

Carole Moore is a writer whose work has appeared in numerous newspapers and magazines. She has also served as a bureau chief for an ABC news affiliate, a radio news director, and a radio talk show host. She worked as a police officer for twelve years, serving both as a patrol officer and criminal investigator, including a stint on a joint federal task force.